LIFE IN THE U.S. ARMED FORCES

LIFE IN THE U.S. ARMED FORCES

(NOT) JUST ANOTHER JOB

Anni Baker

PRAEGER SECURITY INTERNATIONAL
Westport, Connecticut • London

Library of Congress Cataloging-in-Publication Data

Baker, Anni P.
    Life in the U.S. Armed Forces : (not) just another job / Anni Baker.
        p. cm.
    Includes bibliographical references and index.
    ISBN-13: 978–0–275–98982–8 (alk. paper)
    1. Sociology, Military—United States. 2. United States—Armed Forces—Military life.
    3. United States. Army—Military life. 4. Soldiers—United States—Social conditions—
    21st century. I. Title.
U21.5.B35 2008
355.10973—dc22   2007034148

British Library Cataloguing in Publication Data is available.

Library of Congress Catalog Card Number: 2007034148
ISBN-13: 978–0–275–98982–8

First published in 2008

Praeger Security International, 88 Post Road West, Westport, CT 06881
An imprint of Greenwood Publishing Group, Inc.
www.praeger.com

Printed in the United States of America

The paper used in this book complies with the
Permanent Paper Standard issued by the National
Information Standards Organization (Z39.48–1984).

10 9 8 7 6 5 4 3 2 1

CONTENTS

INTRODUCTION

In my work as a scholar of the U.S. armed forces, I have found that people often express special interest in what I do because of their personal connection to the armed services. Sometimes it seems like everyone either knows someone serving in the armed forces today or is related to a veteran of World War II, Korea, or Vietnam. If this were indeed so, the contours of military life would be as familiar to us as going to elementary school or filling out tax forms. But in fact, most Americans don't have a clue about what life is like in the armed forces.

Public ignorance about military life is a change from earlier times. In the decades after World War II, it was common for men to have served in one of America's wars or in the peacetime forces somewhere in the world. Many members of Congress were veterans, and aspiring politicians found it difficult to get ahead without a military record. From the 1940s to the 1970s, most Americans did have friends and relatives who had served in the armed forces.

Since the end of the draft in 1973, though, the expectation that young men serve a few years in the armed forces has disappeared, and the peculiar subculture of the military has receded from public consciousness. Unless we have served ourselves, or have been part of a military family, most of us don't know very much about life in the military, why people join and what they do, why they stay in or leave, or what it is like to work, play, grow up, and grow old on a military base. And even those who are familiar with military life don't know how it came to be the way it is today.

This book is an introduction to life in the U.S. armed forces, from the recruitment process to retirement. It describes the society, traditions, benefits, and responsibilities of military life today, and how the most important aspects of military culture developed over the past decades and even centuries. I have written this book with the general reader in mind, and particularly for the friends and relatives of servicemembers who would like to know more about what really goes on behind the walls of a military base. Former or current personnel will probably be annoyed at the generalizations that I've had to make, but they too may be interested in the stories of those who came before them.

I began this project with the confident belief that it would be a simple survey of what I already knew. Aside from my earlier research and writing on military communities overseas, I have personal knowledge of military life as a family member and a civilian employee on Army and Air Force bases during the Cold War. In the years since, I have kept in touch with my friends in the military, and I have maintained the habit of reading military newspapers and journals. My sense of military life has remained fairly accurate.

Or so I thought. Once I started my research on this book, I realized that since the end of the Cold War, the U.S. armed forces had changed in some fundamental ways. Downsizing, reforms, privatization, and policy changes have added up to a major transformation in the institution and the lives of its members. Not only have the armed forces changed over the past fifteen years, but they also went through a transformation fifteen years before that, when the draft ended. And then twenty or twenty-five years before that, at the beginning of the Cold War. And again, on the eve of World War II. And so on. The fact is that the U.S. armed forces have been changing and adapting to new circumstances since they were established at the beginning of our nation's history.

It is worthwhile to ponder this process of change. Every significant transformation in the U.S. armed forces —every "Revolution in Military Affairs," or RMA, as the professionals call it—has been spurred by the appearance of a new threat to the nation's physical, economic, or geopolitical security. New technology, strategic postures, and resources devoted to the armed forces contribute to transformation, but in the United States, the main impetus for change has been a new threat on the horizon. Today's RMA is no different, and a comparison of the old threat and the new helps us understand why the military is changing the way it is.

From the beginning of the twentieth century until the 1990s, the U.S. forces faced adversaries who were advanced, industrial nation-states: Germany, Japan, the Soviet Union. Like every other nation, the United States relied on conscript armies and industrial technology to overwhelm its enemies; the appalling wastefulness of the two world wars was a tragic consequence of this model. During the Cold War, the United States never directly went to war with the Soviet Union, but the two sides eyed each other through extensive webs of military bases and huge garrison forces. Families built air-raid shelters in their backyards, and the doomsday clock pointed at one second before midnight. Everyone knew that a war between the two powerful industrial nations would result in annihilation of the world.

Ah, the good old days. In our post–Cold War world, the most serious threat we face comes from "non-state actors," terrorists, warlords, and criminals who operate in elusive international webs, or, worse, independently and under the radar of international law enforcement. This "asymmetrical" threat cannot be met by the twentieth-century force model; it requires a highly trained, flexible, professional force that can use cultural, political, and economic tools to battle an ill-defined enemy.

In the early 1990s, some military experts began to predict that terrorist groups, organized crime, and failing states would pose the biggest challenges to national security. It took some time to accept, but by the end of the decade, policymakers in the DoD (Department of Defense) recognized the danger and began to plan for a different type of military. When the Bush administration came into office, Secretary of Defense Donald Rumsfeld offered a blueprint for change in his first QDR (Quadrennial Defense Review): "it is not enough to plan for large conventional wars in distant theaters. Instead, the United States must identify the capabilities required to deter and defeat adversaries who will rely on surprise, deception, and asymmetric warfare to achieve their objectives."[1] The QDR was published on September 30, 2001, just weeks after the attacks of September 11 proved the terrible reality of such "asymmetrical" threats.

According to the new plan, the bulk of America's forces will be stationed permanently on bases in the United States, but units will be trained in "rapid response;" that is, they will be prepared to deploy anywhere in the world within hours. Many large bases overseas will be closed or scaled back, with new, slimmed-down versions established nearer to the action.

The new threats are exactly what many experts predicted, and the U.S. military is doing its best to meet them with an expert professional expeditionary force. Unfortunately, the war in Iraq has derailed many of the administration's proposed reforms, and the Army, America's largest military force, is, according to many experts, close to a breaking point. Frequent deployments, obsolete equipment, and lack of time to train between deployments have left the Army in an exhausted state. It remains to be seen how the Army and the Marine Corps, the other branch most deeply involved in Iraq, will recover from the stresses of their commitments in Iraq and Afghanistan.

U.S. MILITARY HISTORY IN A NUTSHELL

Strangely enough, there really isn't a strong military tradition in the United States, or at least there was none until the second half of the twentieth century. Distrust of standing armies played an important role in the colonial rebellion against Great Britain, and many of the nation's founders wanted nothing to do with a permanent military force. Opponents argued that citizen militias were sufficient to defend the nation and reflected the nation's democratic ideals better than a professional army. "In time of peace, standing armies are dangerous to liberty," the 1788 Massachusetts state constitution asserted; other state constitutions adopted similar language. European armies, many Americans believed, were the repositories of absolutist values and culture, and their existence was dangerous to democracy. "History, both ancient and modern, affords many instances of the overthrow of states and kingdoms by the power of soldiers," Massachusetts governor Samuel Adams wrote in 1768, "who were rais'd and maintain'd at first, under the plausible pretence of defending those very liberties which they afterwards destroyed."[2]

It is true, as the colonists knew, that the armies of European monarchies like Prussia, Russia, and Austria, not to mention Great Britain, were organized on principles of absolutist control. European rulers and their aristocratic officers believed that conscript soldiers were naturally lazy, undisciplined, crude, almost animalistic, and that they needed constant control and punishment. In these armies, soldiers spent their days cleaning their uniforms and polishing their equipment, standing in formation for inspection, and practicing endless drills on the parade ground.

Any fighting these armies did was "in line" on the battlefield, and tactics were limited to maneuvers in close rank formation. Because officers believed, with good reason, that the danger of desertion was high, they did not trust troops to carry out small group operations such as ambushes or guerilla raids; the pistol, a traditional privilege of officers, was used in past centuries against shirkers, *"pour encourager les autres."* Often enough, rulers used these armies to control their subjects, as the British did in colonial America.

The American military tradition, such as it was, developed quite differently. White settlers in colonial times organized themselves into militias for defense against Native American attacks; unconventional tactics like guerilla raids and ambushes became the signature of the Americans fighting in the French and Indian War, and later in the struggle against British rule. American citizen-soldiers fought to defend their property and their political system; as such, they were the antithesis of European conscript armies acting out the squabbles of ruling dynasties.

Many founders wanted to preserve the militia system, and rules for its organization and use are included in the Constitution of the United States and the Militia Act of 1792 (in 1903 the militia was renamed the National Guard). Others, however, such as George Washington, did not trust the abilities or the discipline of militias, and insisted that a permanent federal Army and Navy would better serve the interests of the entire country. Some ex-officers from the Continental Army, which had been disbanded after its victory over the British, went even further, advocating a heredi-tary officer class along European lines.[3] After much wrangling, Congress authorized the creation of permanent armed services: the Revenue Cutter Service and the U.S. Army (1790), the U.S. Navy (1794), and the U.S. Marine Corps (1798).

America's armed forces were small and underfunded in the first deca-des of their existence. The Revenue Cutter Service, later renamed the Coast Guard, patrolled coastal areas. The Army, a ground force based on infantry (foot soldiers), cavalry (mounted soldiers), and artillery (can-non), was used to guard coastal settlements and to push back Native American tribes in the interior, while the Navy fought North African pirates and protected American shipping. In the early days, the Marines were essentially soldiers on ships, and every naval vessel carried a Marine guard.

None of the services were especially popular or well-regarded by civil-ian society. Civilians viewed the "Regulars," or full-time soldiers, sailors, and Marines, as riff-raff incapable of finding gainful employment else-where. When the country became embroiled in a conflict, Congress would authorize the mobilization of volunteer militia regiments, which fought alongside the regular forces. When the fighting ended, the volunteers went home, Congress cut funding, and the Regulars reverted to their tra-ditional status on the margins.

After the Civil War, the Regular Army served as a constabulary force in the trans-Mississippi West, protecting white settlement from Native Americans who resisted encroachment on their land. This mission ended by the 1890s, but in 1898 the United States defeated the Spanish in the Spanish-American War, and the nation acquired its first overseas colonial possessions: the Philippines, Guam, Hawaii, Panama, Cuba, and Puerto Rico. The Army and Marines took on a new mission, quelling rebellions and unrest in the new possessions, while the Navy kept shipping lanes open.

The U.S. armed forces had their first foray into European affairs when President Woodrow Wilson brought the United States into World War I on the side of Britain and France. Almost 5 million Americans served in uniform between July 1917 and the Armistice in November 1918, many of them conscripted. After the war ended, the United States reverted to its traditional isolationist stance, and the armed forces shrank accord-ingly. The two decades before World War II were the twilight of the old-style Regulars. Insular and close-knit, military men and their families spent their lives within the institution and had infrequent contact with civilian society.

On the eve of World War II, the Selective Service Act of 1940 brought millions of draftees into the military, most of whom did not want to be there and had little regard for the spit-and-polish traditions of the professionals. Tough adjustments were inevitable; the career NCOs (Non-Commissioned Officers) and naval CPOs (Chief Petty Officers) gritted their teeth and allowed more laxness in the barracks, while the draftees reluctantly conformed to military standards. By the end of the war, over 16 million Americans had served, and neither military culture nor civilian society would ever be the same.

From the onset of America's involvement in the war, President Franklin D. Roosevelt made it clear that the country would not follow its traditional pattern and disengage from the world when the fighting ended. By 1945, theUnited States was the only industrialized nation not devastated by the conflict, and the world needed its leadership to recover. More significantly for the U.S. forces, tensions between the United States and the Soviet Union began to escalate. The 1950 invasion of South Korea by communist North Korea was the last straw. The American forces, which had shrunk from a high of almost 12 million in 1945 to less than 2 million by 1949, began a rapid buildup. After the end of the Korean War, the U.S. armed forces remained at a level of about 2.5 million.

The draft helped keep the numbers high. In 1948, Congress extended the Selective Service Act that had brought millions of men into the U.S. Army during the war. Between 1955 and 1964, the draft added about 120,000 men to the Army each year, a tiny percentage of the 17 million who were eligible.[4] Many young men also volunteered to serve in the Army or in the Navy, Marine Corps, Coast Guard, or Air Force, a new branch created in 1947 from the Army Air Forces.

The first decade of the Cold War saw a number of crises in world affairs, but the American armed forces managed to stay out of the fray until President Lyndon B. Johnson began sending ground troops to Vietnam in 1965. A total of 8.7 million Americans served during the eight years of that unpopular war. Only about 16 percent of them had been conscripted, but by the end draftees made up almost 90 percent of the infantry and a disproportionate number of the more than 56,000 war dead. Although only the Army used the draft, the other services benefited indirectly, as many young men enlisted in another service to avoid the Army.

Conscription proved to be both divisive and ineffective; the low morale of draftees and "draft-motivated" volunteers contributed to military unreadiness. As American involvement in Vietnam drew to a close, so did the draft era. The administration of President Richard M. Nixon abolished Selective Service in 1973 and the era of the AVF (All-Volunteer Force) began.

To attract qualified volunteers, the armed services boosted pay rates, improved the quality of life of personnel and families, and began "selling" military service.[5] An important element of the AVF plan, and one that until recently has been overlooked, was an increased reliance on part-time troops from the Reserves and National Guard. Their numbers grew, and military leaders at the Pentagon counted on them as they developed doctrine and strategy. After a rough start, the AVF became the best-trained, best-qualified military force in the world. They were also superior in an historic sense—never before had the American military been more professional.

The sudden end of the Cold War has given historians much to argue about, but one thing is certain. The fall of the Berlin Wall in November 1989 and the collapse of the Soviet Union a few years later compelled the U.S. forces to downsize and reconfigure their role as protectors of the nation's security. During the 1990s, the military shrank from about 2 million active duty personnel to 1.4 million, and hundreds of bases all over the world closed their doors. The forces were far from idle; after winning the first Gulf War in 1991, they performed humanitarian missions in Haiti, Somalia, Bosnia, Kosovo, and over a dozen other countries. But to what end? Many worried that the armed forces were becoming a global police force with no clearly defined mission. Equally frustrating, they were still burdened with a Cold War garrison mentality, an assumption that numbers and overwhelming force would win the day.

In the years since September 11, the U.S. forces have come a long way toward the transformation envisioned by the Pentagon, but operations in Afghanistan and Iraq have pushed the resources and capabilities of the armed forces to the limit. The military's "operational tempo" or OPTEMPO, the pace at which it undertakes missions, is almost unrecognizable to those of us familiar with life in the Cold War military forces. Personnel work 12-hour days, and are deployed away from their families for months or years at a time. Today, many servicemembers can expect to be deployed for as many as 180 days per year. Reserve and National Guard units are mobilized repeatedly, taking a huge toll on their families and civilian careers. The military scrambles to make life bearable for its servicemembers and families, but some observers wonder: how long can it go on?

MILITARY SOCIETY

In spite of major changes over the past few years, some elements of military life endure. The military has always been, and will continue to be, an unusual institution, unlike almost any other in contemporary society. It is a community of values, in which duty, patriotism, and loyalty to the group are paramount. Although many young people are attracted to military service for the steady pay and benefits, they do not join the military expecting to get rich. Its emphasis on the group rather than the individual makes the military an anomaly in contemporary America. Rules and regulations that seem absurd or intolerable to civilians often make sense in the context of the best interests of the community. A vivid example of this is the intense training recruits endure, training that is tougher and more challenging than any civilian job preparation program. In basic training, soldiers learn to act as a unit, not as individuals, vitally important when those troops find themselves under fire in hostile action.

This focus on the group, moreover, can be seen in all facets of military life. When an individual servicemember commits a crime off-base, the whole community may be punished with a curfew or restriction. Families living in base housing must conform to military standards of behavior or lose their housing privileges. There is method to the madness; adherence to common standards is the only way that people from a variety of backgrounds can tolerate life in a close and often stressful environment.

Along with its group orientation, the military also places a higher value on hierarchy and obedience than civilian organizations do. From their first days in basic training, recruits are taught to acknowledge their (lowly) place in the military hierarchy with salutes and formal responses to superiors. They are also taught to obey orders immediately, unquestioningly, and exactly as they have been given. Resistance to discipline and orders can earn a recruit endless PT (physical training), a bus ticket back home, or even a jail sentence.

Everyone in a military community has a clearly defined role. Enlisted personnel are the soldiers, sailors, airmen, and Marines who make up about 85 percent of the active duty and reserve forces. Junior enlisted personnel are supervised by experienced NCOs and CPOs, the sergeants and petty officers who form "the backbone of the armed forces," as the traditional expression puts it. Commissioned officers, from lieutenants and midshipmen to generals and admirals, command units of varying sizes as line officers, and serve as administrators, or staff officers. An officer will serve in both capacities many times in his or her career. Nurses, physicians, lawyers, and chaplains also hold officer rank, but they do not normally command units. There are also warrant officers, usually pilots, medical personnel, or highly trained technicians, whose valuable skills earn them the respect and privileges of officers, but they do not take on the managerial role of commissioned officers.

Aside from those in uniform, there are also civilians in a military community. Family members are the spouses and children of servicemembers. Civilian employees, who may or may not be family members, might be federal employees with GS (General Schedule) rank and the benefits of government workers everywhere. Or they might work for a civilian firm with a military contract. Finally, there are military and civilian retirees who live near military bases. They hold ID cards and have access to base services.

The demographics of military society are unusual as well. First of all, it is overwhelmingly young. The average age of enlisted personnel is twenty-seven, and officers thirty-five, and these average ages are higher than they were during the draft era. Rarely are there active duty servicemembers over the age of sixty, although the many retirees who live around military bases are part of the community. Secondly, although about 15 percent of active duty enlisted and officers are female, and over 60 percent of personnel (male and female) are married, the military workforce is still overwhelmingly male. A third difference is the extraordinary geographic and racial diversity of military society. Military personnel are somewhat more likely to come from the Southern states, and somewhat less likely to come from the Northeast, but they hail from all fifty states, Puerto Rico, Guam and other U.S. territories; some are even citizens of other nations. About one-quarter of the active duty forces are African-American.

A fairly common stereotype of military society is that it is largely lower class, poor, and undereducated. In recent years, this stereotype seems to have faded, and it is a good thing, because it is a cruel distortion. Military personnel are on average more intelligent, as measured by batteries of tests given to military recruits and comparable civilian high school students, and they are more likely to have finished high school and gone on to higher education than comparable civilians. They are solidly working- and middle-class, and studies suggest that they are among the more upwardly mobile members of their original civilian communities.

Although military society is quite different from the civilian world, the principle of civilian control over the armed forces was firmly established by the authors of the Constitution. As commander-in-chief of the armed forces, the president of the United States decides when and where the military will be used, and Congress decides manpower and funding levels. Civilian secretaries run the services through cabinet-level departments; until 1947, the War Department controlled the Army, and the Department of the Navy ran the Navy and the Marine Corps. In 1947, President Harry S. Truman created the DoD, combining all services in one department. The civilian secretaries of the Army, Navy, and Air Force report to the Secretary of Defense, each one administering its respective branch. The Secretary of the Navy continues to be responsible for the Marine Corps. In times of war, the Coast Guard traditionally worked under the Navy (in peacetime it was part of the Department of Transportation), but in 2003 it was permanently transferred to the Department of Homeland Security.

A word on ranks, or rates, as they are called in the Navy: ranks are the terms used for personnel at different levels of responsibility. Each service has its own slightly different ranking system, and careless use of the terms will confuse almost any reader, so I will use the pay grade system to refer to the military hierarchy. Pay grades, standard across all services, constitute the "career ladder" for officers and enlisted personnel. The enlisted pay grades run from E-1 to E-9. Recruits in basic training usually hold the grade of E-1; junior enlisted personnel, the privates, seamen, airmen, and corporals of the services, serve at the E-2 through E-4 grades. E-5 through E-9 comprise the NCO/CPO grades, and there is a special grade of E-10 for the highest-ranking enlisted member of each service. The E-10 acts as a spokesperson for the enlisted force, working with the JCS (Joint Chiefs of Staff), the Secretary of Defense, and Congress on issues of importance to enlisted personnel.

The officer grades advance from O-1 to O-10. Company grade officers, O-1 through O-3, include the junior-ranking ensigns, lieutenants, and captains. Officers at O-4 through O-6 are known as field-grade officers, and flag officers—generals and admirals—serve at the O-7 through O-10 grades. The five-star General of the Army or Air Force and the Admiral of the Fleet, of which there are none today, command the forces during major wars. Finally, the five Warrant Officer grades include W-1 through W-5. A complete list of pay grades and corresponding ranks for each service is included in the Appendix.

The subject of military society and culture is huge, and one of the difficulties of writing a book like this is deciding what to put in and what to leave out. This book does not pretend to be encyclopedic; career personnel and other experts will undoubtedly take issue with many of my choices. Life in each of the five branches of the armed services has its own unique customs and traditions, and while I have tried to include information about each branch, I have focused somewhat more heavily on the largest branch, the U.S. Army. Because the Coast Guard has a unique history and mission, I have, with great reluctance, omitted specific discussion of it. In most cases, however, what is true for the other services is also true for the Coast Guard. I regret this and other exclusions, but I do hope that readers will conclude that I have presented a picture of military life that is balanced, informative, and reasonably accurate.

There are many people who have assisted me with their advice, suggestions, and support. Heather Staines at Praeger suggested I write this book, and I am grateful for the confidence she has had in me. I would like to give special mention to my Wheaton Research Partner Kirsten Schuler, without whom the past two and a half years would have been impossible, and my new assistant Noah Burch; also to Fran Weldon for her help, and to Wheaton College for its generous financial support of my work. Thanks to my sister Maureen and my brother Jim. I would like to remember Michael and Ruth Connor. I would especially like to thank my father, Martin Connor, for his unflagging encouragement and enthusiasm. I cannot hope to accomplish all he has in his eventful life, but I will always try.

.

ACRONYMS

AAFES	Army and Air Force Exchange Services
ACF	Army College Fund
ACS	Army Community Service
AER	Army Emergency Relief
AFAP	Army Family Action Plan
AFPC	Air Force Personnel Center
AFQT	Armed Forces Qualification Test
AFS	Air Force Specialty
AGCT	Army General Classification Test
AIT	Advanced Individual Training
ARC	Army Recruiting Command
ARVN	Army of the Republic of Vietnam
ASVAB	Armed Services Vocational Aptitude Battery
AUSA	Association of the United States Army
AVF	All-Volunteer Force
AWOL	Absent Without Leave
BAH	Basic Allowance for Housing
BAS	Battalion Aid Stations
BCT	Basic Combat Training
BDU	Battle Dress Uniform
BRAC	Base Realignment and Closure
BRM	Basic Rifle Marksmanship
BUD/S	Basic Underwater Demolition/Swimmer
BUPERS	Bureau of Naval Personnel/Navy Personnel Command
BX	Base Exchange
CGSS	Command and General Staff School
CHAMPVA	Civilian Health and Medical Program of the Department of Veterans Affairs
CLEP	College-Level Examination Program
CMTC	Combat Maneuver Training Center
CNRC	Combined Navy Recruiting Command
COB	Civilian on the Battlefield
COT	Commissioned Officer Training
CPO	Chief Petty Officer

CS	Combat Support
CSS	Combat Service Support
DANTES	Defense Activity for Non-Traditional Education Support
DCOC	Direct Commission Officer Course
DDESS	Domestic Dependent Elementary and Secondary Schools
DeCa	Defense Commissary Agency
DEP	Delayed Entry Program
DI	Drill Instructor
DLI	Defense Language Institute
DoD	Department of Defense
DoDDS	Department of Defense Dependents Schools
DoDEA	Department of Defense Education Activity
DOPMA	Defense Officers Personnel Management Act
ELINT	Electronics Intelligence
EPMS	Enlisted Personnel Management System
FAP	Family Advocacy Program
FOB	Forward Operating Base
FSB	Family Support Battalion
FSG	Family Support Group
FST	Forward Surgical Team
GS	General Schedule
HALO	High-Altitude, Low Opening
HRC	Human Resources Command
HVT	High Value Target
ICBM	Intercontinental Ballistic Missile
IED	Improvised Explosive Device
IET	Initial Entry Training
IST	Initial Strength Test
JAG	Judge Advocate General
JCS	Joint Chiefs of Staff
JRTC	Joint Readiness Training Center
KP	Kitchen Patrol
LBE	Load Bearing Equipment
MASH	Mobile Army Surgical Hospital
MCCA	Military Child Care Act
MCX	Marine Corps Exchange
MEPS	Military Entrance Processing Station
MGIB	Montgomery G.I. Bill
MOPP	Mission Oriented Protective Posture
MOS	Military Occupational Specialty
MRE	Meals, Ready to Eat
MWR	Morale, Welfare, and Recreation
NAF	Non-Appropriated Funds
NBC	Nuclear, Biological, and Chemical
NCO	Non-Commissioned Officer
NCOA	Non-Commissioned Officers Association

NCOOC	NCO Candidate Course
NDSP	Non-DoD Schools Program
NEAP	National Assessment of Educational Progress
NEX	Navy Exchange
NOPC	Naval Operational Planner Course
NTC	National Training Center
OCS	Officer Candidate School
OEA	Office of Economic Opportunity
OER	Officer Evaluation Report
OGLA	Officer Grade Limitation Act
OPA	Officer Personnel Act
OPTEMPO	Operational Tempo
OSUT	One Station Unit Training
OTS	Officer Training School
PARS	Personnel Advancement Requirements
PCS	Permanent Change of Station
PME	Professional Military Education
PSTD	Post-Traumatic Stress Disorder
PT	Physical Training
PTRP	Physical Therapy Rehabilitation Program
PX	Post Exchange
QDR	Quadrennial Defense Review
R&R	Rest and Recreation
RDC	Recruit Division Commander
REAL	Recreation Education and Leisure
RMA	Revolution in Military Affairs
ROTC	Reserve Officer Training Corps
RSOI	Receiving, Staging, Onward-movement and Integration
SAASS	School of Advanced Air and Space Studies
SAMS	School of Advanced Military Studies
SAW	School of Advanced Warfare
SERE	Survival, Evasion, Resistance, and Escape
SFAS	Special Forces Assessment and Selection
SGLI	Servicemembers' Group Life Insurance
SOCOM	Special Operations Command
SOF	Special Operations Forces
SOFA	Status of Forces Agreement
SRB	Selective Reenlistment Bonus
TDY	Temporary Duty
TI	Training Instructor
TIG	Time in Grade
TIS	Time in Service
TSP	Thrift Savings Plan
UCMJ	Uniform Code of Military Justice
UMUC	University of Maryland University College
USMA	United States Military Academy
USO	United Service Organization

UXO	Unexploded Ordnance
VA	Veterans' Administration
WAAC	Women's Army Auxiliary Corps
WAC	Women's Army Corps
YATS	Youth Attitude Tracking Study

CHAPTER 1

MILITARY RECRUITING

At some point in their lives, most adolescent boys, and not a few girls, wonder what it would be like to join the military. They may see slick, fast-paced advertisements on television, or watch movies in which soldiers appear to live lives of nonstop danger and excitement. Their interest may be piqued by stories from relatives or friends in the armed forces. They may be inspired by their own sense of patriotism, or the desire to prove themselves. Whatever the source, there is no doubt that many images of the military are attractive and compelling.

For most young people, the thought of joining the armed forces is nothing more than passing curiosity, an idle fantasy that drifts away as high-school graduation approaches. But the armed forces need a total of about 180,000 new volunteers for active duty every year; for military recruiters, every young person with even a vague interest in military service is a potential enlistee.

Recruiting is not just a matter of connecting with those young people who are strongly attracted to military service, or who have already decided to join the armed forces. Recruiters must work hard to develop an active interest in military service among ambivalent young people, especially when economic times are good and there are other options for talented high-school graduates. Recruiters must overcome fear and mistrust among potential recruits and their families in the face of many negative images of the armed forces and of military service. And most importantly, recruiters must find and cultivate adolescents who are likely to succeed in the military. As most recruiters will confirm, there is no shortage of young people who want to join the military, but many of them are not especially promising material. Recruiters must find physically and mentally qualified young people who are willing to take on the rigors of life in the military, for compensation that may be less than what is available in the civilian world.

This is not an easy job even in the best of times, and it has become more difficult in recent years. Despite the surge in patriotism after the terrorist attacks of September 11, 2001, general public sentiment in favor of military service has not increased, and parents, teachers, and other adults are reluctant to encourage their children to join the military. This has become increasingly true as the military continues its involvement in the conflicts in Iraq and Afghanistan, and recruiters face suspicion and even hostility from many civilians. To make matters worse, as lower-skilled military occupations are contracted out to civilian companies and military technology becomes more sophisticated, the military needs larger numbers of well-educated, highly intelligent recruits, the very type of young people who have numerous choices in the civilian world.

MILITARY RECRUITMENT, PAST AND PRESENT

Most people would be surprised by the complexity and sophistication of the field of military recruitment. They shouldn't be, though. Military recruitment is, more than ever before, the linchpin of the AVF. Since its inception in 1973, the success of the AVF has depended on the persuasiveness of recruiters, because there is no longer a draft to compel young men to serve. If enough men and women don't sign up, the military is understaffed, quality of life declines, and readiness is threatened—and then, often enough, recruiting becomes even tougher.

Equally important in the modern military, with its high-tech weaponry and politically sensitive missions, is the "quality" of personnel, which includes factors such as intelligence, motivation, self-discipline, and maturity. As General Evan R. Gaddis, former commander of the U.S. Army, said in a 1999 speech, the post–Cold War Army faces a number of challenges, but "one of the most critical is our recruiting mission, that is, providing the force with young men and women committed to their country, their Army, and their fellow soldiers."[1] Gaddis highlighted the importance of recruiting almost two years before September 11; the need has only grown more urgent since then.

Recruitment is so important that each branch of the armed forces has its own department for the task. The largest of these organizations is the USAREC (United States Army Recruiting Command), which oversees recruitment for the U.S. Army and the Army Reserve. As the largest branch of service, the Army must recruit about 80,000 men and women each year for active duty (in January 2007 the Pentagon announced plans to add more than 90,000 soldiers and Marines over the next four years). The ARC includes a staff of 15,000 recruiters and 1,700 recruiting stations across the United States, in U.S. territories, and even on overseas military bases in Europe and Asia. The other branches have smaller but no less committed recruiting organizations: almost 8,000 recruiting personnel in the CNRC (Combined Navy Recruiting Command) work to sign up almost 39,000 enlisted personnel from 1,600 stations.[2] The Air Force Recruiting Service, with about 3,300 personnel and 1,500 stations, recruits 19,000 new airmen and women every year, and Marine Corps recruiters attract an additional 33,000 annually. Like the men and women of ARC, recruiters for other branches enlist personnel for both active duty and the reserve forces; the services together need over 138,000 Reserve and National Guard personnel each year.

Recruiting for the U.S. forces has never been easy. When the permanent Army and Navy were founded in the 1790s, recruiting was left to commanding officers, who had the unenviable chore of rounding up men to serve in their companies.[3] Later, companies or regiments would send recruiting parties of an officer or two to enlist new men, usually in poor sections of Eastern towns and cities where new immigrants and the unemployed congregated. Recruiting was easier in times of hardship than it was in years of economic expansion, but in any case, recruiting officers had little to choose from. Throughout the nineteenth century, officers and civilian observers characterized recruits as petty criminals or chronically unemployed, desperate men fleeing from financial or personal crises, illiterate, unable to speak English, alcoholic and in poor health—from "the most worthless class of our native population," according to one critic. [4] The poor reputation of recruits was exaggerated but whatever the economic situation, recruiting officer struggled not only to induce capable men to enlist but also to keep them from deserting until they reached their regiments, a constant problem in both the Army and Navy. [5] Recruiters were officially prohibited from enlisting men who were drunk, enlisting "negro, mulatto or Indian" men, non–English speakers, and men in physically poor condition, but they also had quotas to fill, and ignored the rules when they had to.[6]

The image of soldiers as the dregs of society persisted into the twentieth century, improving only during wartime when large numbers of citizen soldiers swelled the ranks. On the other hand, in spite of many disincentives to enlist, including arduous working conditions, low pay, squalid living standards, and brutal discipline, not to mention low status in civilian society, men did join the Army and Navy, and many made a career of it. Some had no other choice, but many were enticed by the chance for adventure and a change of scenery, or the pay and benefits, which, while not overly generous, at least met basic needs. Recruiters then, as now, did their best to downplay the negative aspects of military life, and emphasize the positives.

Recruiting has become much more sophisticated since the early days when officers patrolled bars and taverns trying to persuade local vagrants to join their companies. The basic reasons for enlisting are similar to those of 200 years ago, but recruiters have more tools available to highlight the advantages of service. One attraction is the image of military service as an adventure, a personal challenge, or an exotic way of life. Clever marketing campaigns portray servicemembers (or actors portraying them) rappelling out of helicopters, diving under ships, or flying jet aircraft. Media-savvy teenagers surely must know that there is more to military service than what is shown on television, but the images are powerful nonetheless. Another enticement is the quality of life package offered by the military: reasonably generous pay and benefits, job security, housing, pensions, and health care in retirement. Many young people, especially those from lower-income backgrounds, find the stability of a military career extremely desirable. Finally, recruiters can offer a number of incentives, such as money for college, enlistment bonuses, guaranteed occupations or postings, and accelerated promotion. Some of these, like college funds, are standard inducements for all enlistees, while others are offered only to especially qualified young people or those choosing certain hard-to-fill job specialties.

But these incentives only work when they are targeted at the right people, and with the right approach. The men and women who plan recruiting campaigns must have an accurate understanding of who is most likely to join the military and why, so that advertising and incentives can be targeted most effectively. To this end, recruiting commands employ a vast number of social scientists and market researchers to collect and analyze crucial demographic information. They also maintain staffs of expert recruiters who can convey a positive impression of military service and convince the right sort of people to join. Military recruiters go through a rigorous training course before they begin their work, and throughout their tours of duty they hone their sales skills. Recruiting, after all, is an especially challenging form of salesmanship.

The recruiting commands of the various branches have a great deal of control over their publicity, incentives, demographic research, and recruiter training. But in the end, they are at the mercy of other societal factors over which they have no control. If the economy is robust and well-paying civilian jobs are plentiful, qualified young men and women will consider options other than military service, and recruitment is likely to suffer. Recruiters cannot (and, one hopes, would not) induce economic growth to stall and unemployment to rise simply to increase their recruiting success.

More important in today's environment are the ongoing wars in Iraq and Afghanistan. The prolonged conflicts have made recruiting not only more difficult but also more contentious. Parents and other adult "influencers," as recruiters call them, discourage young people from enlisting, and sometimes engage in "counter-recruiting" activities, providing negative information about military service and alternatives to enlisting. When public opinion has turned against a military mission, as it seems to have done today, the military by itself can't do much, even with all the slick advertising money can buy. So even when recruiting commands are putting their best efforts into recruiting, they may still come up short. At such times, even if they reach their monthly or yearly goals, recruiting commands may be forced to spend more money per recruit than they would if external factors were more favorable. Today, the cost of recruiting one enlisted man or woman has risen to almost $14,000, and the DoD's total recruiting budget is close to $4 billion.[7]

SELLING THE MILITARY

For those who are too young to remember the draft, it may seem that military advertising on television, on the Internet, and in the print media is a pervasive and permanent fact of life, like death and taxes. But it wasn't always so. Before the end of the draft in 1973, military advertising, to the extent that it existed at all, was developed by ad agencies on a pro-bono basis and run on television as a public service. These messages were not particularly inspiring, and they didn't have to be. The Army, the branch that had the most trouble filling its ranks, could enlist all the personnel it needed through the draft.

The slick and expensive Madison Avenue-style advertising campaigns that are so familiar today were developed after the Pentagon created the AVF, and all branches of the armed forces began to rely on volunteers. The AVF got off to a rocky start; for most of the 1970s, high-quality volunteers were in short supply. Experts criticized the armed forces, especially the Army, as a "hollow force," on paper fully staffed but in reality unready to fight. Troops were poorly trained and equipped and endured a shoddy quality of life. To make matters worse, military leadership floundered in a crisis of confidence. It is no wonder that morale and discipline were disastrously low. If the situation hadn't changed quickly, the Pentagon probably would have pushed for a return to the draft. As it was, some critics were already calling the AVF a failure.

Responding to pressure to improve the forces, each branch hired civilian advertising firms to develop ad campaigns. The services quickly picked up the language and rhythm of Madison Avenue, as officers in the various recruiting commands took internships with major advertising firms to learn the ins and outs of marketing and advertising. Combat officers with experience in Vietnam helped create ad campaigns for candy and other consumer products before moving back on base to direct military recruiting efforts.[8]

The marketing campaigns were one reason why the quality of the armed forces rose dramatically between the late 1970s and the mid-1980s. Advertising campaigns, along with hefty pay raises and a shift in popular culture away from the antiwar sentiment of a decade earlier, made military service an honorable vocation once more.

Success came at a price, however. Between 1979 and 1986, the military's overall recruitment budget increased by 85 percent, most of it for television advertising. In 1977, Congress allowed the armed forces to pay market rates for broadcast television airtime, so the armed forces could compete with Budweiser, Gillette, and Pepsi for viewers' attention. The Army, in particular, realized that television was by far the most effective medium in generating "qualified forwardable leads," that is, phone calls or coupons requesting more information from a recruiter. Its advertising budget increased from $10 million in 1973 to over $100 million in 1984, with 60 percent or more of that spent on television.

The Army got serious about marketing in the late 1970s when its advertising agency, N.W. Ayer ABH International, developed a massive campaign used to recruit for the active duty Army, the Army National Guard, the Army Reserves, and Army ROTC (Reserve Officer Training Corps). Ayer created the famous "Be All You Can Be, 'Cause We Need You in the Army" slogan, certainly the best-known of all modern military advertising campaigns and the first to air extensively on network television.[9] It debuted in January 1981, during commercial breaks in "every bowl game known to man," according to H. Nelson VanSant of Ayer.[10] The catchy jingle ran during sports events and other highly rated television programs watched by young people, and was played on radio in a number of different genres—soul, country, and the ear-splitting electric guitar of arena rock. It also appeared in mass-market periodicals and local newspapers. The Army committed massive resources to the "Be All You Can Be" campaign, $33.5 million with Ayer during its first year, out of a total recruiting budget of $54 million.[11]

Some observers criticized "Be All You Can Be" for emphasizing "instrumental" rewards such as travel and educational opportunities, rather than focusing on duty, patriotism, and service. It was likely to result in "a corps of Yuppies in uniform," one critic predicted.[12] ARC officials didn't disagree. "The thrust is that the Army increases your chances of doing well in your future life," said Lt. Col. John Cullen, chief of public affairs for the ARC. Despite these qualms, after a few years everyone familiar with the campaign agreed that it was extremely successful, and demographic data supported the consensus view.[13] In 1980, for example, only 54 percent of Army enlistees had graduated from high school; by 1986, the percentage had risen to 92 percent, an indication that better-qualified young people were signing up. Even in 1984, when the expanding economy created many new jobs and unemployment dipped, recruiting continued to be relatively easy and successful.[14]

The "Be All You Can Be" campaign was the high point of a long relationship between the Army and Ayer. The firm had held the Army account since the late 1960s, when no one else was interested. But over the years it began to take the Army's business for granted, and in 1986 one of its executives pled guilty to charges that he had accepted kickbacks from outside vendors. By then, the enormous amount of money spent on "Be All You Can Be" had attracted the attention of other advertisers, and when the Army opened competition for the account in late 1986, several major firms submitted bids.[15] Young & Rubicam, Inc., a major New York advertiser, won the project away from Ayer in 1987; by then, it was worth $100 million a year. Better yet, Young & Rubicam didn't have to come up with a new concept; they retained the successful "Be All You Can Be" slogan.

The Marine Corps' advertising firm, J. Walter Thompson, soon picked up the television bug. Between 1977 and 1984, it experimented with the theme "The Few. The Proud. The Marines," but in October 1984 it returned to its older campaign, "We're Looking for a Few Good Men," using the familiar slogan in television ads on sports and action shows.[16] ("The Few. The Proud." remains a Marine Corps slogan on Web sites and promotional materials, however.) During Super Bowl XIX in January 1985, the Marines spent close to $1 million for several half-minute spots featuring "A Few Good Men." The ads, which had been tested in focus groups, showed a piece of steel being forged into a sword, which was carried by a Marine at attention.[17] The campaign eschewed appeals to personal gain and deliberately focused on the military discipline and toughness of the Marines. It challenged viewers to wonder if they could live up to the standards of the Marine Corps, and not-so-subtly suggested that most would not be able to do so.

By the late 1980s, the military's sophisticated marketing seemed to be a stunning success. Whether using the Army's "instrumental" approach, emphasizing how an enlistee could benefit from a stint in the armed forces, or the Marines' "intrinsic" approach, highlighting traditional military values, military service was back as a career of choice for talented young people.

The drawdown of the 1990s gave recruiters a break as the numbers of new people needed each year decreased. By the late 1990s, however, the Internet economy was roaring, the military had completed its downsizing, and fewer young people were signing up. In 1998 and 1999, the Army, Navy, and Air Force missed their recruiting goals. Some branches of the Reserves and National Guard missed targets on both numbers and quality, that is, they were able to sign up neither sufficient numbers of high-school graduates nor in particular the highly qualified young people they needed for certain occupational specialties.

The Air Force shortfalls were a rude shock for the prestigious branch, which had always been popular enough to turn applicants away. "We essentially stopped advertising because we were doing well," Air Force Col. James R. Holaday, a Pentagon official involved in manpower management, told a reporter. "We learned that's the wrong thing to do." In 1999, the Air Force paid for television advertising for the first time in its history, driven by the fact that public recognition of the Air Force slogan, "Aim High," had fallen to a measly 17 percent. Even so, the Air Force missed its target of 32,673 by 5 percent. In February 2001, the Air Force awarded GSD&M, an advertising agency from Austin, Texas, a 7-year, $350 million contract to come up with a new campaign. GSD&M developed a series of "Cross into the Blue" ads featuring young people metamorphosing from playful teenagers to military pilots or special operations troops.[18]

A decade after the end of the Cold War, new campaigns in all the services cost about $268 million, including $95 million for the Army alone.[19] But "Be All You Can Be," which had worked so well for the Army since 1981, seemed to have lost its magic. At the end of 1999, after two years of disappointments, it announced that it would not renew its contract with Young & Rubicam. After a lengthy search for a new agency, the Army settled on Leo Burnett U.S.A. of Chicago, and in January 2001 rolled out a new campaign slogan, "An Army of One." Market research conducted by Burnett suggested that young people saw military service, particularly in the Army, as dehumanizing and monotonous, so the new campaign emphasized the personal benefits that a young person might receive from military service, including "contemporary leadership and personal empowerment."[20] The "Army of One" campaign, inspired by a poem written by a Burnett copywriter, certainly did focus on the individual. "I am my own force," the new ad said. "Who I am has become better than who I was.... The might of the U.S. Army doesn't lie in numbers. It lies in me. I am an Army of One."[21]

Interestingly, the "Army of One" ads debuted on the hit sitcom "Friends," and shortly afterward ran on "The Simpsons" and "Buffy the Vampire Slayer." This was a startling move away from the Army's long-time reliance on sports broadcasting; one of Burnett's new ideas was to focus television spending on carefully targeted audiences rather than the mass audience of mega-sporting events. Superbowl audiences, researchers discovered, did indeed number many young people but also included older men and women who were not potential recruits for the military, so the message was, in a sense, wasted on them. Burnett advertised on programming that reached the target audience more exclusively.

Initial reviews of "Army of One" were lukewarm, to say the least. The new ad "shows a bit of desperation," wrote Lucian K. Truscott, an author and graduate of West Point.[22] "Too mystifying to make anyone dash to the nearest enlistment center," said another media critic.[23] "Substantially dishonest," was a harsher judgment from Bob Garfield, ad expert for *Advertising Age*, who observed that the U.S. Army was, in fact, decidedly not an "Army of One." Commentators criticized the entire campaign for attempting to "connect with a supposedly new species of extra-selfish young people," but as one reviewer pointed out, the Marines, who continued to stress values of sacrifice and struggle, easily met their recruiting goals even in lean years.[24]

Be that as it may, on September 5, 2001, the Army announced that it had met its own annual target of 75,800 a month before the end of the fiscal year, and recruiters credited the "Army of One" campaign. Responding to criticism of the new slogan by veterans and career service-members, Secretary of the Army Thomas E. White insisted, "I keep telling the old guys like me...we're not recruiting you, we're not recruiting me, we're recruiting the kids that watch Buffy and the Vampire Slayer [sic]."[25]

The Navy launched a similar campaign in March 2001, with a new slogan, "Accelerate Your Life," and ads created by Spike Lee. Like "Army of One," the Navy program was designed to appeal to "Generation Y," born between 1979 and 1994, with a message of self-actualization. "If someone wrote a book about your life," the ad asked, "would anyone want to read it?" The Navy ad debuted during an episode of "Survivor" on CBS, also a shift away from sports programming, but not, perhaps, as remotely distant from the old standard as "Friends." On the other hand, Navy research concluded that, far from being "extra-selfish" as some crusty veterans claimed, Generation Y held values and beliefs— "trustworthiness, self-determination and honor"—that were similar to those of "The Greatest Generation" of World War II.[26]

After the shortfalls of 1998, the Marine Corps was the only branch of the service to stay with its "Few Good Men" campaign, which, USMC marketers believed, continued to project a powerfully attractive image of the Marines. Generally speaking, however, the overall numbers demonstrated the seriousness of the military recruiting dilemma. Advertising spending among all the branches nearly doubled in five years, from $299 million in 1998 to $592 million in 2003.[27]

But perhaps a bigger change in military advertising has been the use of nontraditional methods that appeal to target audiences. Sponsorship of special events and use of the Internet represent new avenues the military has been exploring in recent years in its attempt to reach out to potential recruits.

Probably the most remarkable, and the most remarked-upon, marketing tool in the past few years has been "America's Army," a computer game developed, at a cost of more than $7 million, by designers at the Naval Postgraduate School. In the game, players attend basic training, then participate in combat missions that include targeting enemies and coming under hostile fire. "America's Army" was designed to be extremely realistic—no detail was too insignificant to receive attention from the game's creators. To that end, the Army continues to organize "green-ups" for the game's civilian design team every few months. Programmers ride in helicopters, eat MREs (Meals-Ready-to-Eat), wear night-vision goggles, even get ambushed, so that the game reflects combat experience as accurately as possible.[28]

The game is free to download on the Army's Web site, and recruiters hand out CD versions to potential recruits. It is a huge hit; in the first three years since its July 4, 2002 release, "America's Army" attracted more than 5 million registered users, and it records 100,000 new users every month.[29] The game includes a link to a recruiting Web site, so enthralled players can contact the Army for more information.

In 2005, the Navy released a similar game, "Strike and Retrieve," in which players "locate and secure Top Secret documents from within a downed unmanned reconnaissance plane, all the while battling challenging underwater terrain, deep-sea creatures, and an opposing force also on the trail of the downed plane."[30] Like many computer games, "Strike and Retrieve" contains special codes to help players advance—which can be found on the Navy's Web site, Navy.com.

Another much-discussed tactic used in the past few years is sports marketing—direct sponsorship of athletes and sports teams—which soaked up about $40 million of the Army's $212 million advertising budget in 2003. The Army has taken the lead in sports marketing, sponsoring professional rodeo events, Tony "The Sarge" Schumacher in the National Hot Rod Association, professional rodeo events, and Joe Nemechek in the NASCAR circuit. Nemechek travels with an exhibition of military equipment, uniforms and weapons, which, when on display, cover 12,000 square feet of space at NASCAR events.[31]

Other services are not far behind the Army in their efforts. The Navy, the Air Force, and the National Guard sponsor NASCAR drivers, and the Air Force also sponsors a professional snowmobile team. The return on the investment is hard to quantify, but most experts believe the money is well spent. Rear Admiral Jeffrey Fowler of the Navy Recruiting Command told a reporter that the money spent on the funding for the NASCAR sponsorship results in about three times the exposure of a similar outlay for television ads.[32] Others, however, are not so sure. In 2004, the Marine Corps estimated that the $3.5 million they spent on their car was worth $15 million in television advertising,[33] but in November the Marines, as well as the Coast Guard, announced that they would be dropping their NASCAR sponsorship. According to Drew Johnson, president of a policy research think-tank, "it's a relief that several branches of the military finally wised up to the facts: NASCAR sponsorships are not an effective way to get people to join the armed forces."[34]

The military is also shaping its marketing campaigns to appeal to a more diverse range of potential recruits. Focus group research has driven campaigns to appeal to women, for example, through a more feminine presentation in magazines like *Seventeen* and *Self*.[35] The Army is now increasing its efforts to attract Latino enlistees with the motto "Yo Soy el Army," while the Navy has created a Spanish-language Web site to appeal to Hispanic recruits. In another version of the NASCAR team, the Army sends a "hip-hop hummer" into African-American neighborhoods to drum up interest.

But so what? Does all this marketing really make a difference? Probably, but it's hard to say how much. The General Accounting Office has been a persistent skeptic of military marketing, noting in a 2003 report, for example, that while almost all the branches and components were meeting their goals, it wasn't clear that the $592 million spent on advertising really had made the difference. The DoD has not yet been able to create evaluation processes to separate out the impact of advertising from other factors, so they cannot say with certainty that the advertising works in the way they hope it does. Marketing is only one of the many factors that lead a young person to join the military.

THE MILITARY RECRUITER

Perhaps a more important factor than marketing in a young person's decision to enlist is the military recruiter. An energetic recruiter can convince a doubtful prospect to join the military instead of taking a civilian job, or he or she can convince a prospect to enlist with one branch rather than another. For the skilled recruiter who believes in the advantages of military service for young people, the task is immensely rewarding.

But, outside of actual combat, military recruitment duty is probably the toughest and most stressful job in the armed forces. In fact, it is quite difficult to recruit the recruiters. As the authors of a study on youth and military enlistment write: "Military recruiting is among the most challenging human resources staffing operations conducted by any large-scale organization."[36] Recruiters are essentially salespeople whose product is military service, and most servicemembers do not join the armed forces to become salespeople.

Although recruiting commands welcome volunteers, the majority of military recruiters are assigned to the duty from other specialties.[37]

They are chosen based on performance in their assigned military specialty, which means that although they may be skilled in their "real" occupation, they do not necessarily possess either the talent or the desire to recruit. They must have clean records, a stable family life and no financial problems. In other words, they must be ideal representatives of the armed forces. The services cannot choose recruiters based primarily on their aptitude or potential for success in recruiting, which is unfortunate; studies show that the characteristics of a good salesperson are relatively constant, and it would not be especially difficult to profile potential recruiters to identify those most likely to succeed.[38]

Before they start visiting high schools and job fairs, military recruiters go through approximately seven weeks of training. They must be completely familiar with the numerous programs and occupational specialties available in their branch of service and how an enlistee might qualify for a specific program; what kinds of enlistment incentives are available at any particular time; and how to answer questions about life and work in the service. They also master the skills of salesmanship: how to contact prospects; how to discern a prospective enlistee's interests and motivations; and how to canvass an area, develop contacts, and follow up on leads. For example, in "The Magic of Rapport," one of the lessons in the USMC recruiting course, students learn to use body language, tone of voice, expressions, and approaches to develop a relationship of trust with prospects: "As recruiters, we need to establish rapport with everyone that we meet. If you realize that people are your most important resource, and that everyone you meet can provide something for you, then rapport is the way that you tap that resource."[39] Recruiters also learn to deal with the frustration of putting hours of time into a promising prospect only to lose out to a more attractive college or work offer, and they learn to remain unflappable in the face of antagonism from opponents of the armed forces.

A good recruiter never stops working. He or she may go to a restaurant for dinner and leave with the names and phone numbers of several prospects from among the servers or kitchen staff. Recruiters hand out their cards to young people in schools, churches, shopping malls, fast-food restaurants, local sporting events, beaches, and recreational areas. They spend hours "cold-calling" high-school students, hoping for just one or two positive responses out of dozens of attempts. They drive hundreds or thousands of miles each month pursuing the most tenuous leads.

In spite of recruiters' best efforts, the payoff is small. Studies show that for every one successful enlistment, Army recruiters make between 120 and 150 initial contacts, schedule 17 appointments, and conduct 10 of the 17 appointments (the rest are skipped or missed by the prospect). For each of those 10 appointments, only 1.5 applicants actually pass all the tests and meet the physical standards, and only 1 recruit will join the Army. And this discouraging percentage does not take into account the number of recruits who fail to complete basic training or drop out further along the training pipeline.[40]

Selling is high-energy work that depends a great deal on personal drive and initiative. Civilian salespeople receive commissions as incentives to succeed. Military recruiters are salespeople as well, but by law they cannot receive financial incentives for performance, so the military rewards them with symbolic items like plaques, watches, certificates, medals, and ribbons. In the Army, the highest awards for recruiting success are the Glen E. Morrell Award and the Army Recruiter Ring, similar to a class ring. While ambitious recruiters appreciate these symbols of recognition, awards do not make the job easier, especially in more difficult recruiting environments such as large cities or affluent parts of the country. Recruiting duty is "career-enhancing;" that is, advantageous, if not mandatory, for promotion, and recruiters receive special duty pay of up to $450 extra a month. Many recruiting stations are found in places where military personnel do not normally live, such as large cities, which can be attractive to some recruiters and their families. Recruiters earn points for promotion and are favored in future assignments after they have successfully completed a three-year tour of duty.[41]

Recruiters may earn extra money and preferential treatment, but they hardly come out ahead. For one thing, recruiters often experience financial difficulties during their tours because the cost of living in many urban and suburban areas is higher than it is around most military bases. Recruiters and their families may also forego the use of budget-friendly military shopping facilities and housing if they are too far from a base. In spite of the special duty pay, many recruiters have trouble making ends meet.

Recruiting is also enormously stressful. Recruiters have "missions," or quotas they must meet each month and each year. The quotas are set by a complex calculation of the local population size and "propensity," and change with circumstances. But the bottom line is that the military needs personnel, and a recruiter's failure to "make mission" or fulfill quotas can dead-end his or her career. Evidence suggests that although most of the time the military services are meeting their recruiting goals, it is getting harder and harder to sign up the quality enlistees they need.

For one thing, the percentage of young people who say they are "likely" or "very likely" to join the military has gone down steadily for the past fifteen years.[42] Fewer young people know someone who has served, so role models in uniform are scarce. More young people are going to college. Many adults—teachers, parents, church leaders—are not enthusiastic about their children, or any children, performing military service in a time of war.[43] Under the No Child Left Behind Act of 2001, high schools receiving federal funds must turn over student contact information, and some school districts have tussled with the DoD over the issue.[44] Recruiters have also struggled to gain access to colleges; some institutions have banned recruiters from their campuses because of the military's stance on homosexuality.[45] While it is hard to know to what extent philosophical opposition to military recruitment affects the work of military recruiters, activism and bad press cannot make it easier.

Today, of course, the most important question recruiters face today is, "will I have to go to Iraq?" Good recruiters face this question head-on, even anticipating it. "I tell them the truth," one Army recruiter says. "Soldiers go to war sometimes." But critics of military recruitment say that recruiters lie about the chances of going to war and downplay the danger.[46] As the war in Iraq becomes more unpopular, recruiters increasingly face organized opposition, even hostility from parents and others. The atmosphere has taken its toll on recruiter morale. "I would rather have him in Iraq," the mother of a recruiter told a radio host, "where he is doing something good and feeling proud of what he's doing than the way he's treated as a recruiter today."[47]

Most recruiters are hard-working and honorable, and try to sign up recruits who will succeed in the armed forces. But because of the pressure to make mission, sometimes they may take shortcuts and behave unethically. Most commonly, some recruiters have urged prospects to lie or omit information in order to pass the screening process. There are dozens of medical conditions that will disqualify a recruit, including common conditions like asthma, flat feet, severe acne, and heart murmur. Some recruiters advise prospects not to mention such ailments, and in recent years a few reports have accused recruiters of urging prospects to stop taking proscribed medications like Ritalin or antidepressants before their physical examinations. Some investigations suggest that recruiters have even advised single mothers, who are automatically disqualified from enlistment, to conceal the fact that they have had children.[48] Doctors can spot most disqualifying medical conditions during physical exams, but there have also been cases of recruiters giving recruits answers on tests, hiding drug use, and falsifying credentials. In fact, in 2005 the Army ordered a one-day nationwide recruiting moratorium to address problems in recruiting procedures after receiving reports of fraud.

Another type of deception occurs when recruiters offer unauthorized incentives, make promises they can't keep, or lie about the terms of the recruit's contract. Recruiters may also pressure recruits to sign up for a particular job specialty even if it is not the best match for the individual, rather than losing the recruit to another service or to civilian life. There are severe penalties for recruiters who are caught lying or falsifying information, and most recruiters obey the rules. Nonetheless, recruiters

will certainly portray military service in the best possible light, and prospective enlistees must listen carefully to what the recruiter says and ask
tough questions.

WHO JOINS THE MILITARY?

The extensive marketing and recruiting efforts described above are
directed toward catching the attention of the target audience and encouraging them to consider volunteering for military service. It seems fairly
straightforward. But why, really, do young men and women join the
military? Do young people join the military out of patriotism and a desire
to serve the country? As a personal challenge, a chance to mature and
toughen themselves? Or is it for the money and benefits? In research-
speak, what are the "economic and attitudinal enlistment motivators for
subgroups of the youth population?"[49] The answer to this question is of
critical importance, because a misunderstanding of enlistee motivation
means that the "product" (military service) might be portrayed in the
wrong way in advertising, or advertising campaigns might be directed at
the wrong people. In today's tough recruiting environment, the military
cannot afford to make such mistakes.

Sociologists have devoted an enormous amount of time and study to
the question of "enlistment motivations," and they have discovered a
few things. First of all, the decision to join the military (or not) is a calculation between the attractiveness of the military and the unattractiveness
of options in the civilian world, and the primary measure of attractiveness is financial—the pay and benefits a recruit will receive. Not surprisingly, recruiters working in affluent, economically vigorous regions of
the country have a more difficult time in meeting their targets than do
those in economically depressed areas.

The attraction of military service is not simply monetary, however.
As one former recruiter put it: "No man in uniform has ever enlisted
because the money was great."[50] Recruits also join for the chance to
develop self-discipline and confidence, to master a challenge, to be part
of a larger organization in which they can take pride. Many recruits are
also motivated by values like patriotism, duty, and the concept of service.

Probably the most important basic document for the study of recruitment and enlistment is the YATS (Youth Attitude Tracking Study) a survey
carried out every autumn since 1975 by the DoD and Westat, a civilian
research firm. YATS researchers interview some 5,000–10,000 youths aged
16 to 24, asking them 200 questions about themselves and their career
goals, including the likelihood that they will join the military.[51] Using
these data, recruiting experts gather intriguing and valuable information,
such as whether young people have discussed joining the military with

parents or other adults, and the advice they were given; how often young people have contact with military recruiters and in what context; and the impressions young people have of life in the military. All this is correlated with data on race, gender, socioeconomic status, geography, military background, and other factors, to get a detailed picture of the "potential supply," or the subpopulation most likely to join the military. The young men and women in the "potential supply" have a "basic propensity" to join the military, and the job of the recruiter, armed with pamphlets, posters, hats, and T-shirts, is to "convert" the "supply" into "enlistments," in other words, to convince young people who already have positive images of the military to sign up. Research shows that young people who tell the YATS interviewers that they are "likely" or "very likely" to enlist do in fact tend to sign up. Conversely, when a smaller percentage of young people report that they are likely to enlist, recruiters will have a tough time in meeting their quotas.

As mentioned earlier, the reasons a young person might report that he or she is "likely" or "very likely" to join the military may be *extrinsic,* that is, material, or *intrinsic,* or psychological. The two rationales for enlisting in the armed forces are by no means mutually exclusive, but correctly determining the relative importance of each is essential to successful recruiting.

Researchers know that extrinsic reasons are very important for enlistment motivation; when youth unemployment rises, so does "propensity" to join the military. For young people without attractive options, the relatively good pay and benefits of the military provide an alternative to low-paid part-time work or no work at all. Young people who cannot afford college, or do not want to attend right away, are also more likely to consider joining the military. One of the biggest challenges to military recruiting today is that an increasing percentage of young people in the United States plan on attending college, which means they are less likely to enlist in the armed forces.

Another part of the extrinsic motivation consists of onetime inducements to enlist. The most important of these, in terms of making the difference to potential recruits, is help in paying for college tuition. Recruits are eligible to receive money for college under the MGIB (Montgomery G.I. Bill), a VA (Veterans Administration) program that provides $30,000 or more for college tuition. Personnel tend to use the MGIB after they leave the service; servicemembers receive 100 percent tuition assistance for attending college courses while on active duty. There is also a college loan repayment program, and enlistees in certain job specialties are eligible for additional money for higher education under programs like the ACF (Army College Fund). Other inducements include cash enlistment bonuses, currently up to $40,000 for six-year commitments in certain occupational specialties; guaranteed assignments and job specialties; and accelerated promotion, usually given to recruits with some college credit. Some services even offer recruits referral bonuses for every friend or acquaintance they bring into the service.

Analysis of YATS data suggests that inducements can increase the "conversion" rate, or the percentage of prospects who actually enlist. But inducements are expensive, and must be used carefully. If they are offered to prospects who already intend to join the military, they are, like advertising to middle-aged people, wasted. Certainly recipients appreciate enlistment bonuses and other perks, and they may temporarily boost morale, but from the point of view of cold, hard financial calculation, they are better used to encourage waverers than to reward those who have already committed.

Extrinsic factors are important, to be sure, but intrinsic or "attitudinal" factors also play an important, and, in the opinion of many, underappreciated role in enlistment. "What draws young men to join the military," wrote a Marine Corps recruiter, "has everything to do with the adventure and the challenge and the chance to prove one's worth in an extremely disciplined endeavor."[52] A major study published by the DoD in 2003 showed that a surprisingly high percentage of young people are attracted to military service for such intrinsic reasons, although the advertising currently in use tends to emphasize extrinsic benefits.[53] As has been seen, the Marine Corps uses intrinsic factors such as patriotism and personal challenge in its marketing campaigns to great effect, while some of its other efforts to attract recruits through inducements have stumbled. Recruits often say that they are enlisting in order to get tuition for college, or to learn a specific skill, but they are also influenced by values like duty and self-sacrifice. "They may not say they're enlisting to serve their country," noted one Army recruiter. "They talk around the question and mention the financial benefits. But I believe if we just gave them a chance to serve and nothing else, most of them would still enlist."[54]

Recruits motivated by intrinsic factors may be more inclined to military service than they would be to a similar civilian job offering roughly equivalent benefits and pay (and no basic training to endure). A recruit's attitudes can be influenced by community opinions toward military service, the views of influential adults, and, of course, effective military advertising campaigns. National or international events such as the September 11 attacks also inspire patriotism and a sense of duty, resulting in a temporary rise in enlistments. "It's service to country, now," said an Army recruiter working in the Times Square station, who noted that "lawyers, stockbrokers and business people" came to the office inquiring about enlisting in the wake of the attacks.[55]

Intrinsic factors may play a larger role in enlistments than many experts suspect, but it is difficult to get an accurate measure of the phenomenon. Recruits may over- or underreport their feelings on the importance of values; they may indeed not know their true feelings at all; and finally, they often enter military service with one perspective but find that their attitudes change over time.

THE PERFECT SOLDIER (SAILOR, AIRMAN, MARINE)

Every branch of the armed services hopes to attract the brightest, most motivated, and mature young men and women from across America. Unfortunately, so does every college, university, and technical school, and, for that matter, every employer, public or private. Moreover, the military is not the right place for every bright and motivated young person, even those interested in military service. Is there a "type" of person who will adjust especially well to military life? Is there a level at which young people might be "too smart" for the military—too bright, inquisitive, and independent-minded to handle the discipline of military service? In recent years personnel experts have tried to determine what qualities characterize the "ideal" soldier, sailor, airman, or Marine and the implications for the armed forces if standards rise or fall.

Political leaders have fielded armies for thousands of years, since humankind began to organize itself into distinct societies, but until a few centuries ago, any discussion of qualifications for military service, especially mental qualifications, would have seemed absurd. Standards in most armies were physical in nature—soldiers had to be young, male, and relatively healthy. Traditionally, height was the most desirable quality in a recruit,[56] and there was some sense to this because height was and is closely correlated with nutrition and good health. Some European kings created special elite units of tall men, who were regarded with fear by their adversaries. In some cases, ethnicity was a plus or minus for military service. Many societies shared stereotypes that certain ethnic groups harbored an especially warlike spirit. In the nineteenth-century United States, for example, the Irish were thought to have a propensity for military service, while most officers believed that African-Americans made inferior soldiers. During World War I, combatants on all sides held that Native American "warriors" were especially ferocious fighters, and when German troops heard rumors that an opposing force included Native Americans, panic would ensue. In the United States, a land of immigrants, regulations required recruits to be able to understand English. The rule was often waived, however, and until the 1890s immigrants made up between one-third and one-half of the American Army.[57]

At the end of the nineteenth century, as more complex weapons systems came into use and officers paid more attention to tactics and strategy, recruiters began to look for signs of "trainability" and "aptitude" in their recruits. When the size of the armed forces ballooned during the two World Wars, such qualities became all the more vital. In 1917, the Army developed two aptitude tests to measure the general mental ability of conscripts and volunteers. The "Army Alpha" test was a forerunner of later tests, while the "Army Beta" was an intelligence test for illiterate or non–English speaking recruits that used only images. During World War II, the Army used the AGCT (Army General Classification Test), similar to the earlier Army Alpha test, on the millions of citizen soldiers conscripted between September 1940 and April 1947, when the wartime draft ended. As part of the new conscription law of June 1948, Congress mandated that the DoD develop the AFQT (Armed Forces Qualification Test), which measured not only general ability and trainability, but also particular aptitudes of special importance to the branches of service. Over the years, as the range of occupational specialties within the armed forces increased, tests like the AFQT helped recruiters screen for qualified recruits and identify the best position for each individual.

Generally speaking, the stringency of recruiting standards varies depending on the urgency of personnel needs. During World War II, when the enlisted force reached a peak of almost 12 million, standards were relaxed such that 100,000 illiterate men were able to join the Army. Likewise, during the Korean and Vietnam Wars, standards were lowered as the demand for manpower rose. In 1966, Secretary of Defense Robert McNamara initiated an experiment called "Project 100,000," which opened the door to enlistment for men who would have been disqualified under normal standards. The idea, according to McNamara, was to fill the ranks while giving the men, mostly African-American, an opportunity to benefit from Army training, which would serve them well later on. As it happened, however, Project 100,000, or "McNamara's Morons," as the cruel joke went, was a disaster, benefiting neither the men nor the armed forces.

Project 100,000 was not the only blight on military readiness during the Vietnam era. For new enlistees and more experienced personnel alike, discipline, morale, and training standards disintegrated. Some studies show that it was in fact the more intelligent draftees who had the greatest difficulty adjusting to military life.[58] After the draft was abolished in 1973, average aptitude levels dropped even further as qualified men avoided military service. The Army responded by allowing more women into the ranks. Although women remained a small percentage of the Army, their test scores were so much higher than average that they brought overall average scores up to levels that were on paper, at least, minimally acceptable. It was this statistical quirk, some sociologists assert, that saved the AVF during the years of the "hollow force" of the 1970s when skeptics pushed for a return of the draft. "Had the Army not expanded the opportunities for women soldiers," sociologist Martin Binkin writes, "it is doubtful if the all-volunteer force could have survived the 1970s."[59]

In any case, something needed to be done quickly. Planners and analysts debated whether the problem was "smarter weapons or smarter people," and whether the answer lay in better equipment, tougher training, improved quality of life, more attention to recruiting quality enlistees, or more likely, in some combination of solutions. In 1976 the armed forces introduced the ASVAB (Armed Services Vocational Aptitude Battery), a set of tests measuring both innate ability and specific knowledge. Of the nine sections of the ASVAB, four (Word Knowledge, Paragraph Comprehension, Arithmetic Reasoning, and Mathematics Knowledge) are used to determine an "AFQT score," a percentile ranging from 1 to 99, which is considered to be an indicator of trainability. The AFQT score is used to determine whether a recruit is eligible for military service.

The range of AFQT scores is divided into five main categories, I through V. The goal of the armed forces is to have as many recruits as possible from categories I, II, and III, representing the top half of AFQT scores. In 1981, the National Defense Authorization Act limited scorers in Category IV to 20 percent of the entire force; scorers in Category V are ineligible for military service. Individual services have higher standards, however; the Air Force requires a score of at least 36, the Navy 35, the Marines 32, and the Army 31, although recruiters sometimes give exceptions.

As it happened, the introduction of the ASVAB system did not immediately lead to an improvement in the average mental quality of recruits. From 1976 to 1980, an error in calibration—the calculation that determines the category in which a test-taker's AFQT score belongs—pushed thousands of low-scoring recruits into higher categories. By the end of the 1970s, military planners believed that only 5 or 6 percent of new enlistees had fallen into Category VI, but in reality the proportion reached almost 33 percent.

In addition to high AFQT scores, the armed forces prefer to have recruits with high-school diplomas. Studies show that they develop fewer disciplinary problems, having demonstrated more self-discipline and perseverance than high-school dropouts or those with GEDs. Depending on the general recruiting environment, recruits without a high-school diploma are rejected entirely or accepted only with an AFQT score of at least 50 (the Air Force will only consider GED holders with scores of at least 65). Recruits must be U.S. citizens or permanent residents, and between the ages of 17 and 35 (the Army allows recruits as old as 42), but 17 year olds must have their parents' permission to enlist. Recruits must also be free of infectious diseases and other medical conditions that would affect their service, and be physically capable of performing military duties. Normally, if married, they cannot have more than two dependents under the age of 18; unmarried recruits may not have any dependents. Recruits with serious criminal records or histories of major behavior problems are prohibited from enlisting.

In 2005, the Army and several of the reserve branches fell short of their annual recruiting goals, at a time when troops were urgently needed for the wars in Iraq and Afghanistan. All branches met their goals the following year, but it was thanks in part to lower standards. In 2006, about 17 percent of active duty recruits received waivers so they could enter the service—either medical or "moral character" waivers involving misdemeanor crimes or substance abuse.[60] The Pentagon claims that the 65 percent increase in waivers over the past three years will not hurt readiness, but there is no question that the projected expansion of Army and Marine Corps personnel will result in the trend continuing. Not only may less-qualified recruits be accepted, but also the military, especially the Army, is opening the doors to more immigrants, who receive citizenship in return for their service. Currently, about 5 percent of the total active duty force is foreign-born, and over 40 percent of those are not citizens. Some experts have raised questions about a potential risk to national security, but studies show that noncitizen troops have lower attrition rates and are better soldiers than American-born recruits.[61]

MILITARY OCCUPATIONAL SPECIALTIES AND OTHER DECISIONS

The MOS (Military Occupational Specialty) is the term that the Army and Marine Corps use for the specific work an enlistee will perform after basic training. In the Navy, job specialties are called ratings, and AFS (Air Force Specialties) in the Air Force. Some job specialties, such as medical technician or computer specialist, can be very directly practical to a civilian career; others are unique to the military, even unique to one branch of service.

Recruits must take a number of factors into account when deciding on a job specialty. One of the first considerations is gender; most job specialties are now open to women, but those in the combat arms, such as infantry, armor, and artillery, are not. The second factor influencing the selection of a job specialty is the recruit's performance on the ASVAB tests. Some specialties are open to all, while others require a very high score on specific sections of the test. A third factor is the recruit's personal history. Some sensitive specialties requiring security clearances, such as military intelligence, are closed to recruits with financial troubles, drug or alcohol infractions, even extensive traffic violations. A final factor is whether positions in the specialty are available at the time a recruit is planning to join the service. If the service has enough recruits for a particular job specialty, the field may be closed temporarily. A recruit can decide to wait until the specialty opens up again, but the recruiter is likely to push the recruit to choose another job. Like all good salespeople, recruiters want to close the deal.

THE PROCESS

The first step in joining the military is speaking with a recruiter. This can be done over the phone or in person. The recruiter provides some basic information about military service, and asks about the prospective recruit's level of education and health, including possible medical issues, and whether the prospect has "good character." What this means is that the prospect should have no problems with drugs or alcohol and no serious run-ins with the law. Recruits are well-advised to be honest about their backgrounds, because at some point the truth will come out. Recruits are no longer asked about their sexual preference, but if they voluntarily acknowledge homosexuality they are barred from enlisting.

If a prospect passes the initial screening, and many do not, the recruiter and the recruit will discuss options for military service, such as what skill the recruit might like to learn, the length of time the recruit plans to sign up for, when the recruit will begin training, and even, depending on what education the recruit has completed, what rank he or she will hold during training. The recruiter might also discuss enticements such as enlistment bonuses and "kickers," or extra money for education. The recruiter can't make promises, however, because the recruit has not qualified for anything yet.

After the recruit has decided to go further, the next step is a daylong visit to a MEPS (Military Entrance Processing Station). This is a facility where recruits receive entrance physicals and take the ASVAB. The recruiter schedules the recruit's visit to the MEPS, which is usually within a few hours drive from the recruiting station. Often, however, the MEPS is far enough away that the recruits arrive by bus the evening before and spend the night in a nearby motel. The MEPS visit starts as early as 4:30 A.M. with a wake-up call and breakfast, and continues with hours of filling out forms and providing medical histories. Recruits take the ASVAB test, and afterwards, at around midmorning, receive physical examinations. In the afternoon they meet with job counselors, who help them choose job specialties based on their ASVAB scores. At the end of the day, recruits take a preliminary oath of enlistment.

In most cases recruits are then officially enrolled in the DEP (Delayed Entry Program), which means they return home for a period ranging from a few days to a year before going to basic training. Recruiters must control the number of recruits going through the testing and training pipeline so that the military receives a steady supply of recruits; the DEP helps recruiters manage the process, putting recruits "on hold" until there is space for them. For many recruits, training and active duty must wait until they have finished high school. For others, a desired job specialty is not immediately available and the recruit is given the option of waiting.

The recruits are now in the pipeline, and will receive monthly pay stubs, even if they are earning no money. But the final firm commitment to the military comes when the recruits return to the MEPS just before they leave home for basic training. They receive another physical exam, review and validate the personal information they gave to their recruiters earlier, and take a second oath of enlistment. This oath legally binds them to enter military service.

CHAPTER 2

TRAINING

Aside from the possibility of getting wounded or dying in battle, probably the most frightening thing about joining the armed forces is the prospect of basic training, or boot camp, as it is often called. Movies and television programs occasionally show basic training as a series of humorous mishaps, as in the films *Private Benjamin* and *Stripes*. Usually, however, the experience is depicted as brutal and cruel, unbearably harsh for anyone of normal sensitivities. Drill sergeants appear to be insane, conditions in the barracks are medieval, and the physical training is dangerous, even life threatening. In the most extreme depictions, recruits are tortured and humiliated by sociopaths until they become mindless automatons, all humanity beaten out of them.

This is a satisfyingly dramatic way to think about basic training, and military personnel may well receive some additional respect from civilians for having survived such an ordeal. Basic training is certainly one of the most challenging experiences young people can endure. But while a basic training camp may seem to its inhabitants like a refuge for sadists, every step of the training process has been carefully planned and evaluated for its effectiveness in turning civilians into soldiers, sailors, airmen, and Marines.

Basic training is only the beginning of years of training and education for those who choose a military career. After boot camp, recruits attend an advanced training course in their job specialty. The advanced course can range from a few months to over a year, depending on the specialty. Taken together, basic and advanced training are known as IET (Initial Entry Training), and military personnel in all branches go through it. After that, each branch offers a bewildering number of additional courses and camps, many of which involve specialized combat training of some sort and are attended by personnel in combat specialties. Some of these additional courses, such as Airborne training, may be part of a recruit's IET; others, like Special Forces training, usually occur later in a soldier's career, after he has shown particular potential. In the armed forces, training never really stops, but continues on throughout all phases of the career cycle.

THE PHILOSOPHY AND HISTORY OF BASIC TRAINING

Although basic training is a valuable experience and one that can lead to tremendous personal growth, it is true that almost every moment of it is "highly uncomfortable for the individual," as one guide nicely puts it.[1] During boot camp, all aspects of the recruit's life are regimented. He or she is shouted at, ordered to do things that don't make sense or are impossible and then berated for not following orders, hurried along and then told to wait, held responsible for others' mistakes, made to march, run, and do thousands of sit-ups and push-ups, forced to sit through hours of tedious lectures, allowed no privacy, and forbidden almost all contact with the outside world. Trainees feel helpless, and for good reason: they have little or no control over their lives during basic training. It's a wonder that anyone agrees to put up with this treatment.

The purpose of it all is to train soldiers to react instinctively the way they will need to in combat—immediately, precisely, without personal preferences or doubts getting in the way. The only way soldiers will have any hope of surviving the chaos of battle is to act together as a team, unquestioningly obeying the commands of a leader exactly as received. Both advocates and critics of the philosophy call this "indoctrination," and it is true that recruits learn, in an intensive, stressful environment, to think as soldiers, not as individuals. Instilling the habit of immediate and unquestioning obedience is at the heart of basic training. Without it, no modern military force could exist.

Another goal of basic training, especially during the past few years, is to help enlistees develop a sense of ethical standards that reflect well on the armed forces. Military leaders believe that the individualistic norms of civilian society are very different from the communitarian ethic needed for a life in the armed services; they believe that not only are civilian values different from military ones, but the two are in some cases directly opposed. In the past decade, each branch of the armed forces has implemented or expanded its emphasis on teaching "core values" to recruits. In Army Basic Combat Training (BCT), for example, recruits are taught the seven Army core values: Loyalty, Duty, Respect, Selfless Service, Honor, Integrity, and Personal Courage, which form the somewhat tortured acronym LDRSSHIP. In the Air Force, core values are stated as: "Integrity first, Service before self, Excellence in all we do," and the core values of the Navy and Marine Corps are expressed in three words: "Honor, Courage, Commitment." The intensity of the basic training experience naturally brings forth a sense of these values during the training period, but experts have long known that most servicemembers revert to a more civilian outlook after they leave camp. The goal in core values training is to inculcate these values permanently, so that they become a larger part of military culture in general.

The military's emphasis on "core values" is in part a large extent a response to the fact that during the Cold War, all-too-frequent episodes of sexual misconduct, negligence, and arrogant behavior earned the U.S. forces a bad reputation among civilians, especially overseas.[2] Military leaders realize the importance of cultivating a positive image, especially in areas where the United States or U.S. foreign policy is unpopular. Core values training is also a reaction to the military's perception of widespread permissiveness and self-centered behavior in the civilian world since the 1960s, as well as an attempt to instill in military personnel from widely different backgrounds a sense of consideration for each other. A spate of racial incidents and sex scandals in the 1990s prompted even more focus on the values of respect and integrity.[3] Finally, perhaps, it is an acknowledgment that in the counterinsurgency missions of the present and future, ethical behavior on the battlefield is a delicate, easily lost commodity. Revelations of prisoner abuse in Iraq, Afghanistan and Guantanamo Bay, Cuba, and more recently, allegations of massacres of civilians by American military personnel in Iraq demonstrate how easy it is for troops in stressful situations to behave in ways they would never dream of in peacetime.

Generally speaking, basic training involves a lot of physical conditioning and practice in specific skills such as map reading, basic first aid, and weapons care and use. Tough training is, obviously, most important for enlistees in combat specialties such as infantry, artillery, or armor, and boot camp for combat troops has always been intense. During the Cold War, however, basic training for those in noncombat job specialties, such as that at the Army's Fort Jackson, known as "Relaxin' Jackson," acquired the reputation of being less rigorous than at Fort Benning, where the infantry trains.

Since September 11, the DoD's policy has been to emphasize combat readiness for all troops, regardless of job specialty. Given the likelihood that military personnel, whatever their job specialties, will be deployed to a combat theater, the DoD has required basic training courses in all branches of the service to teach combat skills more intensely to all personnel than was the case in the past. Training in the Marine Corps has always included thorough combat training, illustrated by the USMC motto, "Every Marine a rifleman first"; now the other services have also reformed their basic training regimens to include more realistic battlefield and weapons practice. Extended field exercises test trainees on skills that they will need in missions in Iraq, Afghanistan and other combat theaters. The services are also incorporating anti-terrorism and force protection training into all phases of basic training. "It is important we bring as much realism and intensity to boot camp as possible. It's the only way to mentally and physically prepare our new Sailors for their roles on the front lines in the war on terrorism," explains Rear Adm. Ann E. Rondeau, Commander of the Naval Training Center at Great Lakes, Illinois.[4]

The most important lesson of boot camp training is to listen and obey. Trainees learn to listen to an order and do exactly as they are told, not to discuss or raise objections to the order. Equally vital and perhaps more difficult for intelligent, motivated recruits, they must learn not to add anything extra to orders they receive, even additions that might appear to be entirely reasonable. Recruits who have the toughest time are those who respond to orders with resentment or defensiveness, and those who tend to get discouraged, give up easily, or break down when they are challenged. Drill instructors know how to spot at a glance individuals with these and other attitude problems, and they direct most of their venom on such unfortunates. Trainees who understand the rules of the game, and realize that it is a game, are left alone for the most part. They are required to carry out all orders and punished for infractions, but they escape the drill instructor's most severe harassment.

To achieve the transformation from civilian to soldier, one commentator notes, "no psychological weapon is neglected. Group shame, individual guilt, pride of accomplishment, ridicule, fear of failure and suffering, hope of improvement—all are applied to produce quick and automatic compliance with orders."[5] Basic training may sound unendurably traumatic, but one must keep in mind that it is designed to shape 19- and 20-year-olds into soldiers, sailors, airmen, and Marines. If basic training is considered in this light, some elements of it fall into proper perspective. First of all, the amount of physical exercise in basic training is designed for the late adolescent. It is rigorous and best suited for young and healthy people. Older adults might cringe at the thought of all the running, sit-ups and push-ups, but the physical demands of basic training are not impossible for healthy teenagers. Unfortunately, recruiters and drill instructors are finding that more and more recruits are in very poor physical shape; boot camp is so difficult for many recruits because a childhood filled with junk food and television has not sufficiently prepared them for it, not because the physical standards are so unreasonably high.

The mental and psychological challenges of basic training are designed for the same late adolescent: physically out of shape, perhaps unused to taking orders or achieving difficult goals, defensive when criticized. Any high school teacher will recognize how hard it must be to turn teenagers into soldiers. Some of the outcomes of basic training, such as self-discipline, pushing through until a task is accomplished, stifling one's personal feelings in the face of challenges and responsibilities, are skills that many (not all) adults have already mastered to some degree, whether by attending professional schools or job training programs, managing busy careers while raising families, or even through their own experiences in the armed forces. What may appear in popular films and television programs to be a bizarre process of brainwashing and mental stress is actually an excellent preparation for adult life. The habits of mind taught in basic training are common to successful people in every profession. In the military, the instilling of such habits comes about in an unusual way, but it's not wrong to think of basic training as an arduous but effective preparation for adulthood.

That being said, the rigors of basic training are probably unique in the modern industrialized world. Nowhere else are novice employees regimented so thoroughly, with so little choice over their daily actions. The physical training of a professional athlete is certainly at least as rigorous as that of basic training, but athletes can quit without legal penalty, they are not subject to the intense mental pressure of a drill instructor (coaches and trainers might approach those levels at times, but on a regular basis they are no match for their military counterparts), and the rewards of military service, financial or otherwise, are nothing like that of successful professional athletes. No other institution would dare to challenge trainees the way that basic training does. Basic training has to be unique. Trainees are taking the first step toward becoming professional warriors; the skills and mental habits learned in boot camp may be useful in the civilian world, but they are matters of life and death in battle.

The extensive and carefully designed training that today's recruits experience is a far cry from the traditional preparation the services gave their new enlistees. During most of the nineteenth century, training was haphazard at best, and often enough, virtually nonexistent. Recruits spent a few weeks at one of the recruiting depots like Carlisle Barracks in Pennsylvania or Jefferson Barracks in New York, trying to learn close-order drill or marching in formation around a parade ground. Soldiers were not trained in marksmanship until the late 1850s, and those joining cavalry regiments often reported to duty without ever having mounted a horse. Soldiers and sailors learned almost all of what they knew through on-the-job experience.

In those days, the main barrier to training was finding the time necessary to devote to it. Manpower levels in the nineteenth-century armed forces were so low that neither the Army nor the Navy could afford to give recruits several months away from their regiments or ships. By the end of the century, however, the Army had developed a program of drill, target practice and physical training. Recruits, then as now, also learned military courtesies and behavior and spent hours each day on "fatigue duty," working in the mess halls and kitchens; maintaining grounds, buildings, or vessels; or other labor. During the years before World War II, PT and athletics became a bigger part of training, both at the beginning and throughout military service. Recruits also learned to use basic military equipment and practiced military skills. Even so, in 1917 General John J. Pershing, commander of the American Expeditionary Force during World War I, saw that the soldiers under his command were poorly prepared, and he refused to allow them into the trenches until they had finished more extensive and realistic training in France. His stubbornness delayed American participation in the war but certainly saved many lives.

Today, basic training is more or less the same in each branch of the service, but there are also significant differences. For one thing, the duration of basic camp is different in each branch. Air Force basic training lasts six and a half weeks, Navy training for eight, and Army training for nine weeks. Marine Corps boot camp is the most intensive, lasting thirteen weeks. Each branch of service has its own training bases. The Air Force conducts its training at Lackland Air Force Base, Texas, and the Navy at Great Lakes Naval Training Center in Illinois. Marine Corps recruits east of the Mississippi River train at Parris Island Recruit Depot in South Carolina with its famously brutal weather, and those in the West at the Recruit Depot in San Diego, earning the nickname "Hollywood Marines" from their Parris Island comrades. The Army has five basic training bases: Fort Benning, Georgia; Fort Jackson, South Carolina; Fort Knox, Kentucky; Fort Leonard Wood, Missouri; and Fort Sill, Oklahoma. Every American servicemember, whether on active duty or in the Reserves or National Guard, has trained at one of these bases.

PREPARING FOR BASIC TRAINING

Heading off to basic training has to be one of the most nerve-wracking experiences of anyone's life. Usually, recruits have enlisted weeks or months before; they either have signed up to go on a specific date, or they are waiting until a billet opens up. During the time between signing up and shipping off, they are enrolled in the DEP. As described in the previous chapter, recruits take an oath of enlistment when they visit the MEPS to take the qualification tests, get their physicals, and choose their job specialties. But they aren't truly, legally committed to serving until they take the final oath of enlistment at the MEPS right before going to boot camp. During the recruit's time in the DEP, it's up to the recruiter to keep him or her focused on joining the military. A lot can happen between the first MEPS visit and getting on the bus or plane: a new job, a college opportunity, a marriage or engagement, a child on the way, or simply second thoughts about joining the service. The attrition rate during the DEP is one of the problems that bedevils recruiters, and they try to ensure that the time their recruits spend in DEP is as short as possible.

Wise recruits use their time in the DEP, however long it may be, to prepare for basic training. Preparation includes both physical and mental pretraining. One advice guide, Peter Thompson's *An Insider's Guide to Military Basic Training*, suggests the following steps:

1. Get used to going to bed at 10 P.M. and getting up at 5 A.M.
2. Phase out junk food, eat a more nutritious diet and get used to drinking water.
3. Quit smoking—the best advice anyone can give a recruit. (It's also a good idea to give up caffeine.)
4. Start physical training—sit-ups, push-ups, running.
5. Get a copy of the IET book and begin memorizing it—including materials like military ranks, the military alphabet system, marching orders, etc.
6. Develop a strong, positive attitude and focus on personal reasons for joining the military.[6]

Recruits are well advised to learn as much about basic training as possible before going, so there will be fewer surprises. There are several excellent guides available, and it is helpful to talk with those who have been through it, especially for "non-traditional" recruits; older men and women or those with families may face different challenges than the younger, single recruits just out of high school.

If recruits don't prepare systematically, however, and probably most of them do not, they might still get a little taste of PT before they go if their recruiter organizes workouts for recruits during the DEP. Recruits may go to a nearby base to train, or go on group runs. But they return home afterwards, so it cannot be the same as the real thing.

Before recruits go to camp, they visit the MEPS one more time to take an AIDS test, review their paperwork, and take the final oath, the one that legally commits them to join the service. Then, within a day or so, they fly on a civilian airline to the airport nearest the training camp. They gather at the airport, often at a room at the USO (see Chapter 6), and are collected by a receiving sergeant who herds them onto a bus. The bus trip is where the atmosphere begins to change. The recruiter's joking and encouragement is a thing of the past, replaced by the gruff orders of the receiving sergeant.

THE DRILL INSTRUCTOR

During basic training, recruits' lives are dominated by a staff of instructors known as drill sergeants, drill instructors (DIs), Training Instructors

(TIs), or Recruit Division Commanders (RDCs, or "Red Ropes"). DIs, who are experienced NCOs with outstanding career records, are specially trained for this grueling work. The recruits learn to hate, fear, respect, and eventually admire the DIs, although most will always cherish the belief that their own DI was uniquely sadistic. No one who has ever been through basic training forgets his or her DI's name.

Drill instructors are selected for the duty after they have served in the military for several years, attained the grade of E-5 and in some services have attended the basic NCO course, an intermediate-level school for career servicemembers. Many drill instructors volunteer for the arduous duty because they remember the impact their own DIs had on them, and they want to act as be role models for new recruits the same way. It is also, like recruiting duty, a "career-enhancing" step.

Drill instructors go through a tough course of training. It is difficult to qualify for Drill Instructor School and applicants must be the best of the best: no disciplinary problems, extremely physically fit, orderly and stable personal lives. Candidates are selected from bases all over the country for DI duty; about half volunteer, and half are assigned by their commanders. Volunteers are more motivated, obviously, and fewer drop out of Drill Instructor School, but overall up to 50 percent of DIs trainees fail to complete the course.[7] Training lasts about twelve weeks, and much of the course reviews boot camp material such as basic military subjects, weapons and marksmanship, close-order drill, and individual combat training.[8] Trainees also learn how to handle and motivate recruits, and they are pushed harder than basic trainees ever will be, so that they can serve as role models for their charges. In the Marines, for example, DI trainees are deliberately given too much to do so they skip meals, and it is normal for them to lose twenty pounds during Drill Instructor School.

During their two or three-year tours, DIs usually work 100 or more hours a week. They receive perks, like superior-performance pay and preferential consideration for their next duty station, and being a successful drill instructor helps in the promotions game. However the work is extremely stressful, not only because of the physical and mental challenges of the job but because today's DIs must walk a careful line between being tough and being abusive. DIs are not allowed to physically or verbally abuse recruits, and a mistake, no matter how well-intentioned, can cost a motivated lifer his or her career.

Today's DI is not the martinet of old. Experts have realized that, far from motivating recruits, the system of deliberate terrorization simply made them "want to jump the fence and quit," says one commander.[9] So the intimidation model is out, and positive motivation is in. But even in the old days, DIs were more than martinets. In his account of Navy basic training, author J. F. Leahy recounts a story he heard from John Hagan, Master Chief Petty Officer of the Navy (Ret.):

> On one occasion during an outbreak of spinal meningitis we were all given preventive medication daily to take after meals. When BM1 [RDC] Jones found several of the yellow pills on the head [latrine] floor he was enraged, and we all began to anticipate the rifle drills or other such punishment in store for us. Instead he made us all take a sheet of stationery and write a brief letter. Beginning "Dear Mom and Dad," he dictated a short note on the facts of the meningitis outbreak and the several deaths that had already occurred. His dictation noted that the Navy was conscientiously providing lifesaving medicine to us every day and concluded by informing them that we threw our medicine away instead of taking it as ordered. He had us conclude, "With love, your son" and sign our names. He then collected the letters and stamped the addressed envelopes. He apparently never mailed the letters, but nearly all our mothers received a strange letter we wrote later that night attempting to explain. No more discarded medicine was ever found on the deck.[10]

THE RECEPTION PHASE

The recruits take the bus to the training camp, but they are not at basic training yet, strictly speaking. The first week or so after arrival is taken up with processing paperwork, collecting equipment, and being introduced to military regulations and behavior. This pre-phase in basic training, which, to the chagrin of many recruits, does not count toward the weeks of official basic training, is called Recruit Receiving, Reception Battalion, Recruit Inprocessing, "P-Week," or Zero Week, depending on the branch of service. The recruits stay in a separate reception barracks before transferring to the barracks or dormitory that will be their home during their training. In every branch except the Marines, Reception isn't quite as exhausting as basic training, but it may be more frightening because it is here that the recruits realize there is no turning back; they cannot change their minds and go home.

As soon as they step off the bus, recruits get a quick lesson in military discipline. If they are typical teenagers, they will slouch down the bus stairs, drop their bags to the ground, whisper nervous jokes or comments to their neighbors, grin and look for approval in the eyes of their drill instructor, whom they have just met. This behavior will earn them an annoyed, high-volume harangue. They were told to hustle, the DI shouts. Were they told to put their bags on the ground? Then why are the bags on the ground? They were ordered to be quiet, to look straight ahead, to not giggle like idiots. What part of the instructions didn't they understand?

Depending on what time of day the recruits arrive at Reception, the DI might spend a few minutes or a few hours teaching them to stand at attention, eyes forward, chins and elbows in, knees not locked. It will be a long while before they really look like members of the military, so they may as well start right away. Over the next few days, they will practice standing at attention, learn how to salute and who to salute, and how to reply to an order. They will learn to shout out responses: "YES, Drill Sergeant Smith! NO, Drill Sergeant Smith!" They will learn to call everyone by their last names, even their best friends.

But in the first nerve-wracking hours of Reception, recruits forget their own names, turn left instead of right, and call their drill instructor by the wrong name or title (Each branch has a different custom. DIs are never addressed as "Sir" or "Ma'am" in the Army or Navy, but they are in the Air Force and the Marine Corps.) When DIs disgustedly call them the worst bunch of recruits they've ever seen, something they say to every class, it isn't hard for the hapless recruit to agree.

During Reception, recruits give up most of their civilian belongings. Clothes are put in a sealed envelope to be returned after graduation; socks and underwear are tossed out (in the Navy, civilian belongings are not stored; they are either mailed home or donated to charity). It is essential that recruits bring only the items that are on the list they have received. Contraband, which includes electronic devices, books other than religious ones, jewelry, food, gum, and tobacco, is confiscated permanently. The DIs inspect everyone's belongings, and personal items, even those that are not specifically prohibited, will be held up and ridiculed in front of the rest of the class.

There is another reason for packing as little as possible. When they arrive at Reception, recruits may be ordered to run with their luggage from the bus to a truck, sometimes several times in an apparently pointless exercise, and the recruit who travels light will be especially thankful. In any case, toilet articles and other personal items can be purchased later on in the post or base exchange. There are several items that survivors of basic training recommend bringing, for example, stamps, envelopes and paper, cotton swabs and balls for cleaning gear. It is a good idea for recruits to find out as much as they can before they leave about what they will need and what they are allowed to bring.

During the first full day of Reception, recruits are issued gear, which may include a Kevlar helmet, a ruck sack, a poncho, and a set of suspenders and belt known as an LBE or Load Bearing Equipment, on which hang a canteen, ammunition pouches, and other tools. Recruits are also issued clothing and uniform items, such as running shoes and sweat suits (called "smurf suits" in the Navy for their shapelessness and blue color), the camouflage shirts and pants known as Battle Dress Uniforms or BDUs (BDUs are being phased out in favor of a lighter, more comfortable desert uniform), combat boots, underwear and socks, T-shirts and shorts, towels, and a duffel bag to carry it all in. They are issued copies of the IET manual for their branch of service, ID cards, and the dog tags that they must wear throughout boot camp. Their records are reviewed one more time, and they are offered an amnesty or a "Moment of Truth," the chance to reveal anything that might affect their standing in the military. This is the last opportunity to tell the military about an undiscovered drug bust or a medical condition. The amnesty is brief and won't come again, and if a falsehood is later detected, the recruit will be heartily sorry.

Perhaps the most famous, or notorious, part of Reception is the military haircut. Male recruits pay eight or ten dollars to have the post barber crudely shave their hair off with an electric razor. Females may get a short haircut as well, although most cut their hair before basic training or keep it pulled back with clips at all times. In the Navy, women are required to have their hair cut by the barber.

The military haircut serves both a hygienic and a psychological purpose—it symbolizes the break between the old civilian and the new military individual more shockingly than anything else. When newly shaved recruits look around at their bald peers, they can't help but see themselves in a new way. For some, the transformation in personal appearance continues when they are fitted for shatterproof eyeglasses. Contact lenses and civilian eyewear are prohibited; the heavy black plastic military-issue "boot-camp glasses" are known as "birth control glasses" or BCGs for a reason.

Whether or not they are wearing BCGs, it is very unlikely that recruits of either gender will have any time or energy for romantic matters, even though they will be training with members of the opposite sex. All branches of the military except the Marine Corps have been training men and women together since at least the mid-1990s. This is a complex and controversial issue, and few people in the military have no opinion on the subject. On one hand, women now make up about 15 percent of the U.S. forces and are found in most job specialties and at all ranks; segregation in basic training tends to set a pattern for second-class status. As proponents of gender-integrated training like to say, the first time a male is under the command of a female should not be in a war zone. The sooner male recruits get used to working with female recruits, the sooner they will learn to deal with women as equals. Research also shows that women do better at PT in gender-integrated classes. Men tend to push each other to succeed in challenging physical tasks like obstacle courses, while women do not challenge each other as much, nor do they establish pecking orders based on physical prowess.

On the other hand, the differing physical standards for men and women have led some men to conclude that women don't "pull their own weight" in training, and thus perhaps are less likely to do so on the job. Resentment and suspicion does not disappear when men and women train together, and after the Army instituted integrated training in 1994, many men felt that unit cohesion, discipline, and esprit de corps suffered. In the mid-1990s, when drill instructors at the Army's Aberdeen Proving Ground were accused of sexually harassing and even raping female recruits, criticism of gender-integrated training grew louder. In 1998, a civilian panel appointed by the Pentagon recommended that there be some gender segregation in basic training, and Congress introduced a bill that required separate training for men and women. Army, Navy, and Air Force leaders, however, argued that integrated training worked well in almost all cases, and rejected calls for segregation. In time, the issue died down. The military expanded its corps of female drill instructors, women became a larger and more integral part of the armed forces, and many of the adjustments and initial discomfort of gender integration faded.

Recruits begin to get paid during Reception. That is, they fill out the paperwork to have their paychecks directly deposited in their bank accounts. If they do not have a bank account, they must open one. Military personnel are paid on the first and fifteenth of each month, but it can take up to two pay cycles before the processing is completed and recruits see new funds in their bank statements. Most recruits in basic training are at the lowest rank, E-1, and will receive base pay of almost $1,200 a month; married recruits will also receive a BAH (Basic Allowance for Housing), which is calculated according to where their families live. BAH can range from less than $600 if a recruit is from rural Oklahoma or Alabama to almost $2,000 in New York City. Recruits often find that at the end of their IET period, they will have accumulated quite a nest egg, because there are so few opportunities to spend money while in basic or advanced training.

In Reception, recruits are also given the opportunity to sign up for SGLI (Servicemembers' Group Life Insurance), the most inexpensive type of life insurance available to anyone. Most recruits take it, and they should; they can get $250,000 of life insurance for less than $17 a month. Recruits can also enroll in an automatic savings bond plan. Smart recruits will sign up for both programs; the military paycheck may seem huge to a young person fresh out of high school, but there are too many ways for it to disappear without a trace once they are out of IET. These elementary financial planning steps can go far in preventing heartache down the road.

An important part of Reception is the battery of physical tests and procedures recruits undergo. They get another medical exam, including pregnancy tests for women and blood typing. They also receive a series of immunizations, standing in line while a doctor or nurse shoots a dose into each recruit's arm and buttocks with a frightening steel injection gun.

Recruits have probably already received most of the immunizations at some point in their lives, but the military does not take chances. Sometimes recruits get a penicillin shot to help guard against bacterial infections that spread through the crowded barracks, finding vulnerable hosts in the physically and mentally exhausted recruits. Recruits also see a dentist, some of them for the first time in their lives.

At the end of Reception week, recruits take their first fitness test, consisting of running, sit-ups, and push-ups. In the Marines, the IST (Initial Strength Test), which is given on the first day, also includes pull-ups. In all branches, the test is relatively easy, compared to the physical standards required by the end of basic training. In the Army, for example, men must run a 9-minute mile, do 25 sit-ups and 13 push-ups, and women must do one pushup. In the Marines, men must do two dead-hang pull-ups, 44 crunches in 2 minutes and run 1.5 miles in 13.5 minutes. Recruits who fail the test or are overweight are sent to a special physical fitness unit where they train until they can pass the test. There are several nicknames for this "remedial" unit, all of them humiliating, and recruits should do whatever they can before they arrive to avoid the experience.

During Reception week, the recruits are frightened and stressed. Many recruits remember Reception as harder than basic training itself, simply because of the uncertainty, fear, and loneliness. Families are especially likely to receive desperate letters written during this phase. Recruits may have small pockets of time to themselves, and during Reception they spend a lot of time waiting in lines, so in one sense they won't be working as hard as they will be later on. But the boredom and anxiety can be as deadly as hours of marching in the rain.

BASIC TRAINING

Basic training is generally conducted in several phases. Sometimes the phases are clearly delineated; the Army has three phases, and a colored flag may fly over the camp to indicate what phase the trainees are in. Sometimes the transition from one phase to another is unannounced, and the recruits don't notice the changes immediately. But it is helpful for trainees to keep in mind, especially at the beginning of training, that boot camp will not always be as tough as it is at first.

The initial phase, lasting anywhere from two to seven weeks, is without doubt the harshest. It may be called "Total Control," "Lockdown," "Basic Learning," or "Red Phase." During these terrible weeks, recruits are broken down physically and mentally, pushed harder than they ever believed possible, and controlled every minute of the day. DIs single out recruits who reveal signs of weakness and go to work on them. During the first phase, recruits can do nothing right. They are berated and punished for everything, no matter how hard they try. PT is not as rigorous as it is in later phases, but most recruits are yet not in top physical shape, so they wake up every morning exhausted and in pain. Dropout rates are high during the first phase, but recruits who survive are likely to finish boot camp successfully.

The second phase includes instruction in basic military topics. Much of this instruction takes place in the classroom, but it is not exactly a break from strenuous PT. Chronic exhaustion and boring lectures make it extremely hard for trainees to stay awake, and recruits who engage in "neck PT"—allowing their heads to fall forward or back as they struggle to stay awake—will be invited by their DIs to stand in the back of the room with their arms outstretched. Weapons and equipment training is also part of the second phase.

If there is a third phase, it generally involves long marches and field training. Recruits, who now resemble real soldiers, sailors, airmen, or Marines, are treated with somewhat more respect, although they still must maintain strict discipline with their DIs. In all the branches, there is a several-days long capstone type experience at the end of basic training, where trainees test their skills under simulated battlefield conditions.

The days of basic training are full, and there is no unscheduled time. The general routine begins with a blaring reveille wake-up at 4 or 5 in the morning, running and calisthenics before breakfast, cleaning and inspection of the barracks, classroom instruction before or after lunch, marching and drill instruction, more physical training, dinner, cleaning, study and preparation for the following day, and lights out. There is little time for homesickness or the interests of premilitary life, and no television, radio, or Internet. The highlight of the day is mail call, and trainees look forward to getting letters. Anyone who writes letters to a friend or relative in basic training will earn everlasting gratitude.

This routine is followed in all the services. Some of the skills taught in the Air Force and Navy are different, obviously, than those taught in Army or Marine Corps basic training. Navy recruits practice firefighting, an important skill for all sailors on a ship under attack. Army and Marine Corps trainees spend a lot of time learning infantry skills such as how to use a claymore mine and hand grenades, and how to dig foxholes and go on patrol. There are also important common skills among all the branches, including map reading or navigation, basic first aid skills, and instruction and practice in communicating over the radio. Instruction, whether in the field or in the classroom, is at the most basic level, and for many recruits, one of the more challenging aspects of basic training, and, for that matter, much of military life, is learning to tolerate boredom.

In all services, basic trainees learn how to use a rifle. Usually, recruits receive their rifles—the Colt M16-A2—within the first few weeks of training. The first thing they learn is that the M16 is a rifle, not a gun, and they are encouraged to name their weapons, because "the rifle will be your best friend." During the first lessons of BRM (Basic Rifle Marksmanship), recruits learn to disassemble and reassemble their rifles and to clean them thoroughly. During inspections the insides of the rifles are wiped with cotton swabs to see if they are clean. The recruits then practice long-established principles for holding and aiming the rifle. Only after several weeks do they go to the rifle range to begin practicing with live rounds. As the weeks continue, recruits practice more advanced techniques, like firing at night or with artificial illumination, or using the weapon in urban areas. At the end of marksmanship training, recruits will qualify as marksmen, sharpshooters, or experts, depending on their proficiency with the M16.

The "gas chamber," another infamous experience of basic training, usually occurs around the fifth week. In this exercise, recruits spend a few minutes in a closed room filled with CS ("tear") gas. After several hours of instruction in NBC (Nuclear, Biological, and Chemical) warfare, small groups of recruits enter the chamber, usually a small, low building in an isolated area. Often they are deliberately brought to the chamber just in time to see another group of recruits staggering out, mucus streaming from their eyes, noses, and mouths.

When it is their turn, the recruits enter the chamber wearing gas masks. The DI accompanies them, also wearing a mask. The lights may go out, and CS gas begins seeping out of a canister. The gas reacts to moisture on the body, so recruits who are perspiring will feel it tingle or burn their skin. They move about the room for a few minutes, inhaling through their masks, then the DI orders them to remove their masks. As the gas interacts with the mucus membranes and the recruits struggle to breathe, the DI orders them to repeat their ID numbers, then leave the chamber.[11] According to most who have been through it, the best way to survive the gas chamber without vomiting is to take a deep breath and close the eyes before removing the mask, then, keeping the eyes shut if possible, hold the breath or take shallow breaths.[12] The CS gas is painful although not really debilitating, but the disorientation of the dark chamber and seeing other recruits struggle and panic is an unforgettable experience.

The PT element of basic training is what tends to worry new recruits the most, and it is certainly challenging. Recruits who have been involved in high school sports may have an advantage, but for those who have not been active in sports, the physical discipline is probably new. In recent years PT has gotten more demanding; responding to concerns that training had become too lax, the DoD in the late 1990s ordered the services to toughen up the standards. "I have been rather surprised to find that I perhaps can do more of the physical activity than some of the recruits—even at my advanced age," Defense Secretary William Cohen commented in 1998. "I think that does not bode well for those young people."[13]

PT varies slightly from service to service. In all cases, however, it does not require fancy equipment but is based on old-fashioned calisthenics. All services require pushups, sit ups, and running, and usually other exercises. Every day, trainees may do some variation of the "dirty dozen," a set of exercises that includes jumping jacks, crunches, push ups, flutter kicks, and other drills.

Obstacle courses, today more commonly known as "confidence courses," are another part of physical training. The courses are made up of a dozen or so exercises like climbing ropes, scaling walls, and crawling through tunnels. Confidence courses often include "high" obstacles like the "slide for life," where trainees climb a tower then slide down a rope over a pool. These are designed to help them conquer their fear of heights. Recruits tackle the confidence courses in groups, competing with other groups, and the exercise builds teamwork and self-confidence. For many trainees, obstacle courses are a highlight of basic training, and DIs try to make time for their charges to go through the course more than once.

The most fundamental type of military PT is cardiovascular exercise, mostly road marches and running. Trainees run and march every day, and as the weeks of training go on, the marches and runs get longer and the pace quickens. Today, trainees wear running shoes to prevent injury, but toward the end of training they will complete long marches in their boots, which can be an uncomfortable experience. Swimming is another skill that most servicemembers learn in basic training, if they have not done so already. They must pass a basic swimming test, and in some branches, they must also jump off a diving platform.

Recruits do much more PT than a glance at an official schedule might indicate. DIs use running and calisthenics as punishment for real or imagined infractions. Rare is the trainee who has never been "smoked" or made to do pushups or other exercises as punishment. Units and teams get "smoked" for the mistakes of one member, so it is virtually impossible to avoid the experience.

Most trainees come through the PT element of basic training more successfully than they ever imagined, and emerge in excellent physical condition. The intense levels of physical activity, however, put trainees at risk for injury and illness. Studies estimate that as many as 25 percent of male and 50 percent of female trainees are injured during basic training.[14] The most common injuries include ankle sprains, stress fractures, and torn ligaments, and the most common illnesses are respiratory problems like bronchitis. Another concern, especially in the summer months, is illness from dehydration and heat stroke, and DIs order their trainees to drink canteens of water at regular intervals.

Trainees who are sick or injured may go to a clinic for treatment. Most problems are not serious, but for more severe injuries or illness, recruits may lose time in training. If they are out for too long, they may be "recycled," or forced to repeat sections of training, something no recruit wants to do. In the case of extremely serious injuries, trainees may be sent to a special physical therapy clinic to recuperate until they are ready to return to camp.

In recent years there has been some controversy over the Army's PRTP (Physical Therapy Rehabilitation Program). Until 1998, Army trainees who were seriously injured were given the choice of PTRP or discharge. Most chose discharge, so in 1998 the Army changed the rules to require injured trainees to go to PTRP. Since then, trainees have made numerous allegations of abuse and poor medical care at the PTRP. They say that PTRP is like a never-ending basic training, where they are belittled and controlled for up to a year or more, and not given the chance to recover from their injuries. In March 2006, an Army private died in PTRP after a 13-month stay. Many critics assert that he should have been discharged after months of harsh treatment in the program.[15]

The PTRP death was unusual but not unprecedented. Basic training causes a small number of deaths each year. Precise statistics are hard to come by, but one study of Air Force basic training shows that between 1956 and 1996, 85 trainee deaths occurred at Lackland Air Force Base. Most were from illnesses such as cardiac arrest, infections, and heat stroke. Eleven of the deaths were suicide. Although basic training deaths are shocking and tragic, they are much less common, statistically speaking, than deaths of civilians of the same age,[16] and the armed forces have implemented a number of changes in response to trainee deaths that have reduced them further.

Not all of boot camp training is physical or combat related. Recruits also learn to fold their clothes and arrange their personal belongings according to strict military standards; they spend endless boring hours on guard duty or doing chores like KP (Kitchen Patrol); they learn to present a military appearance at all times. Recruits spend most of their free time polishing boots and cleaning their gear, and memorizing information they have been taught in the classroom. Their appearance and equipment is inspected constantly, and one tiny error will bring grief upon the careless recruit, often for days or weeks, as the DI harasses the offender at every possible moment.

One of the most important parts of basic training in all the branches is learning to work as a team. In the Army, trainees are assigned "Battle Buddies," partners who work together through the weeks of camp. "Battles," as they are called, help one another prepare for inspections, get through PT exercises, and deal with moments of despair. DIs often pair Battles who are very different from one another—a recruit from a large city will be paired with a recruit from a small town in a different part of the country, for example. The obvious point of this is to get recruits accustomed to working with people of different backgrounds, as they will have to do throughout their military service. A more subtle aspect of the buddy system is the punishment that is meted out to both buddies if one makes a mistake. The important lesson is that the recruit is not an "Army of One," but a member of a team, and a mistake of one is a mistake of all. Every service incorporates buddy systems or teams in its training, and recruits learn quickly that they are responsible not just for themselves but for other members of the team. A team that is "smoked" because of the carelessness of one member will not let that member make the same mistake again. Much of the "core values" training centers on examples of successful teamwork and self-sacrifice in combat. The sense of responsibility, of not wanting to let the others down, is a fundamental aspect of training, and it is one of the indelible experiences of soldiers in combat (see Chapter 9).

THE CAPSTONE EXPERIENCE AND GRADUATION

In the past fifteen years or so, every service has incorporated an extended field exercise in basic training, to pull together all the skills and information the trainees have learned in the previous weeks. Before undergoing the exercise, recruits learn about real examples of soldiers, sailors, airmen, and Marines who reacted heroically in crisis situations, part of the core values training and a way of inspiring them with models of behavior. The capstone exercise is designed to be as realistic as possible, similar to emergencies the recruits might experience while on active duty. In the Navy, for example, the set of exercises, called Battle Stations, requires recruits to respond to an attack on a ship or barracks, a fire, an emergency on board a ship, a man overboard, and other scenarios. Recruits are divided into teams and are tested on their responses. If they do not respond appropriately, they get a strike, and if they receive three strikes, they fail the exercise and must repeat several weeks of training before they take the test again.[17] In the Marines, the final exercise is the famous Crucible, a 54-hour endurance course with 32 combat exercises and 40 miles of hiking. One of the main goals of the Crucible is to emphasize the importance of teamwork. Before the exercise begins, trainees get 2.5 MREs, which they have to split with a buddy.[18] Trainees get little sleep during the Crucible, and the exercises become increasingly challenging, but they must work with their teams to complete them.[19] The Army capstone experience is a five-day field exercise and march during which recruits respond to simulated attacks in urban and wilderness environments. In the Air Force, trainees go through "Warrior Week," which includes target practice, a gas chamber experience, and a field exercise similar to those of the ground forces. After trainees finish the field exercise successfully, they get ready for graduation. The DIs ease up on them somewhat, and they may have more free time. They are still in boot camp, but the final week begins their transition to life in the active duty or reserve forces.

Graduation from basic training has become a major event for recruits and their families. Ceremonies can last several days, and most recruits look forward to seeing family members and friends at the festivities. The ceremonies generally begin with an evening retreat. All the units of the basic training class march in formation to the parade ground, and stand at attention during the lowering of the flag. Families and friends watch from bleachers as the men and women in formation demonstrate their new military professionalism. After the ceremony, families can visit with the recruits if they can locate them in the crowds, but the visit is short because the recruits must be back in their barracks before curfew.

The graduation ceremony takes place on the following day, and includes a parade and speeches by the commanders of the training camp. Afterwards, families are allowed to tour the barracks and spend the rest of the day with the graduates. Depending on the service, trainees may also earn passes with which they can leave the base and visit the nearby town or city.

Parents will find that their sons and daughters have changed beyond belief. Not only are they in the best physical shape of their lives, but they also exude self-confidence and pride in their accomplishments. They walk smartly, dress with military precision, and show a new maturity that their families probably have never seen in them. The former late riser with the messy room has been transformed into a professional warrior. Graduates pepper their conversations with military acronyms and call their friends by their last names. They also tend eat ravenously for the first few weeks after graduation—they crave everything that they have been denied for the past few months.

ADVANCED TRAINING

Everyone goes through more or less the same experience in boot camp, but after that, training varies immensely, depending on the job specialty a trainee has chosen. In the Army, the second phase of training is called AIT (Advanced Individual Training); in the Navy it is called initial skill training or "A school"; in the Air Force, Tech School. In the Marines, non-infantry graduates of basic training take an additional two-week Marine Combat Training Course before they go on to advanced training in their MOS.

Usually advanced training for job specialties takes place immediately after boot camp, but sometimes, especially for trainees joining the Reserves or National Guard, training can take place weeks or even months after basic training. Depending on the course, basic training graduates either stay at the base where they trained or move somewhere else. In the Army, soldiers in combat arms branches will complete basic training and AIT at the same time, in what is called OSUT (One Station Unit Training), but most branches require trainees to move to another base.

Advanced training is less regimented and stressful than basic training, but the standards and expectations of basic training continue to rule. During the weeks or months of AIT, trainees advance through a series of phases, during which they receive privileges and increasing freedom. Phase One is very much like basic training, in which trainees are restricted to the base and required to maintain their living spaces according to regulations. By Phase Three, they are allowed to drink alcohol off-duty, leave the base and keep personal items in their rooms. In advanced training, trainees must pass PT tests, but the intense PT of boot camp is no longer required for most courses (combat MOS training is an exception).

Instruction in advanced training occurs partly in the field during exercises, drills and hands-on practice. It is, however, depending on the job, largely conducted in the classroom, although in the combat arms branches most instruction takes place in the field. The training in the more technologically complex job specialties can resemble intensive college courses. The length of advanced training depends on the job specialty. Some specialties, such as the Navy Aviation Structural Mechanic—Hydraulics (AM) or the Army Shower/Laundry and Clothing Repair Specialists (92S), require only five and six weeks of training, respectively. On the other extreme, Army Radiology Specialists (91P) go through forty-six weeks of training.

At some point during or after advanced training, most recruits receive promotions from E-1 to E-2. Some even get promoted to E-3, if they have college credits or other qualifications; accelerated promotions are written in the recruit's enlistment contract. Promotion brings higher basic pay and BAH, and the recruit is no longer the lowest person on the totem pole. After advanced training, most recruits go on to their first assignment. They are no longer recruits or trainees, but soldiers, sailors, airmen, and Marines.

TRAINING FOR THE SPECIAL OPERATIONS FORCES

Among the many job specialties in the U.S. armed forces, SOF (Special Operations Forces) merit a special mention. These are small groups of elite, highly trained warriors who tackle the military's toughest challenges, and they are especially important in current conflicts. SOFs are experts in both "direct action," or combat, and "indirect action" such as advising foreign security forces, reconnaissance, or psychological operations and civilian affairs activities, "winning the hearts and minds" of the civilian population. They include the Army Rangers, Special Forces (Green Berets), and Airborne units, the Navy SEALS, Marine Force Reconnaissance, Air Force and Coast Guard Special Operations units, and Delta Force, a counterterrorism unit that recruits its personnel from all the branches of service. Normally the SOFs remain in the chain of command of their branch of service. During wartime, however, they are placed under the command of the U.S. SOCOM (Special Operations Command) so that they can conduct joint operations.

Altogether there are about 55,000 servicemembers in SOFs. They have been crucial in the Philippines where they have helped fight the Islamist group Abu Sayyef, and they have participated in missions in Southeast Asia, South America, and Africa. The majority of SOFs today, however, are operating in Iraq and Afghanistan, and some critics say that the emphasis on "direct action" in the war zone draws SOFs away from other parts of the world where their "indirect action" skills are urgently needed.

Even though they are vital to contemporary security efforts, the number of SOFs cannot grow quickly or easily. Every member of a special operations unit is a survivor of the most rigorous training in the U.S. military. Today some SOFs will accept candidates directly from civilian life, a change from earlier decades when candidates had to serve several years in the regular forces before applying for special operations training. The reason for the change, military leaders say, is because the applicant pool within the services has shrunk at the same time that the SOFs are more integral to military operations.

Acceptance as a candidate for a special operations school and making it through the many months of training are two different things. Candidates, all of whom are male, must have superior test scores and physical fitness and clean records. Some SOFs recruit only from combat branches, while others will accept candidates from all job specialties. Servicemembers or recruits interested in going to one of the special operations schools must pass a series of challenging tests before they are even accepted into training. The selection and training process for the Army's Special Forces is a good example of the rigor of the SOFs. The primary mission of the Special Forces is to train and work with allied military forces and civilians, so they are trained not only in combat but in language and culture as well. Candidates take a 30-day preparation course to get ready for the SFAS (Special Forces Assessment and Selection) course, the test course for the real thing. Only those who pass the SFAS will be allowed to enroll in the Special Forces Qualification Course (Q-course). The minority of candidates who make it through the Q-course then go to language school for study of language and culture, so intense that when they are finished they can blend into the society in which they are working.

Most of the other SOFs are trained as commando units, able to perform special missions on the ground, in the air, or in the water. All SOFs go through months of training that is unimaginably grueling. The Army Rangers, for example, endure a 65-day course that occurs in four phases. The first phase includes two weeks of very intense basic military and physical skills at Fort Benning. The next three phases, desert warfare, mountain warfare, and jungle warfare, increase in intensity as the days go by. During Ranger training, candidates do not get enough to eat and they usually lose twenty or more pounds. They are allowed only about four hours of sleep a night, so during the final two weeks, it is common for candidates to hallucinate and suffer from paranoid delusions. Only about one-third of the candidates who began Ranger School will finish, and when they graduate, they will be in the worst physical shape of their lives. Most Rangers need at least several months to recover from training. The privations of Ranger School are similar to those of other SOF training as well.

SOFs learn a wide variety of special skills. Airborne School trains personnel in parachuting from aircraft, especially in the risky HALO (High-Altitude, Low Opening) technique used by paratroopers. SERE (Survival, Evasion, Resistance, and Escape) school teaches those tactics to SOF personnel who are inserted behind enemy lines in small teams. SOFs may learn BUD/S (Basic Underwater Demolition/Swimmer) or Combat Diving skills, become Combat Medics, train as Mountain Warfare experts, or go to Sniper School to master the famous "double-tap" sniping technique.

There are too many specialized courses and schools available to the special operations forces to list, but whatever the combination of skills an individual servicemember accumulates, he will be one of the most highly trained military experts in the world.

CHAPTER 3

OFFICERS

When scholars and experts talk about the military as a "profession," they are usually referring to the officer corps. The idea of military officers as professionals, with specialized training and skills similar to those of physicians, lawyers, and college professors, has developed since the late nineteenth century. Today, a profusion of officer training colleges and courses tries to give officers the theoretical knowledge to assume command in an extremely complex organization. In addition, every officer in the U.S. armed forces is a college graduate, and to advance beyond the rank of O-3 (captain or, in the Navy, first lieutenant), officers generally must complete some postgraduate education.

Officers not only receive leadership training and civilian higher education, but they also specialize in a particular branch of their service. Throughout their careers, officers in all branches can expect to be assigned to both staff and command positions. Staff officers are the administrators of the armed forces, while commanders lead units, ranging in size from squad or platoon to Field Army, Fleet, or Major Command. Today, most officers must have experience in both administration and command in order to get promoted to the highest ranks.

Officers are accorded privileges of rank: enlisted personnel and junior officers salute superior officers; officers receive higher pay than enlisted personnel and live in separate housing areas, which are themselves divided between lower-ranking and higher-ranking officers.

The differences between officers and enlisted go beyond training and perks, however. The officer corps has distinct customs, culture, and traditions, and officers tend to embrace a different, more intense identification with the military than the enlisted personnel they command. Career officers, especially those who have trained at one of the service academies, often identify strongly with the values and traditions of the institution. This does not mean that career enlisted personnel don't feel this way as well, but part of the training and socialization of officers involves a sense of becoming part of the history of the military.

LEADERSHIP AND CONDUCT

Officers are, above all, leaders.[1] They issue instructions, orders and policy; even more, the morale, discipline, and atmosphere of a unit is set by its commanders, from the new squad or platoon leader to the head of the JCS. Officers at the highest levels may seem to be invisible to the men and women of the ranks, but virtually all aspects of work and life on a military base are controlled by officers in command. In a very real sense, officers are fundamentally personnel managers. Military leadership is much more than personnel management, however. Good officers, like good personnel managers, develop the knack of placing their subordinates in roles most suited to their skills, but military officers, unlike civilian managers, must be prepared to lead their troops into battle or command them as they undertake life-threatening missions.

Leading men and women into dangerous and chaotic situations where they face injury or death, and where they must kill if necessary, is not easy. Some portrayals of the military emphasize the coercive element, that is, the notion that troops follow their leaders into battle because they are drilled or brainwashed into it. In fact a great deal of battlefield victory comes from successful motivation, rather than coercion. Soldiers are led into battle, not forced into it. Not surprisingly, a great deal of emphasis in training officers is on leadership, and much of officer culture centers on the idea that officers should be inspirational leaders.

There are several principles of military leadership that all officers learn by heart. The most fundamental element of military leadership is looking after the troops. Officers are taught that the troops come first, always. Whether in training in the field, traveling from a base to a deployment area, or in a combat situation, officers are supposed to make sure their troops are safe, housed and fed before they themselves are. Another principle closely related to looking out for the troops is providing a good example. Officers are taught to lead by example and are not supposed to expect more of their troops than they do of themselves. The example an officer sets will influence his or her subordinates all the way down the ranks.

A third fundamental principle of leadership is professional competence. Officers are expected to have the answers to problems, not pass the buck to someone else. The Marines like to say, "You can't snow the troops,"[2] meaning that an officer who tries to bluster and pretend will be spotted immediately. Subordinates look to their commanders to solve problems and provide answers. Officers will not necessarily have the best answers, but they must have a solution that is at least adequate, and much of officer training is intended to accustom officers to make quick decisions under intense pressure.

An important aspect of military leadership that is related to competence is command presence, that is, the sense of leadership and maturity an officer projects. Command presence is a part of the culture as well as the formal training of officers. Officers are expected to behave like leaders, and to know exactly where they stand in the military hierarchy. They must not be overly familiar with their subordinates or their superior officers, nor are they to display indecisiveness or cynicism. On the other hand, they should not be too enamored with spit-and-polish formality either, a sure sign of insecurity. The troops will subtly target any officer who shows symptoms of this failing. One common method of bringing an officer down to earth is for groups of troops to walk in a single line when approaching the officer, forcing him or her to salute each individual soldier separately. The resulting foolishness often teaches the officer to take him or herself a little less seriously. Officers should not be oppressive martinets, but should project self-assurance and military bearing, inspiring confidence in the troops.

The most fundamental concept linking all these elements of military leadership is responsibility.[3] Officers in charge of units are responsible for their troops, period. A newly commissioned O-1 in command of a platoon is accountable for everything that happens to that platoon. The captain of a naval vessel is responsible for the ship and everyone on it. Not only are officers in charge of the conduct and training of their troops while on duty, but they are responsible for what happens off duty as well. Civilians might be surprised at how many issues and problems fall under a commander's purview. When a soldier has family trouble—a messy divorce, a child custody fight, a child with special needs or a rebellious teenager—his or her commanding officer is involved. Officers counsel their troops not only on work-related matters but also on personal issues such as marital problems, personal finance, and health care. If a servicemember gets in trouble with the law, or has a problem with substance abuse or domestic violence, his or her officer is notified immediately.

Officers are also expected to keep their own personal lives in order. Officers whose spouses or children cause problems in a military community can find their careers cut short. Husbands of female officers may have fewer expectations levied upon them, but officers' wives, especially those of unit commanders, have numerous social obligations toward enlisted and junior officers' spouses. This tradition is sometimes resented by wives who feel the burden of being an unpaid appendage to their husband's careers, but it is a hard habit to break. The practice of commenting on a wife's behavior in the annual OER (Officer Evaluation Report) has officially ended; until fairly recently, however, it was normal for an evaluator to discuss a wife's ability to carry out social duties and participate in unit activities. Wives continue to feel pressure to conform to traditional expectations so that their husbands' careers are not imperiled. Officers are prohibited from fraternizing with enlisted personnel, and an officer who carries on a romantic relationship with an enlisted person or even subordinate officer is likely to face disciplinary measures.

Does this mean that all officers in the armed forces behave impeccably as officers and gentlemen, according to cliché? Of course not. Officers, like enlisted personnel, are overwhelmingly younger men, and face the same maturity issues of young men everywhere. Officer culture is by no means immune from corruption and hypocrisy. The notorious Tailhook scandal of 1991, when drunken male officers at a Navy pilots' convention harassed and abused women, including their fellow female officers, is an example of officer culture degenerating into foolish machismo.[4]

Moreover, the immense responsibility placed on officers can lead to individuals abusing their power for personal gain. A notorious corruption scandal among Army commissioned and noncommissioned officers occurred in the late 1960s, when investigators discovered a well-organized system of extortion and theft among managers of servicemen's clubs. The scandal was unusual in its scale and was certainly a symptom of the disintegration of the Army at the time, but it was not unique. Since then there have been other instances of officers court-martialed and convicted of crimes like embezzlement, bribery, and fraud.

Misuse of power in a combat situation can result in the most tragic consequences, such as the notorious My Lai Massacre. On March 16, 1968, a company of soldiers on a "search and destroy" mission entered the South Vietnamese village of My Lai 4, a suspected insurgent stronghold. Under the instigation of their company commander, Captain Ernest Medina, and platoon leader Lieutenant William Calley, the men of Charlie Company killed as many as 504 unarmed villagers, shooting them as they cowered in fear. Afterwards, commanders and staff officers in the brigade tried to cover up the incident, but by November 1969 the American media had learned of the story and reported it. In March 1970, more than a dozen officers were accused of participating in the cover-up, while Medina, Calley and other officers were court-martialed for their roles in the atrocity. Medina, who argued that he did not know what his men were doing, was acquitted; Calley was sentenced to life in prison, but his sentence was later thrown out. All other charges were later dropped.[5]

Against this grim record of abuse and conspiracy, however, stands the story of Warrant Officer Hugh Thompson, an Army pilot who flew over the scene at My Lai on that terrible day. Witnessing officers and soldiers firing at wounded villagers, Thompson landed his aircraft, turned his weapons on the soldiers of Charlie Company, and threatened to shoot anyone who continued the massacre. He then organized an evacuation of wounded villagers and reported the atrocity to his superiors.[6] For years, Thompson's heroic actions went unheralded, but in 1998 he and two of his men were awarded the Soldier's Medal, the Army's highest award for noncombat bravery. Lieutenant Calley and Warrant Officer Thompson represent both the worst and the best of officer culture and ethics.

BECOMING AN OFFICER

In the simplest sense, a man or woman becomes an officer by receiving a commission from the government. At the commissioning ceremony, a higher-ranking officer and sometimes a civilian will say a few words about the honor and responsibility that comes with the position, and family members will pin the badges of rank on the new officer. A tradition at some commissioning ceremonies is that the newly commissioned officer gives a silver dollar to the first enlisted person who salutes him or her, a custom derived from the British military. In the old days of the Royal Army and Navy, officers had enlisted men as servants and advisers; they earned a dollar for the job, and the silver dollar tradition is a useful reminder of the reciprocal relationship between officers and their troops.[7]

A young man or woman can become eligible to receive a commission in the U.S. armed forces in three ways: first, by attending one of the military academies; second, by completing an ROTC (Reserve Officers' Training Camp) program at a civilian college or university; and third, by attending an officer candidate training course either directly after completing boot camp or after serving some time in the enlisted ranks. The academies provide about 10 percent of the officer corps, while ROTC accounts for 40 percent, and officer training courses for 35 percent. In addition, the professional branches of the services—the JAG (Judge Advocate General), the Chaplain Corps, and the Medical Corps—provide about 15 percent of the officer corps, offering training programs through which lawyers, chaplains, and physicians can receive commissions directly.

Service Academies

Many military officers receive their undergraduate education at one of the service academies: the USMA (U.S. Military Academy) in West Point, New York; the U.S. Naval Academy in Annapolis, Maryland; the U.S. Air Force Academy in Boulder, Colorado; or the U.S. Coast Guard Academy in New London, Connecticut. These four-year colleges accept high-school seniors, and the application process is much like applying to any college. Applicants submit SATs, transcripts, letters from teachers and guidance counselors, essays, and other materials. The service academies also require students to submit a letter of nomination from their congressional representative. This obligation is a throwback to when admission to a military academy was based more heavily on social status and personal connections than it is today.[8] The academies are among the most competitive schools in the country to get into, with admission rates of only 10 or 15 percent.

Once a high school senior is admitted into a service academy and decides to attend, his or her experience begins to diverge dramatically from that of students at civilian colleges. For one thing, students do not pay tuition to go to a service academy; instead, they receive a free education in return for five years of military service. And they aren't called students. They are known as cadets or midshipmen, and right from the start they are trained according to the most rigorous military standards.

Academy life starts immediately after high school graduation, in summer camps designed to introduce cadets to military life. At the Air Force Academy, Basic Cadet Training lasts five weeks, while at the Naval Academy, Plebe Summer lasts seven weeks; the six-week USMA program is known officially as New Cadet Barracks but called "Beast Barracks" or "The Beast" by everyone who has survived it. Summer cadet training is similar to basic training for enlisted personnel in its physical and psychological demands. Cadets undergo rigorous PT, learn to obey orders, and begin to strip away their old personalities. As in boot camp, the "stress factor" is a major element of the programs. A quarter or more of the cadets do not make it through the first summer, even though the academies always try to select young men and women who can cope not only with the rigors of the academy but also with the responsibilities of a commissioned officer.[9] By the time cadets and midshipmen begin their official first year at the academy, they have been socialized into the values and standards of the military.

The first academic year for cadets is certainly the hardest. First-year cadets or midshipmen, known as plebes, are at the bottom of the academy pecking order, and they undergo a year of what most civilians would consider an outrageous level of hazing and harassment. The violent hazing of the 1950s and early 1960s has been abolished, but plebes must obey orders from upperclassmen, which include everything from doing personal chores to rounds of pushups and worse. Upperclassmen corner plebes in the hallways and quiz them on rules and regulations or historical trivia. In the dining halls, plebes are subject to the famous "square meal," in which they must move their forks in a 90-degree angle from plate to mouth between each bite.

Every moment of the day is scheduled and regulated. The academic schedule is punishing, and cadets must participate in varsity sports throughout their years at the academy as well. There are hours of military drill and training, and additional hours of unavoidable punishment. The schedule is deliberately overstuffed so that cadets learn to accomplish tasks as quickly and efficiently as possible; the idea is that they are subjected to levels of stress similar to those of leading troops into combat. While in time the pressures ease up and privileges increase, a four-year education at a military academy is nothing like a civilian college experience, to put it mildly.[10]

During their final year, cadets choose the arms branch in which they will receive further training. It is a process fraught with anxiety. As they decide on a branch, cadets are making choices about their future military careers. Many prefer the combat branches, because traditionally the highest-ranking general officers have ascended through the ranks as combat specialists. An officer in a combat branch is more likely to command a unit or a vessel in wartime, an important advantage in the competition for promotions. Other cadets may choose branches that are useful in a civilian career, such as finance or logistics. After they submit their choices, their records are weighed against the needs of the service. Not everyone will be assigned to his or her first choice, and it is a hard blow to receive a second, or worse, third choice. When they have received their branches, they then find out where their first assignments will be. After graduation, they may be sent overseas, or to a base near home.

Although the program at the military academies is admirable in many ways, it has its critics. For example, historian Martin van Creveld notes that selection of officer candidates is made when students apply to the service academies, before they have had any official contact with military life or demonstrated aptitude for military leadership. The only officer candidates with any military background are prior-service personnel enrolled in officer training courses. Thus, the development of America's military officer corps depends, in large part, on the predilections of 18-year-old high school seniors.[11]

Other military experts have observed that the emphasis on "getting the job done," ubiquitous in the pressure-cooker atmosphere in the academies, is diametrically opposed to the traditional goals of higher education: encouraging critical thinking, establishing the habit of reflection, and considering diversity of opinion.[12] Many critics in and out of the military say that what military leaders need are more of these skills, not more PT. The academies' emphasis on completing tasks only because they must be done neglects the development of self-initiative. Cadets and midshipmen hardly have time to finish the work assigned to them, never mind learning something new because they want to. As a result, some say, the education at the academy is somewhat less than it appears; cadets are highly disciplined, but not intellectually mature.

In recent years the academies have been trying to bridge the gap between the norms of professional military training and those of civilian-style higher learning. Recognizing that effective officers will need political, social, and cultural savvy in addition to their military expertise, the academies have been revising their curricula and bolstering their social science and humanities programs. The curriculum at the USMA, for example, revised in 2004, "affords cadets a broad liberal education designed to develop versatile, creative, and critical thinkers who can adapt to the professional and ethical challenges that will confront them throughout their careers," according to a vision statement.[13] But the fact remains that military academies train cadets and midshipmen for the rigors of military service. The methods and outlook of the academies cannot help but be somewhat different from those of civilian universities.

Reserve Officers' Training Camp

ROTC is an elective program of classes and military training for students attending civilian colleges and universities. Upon successful completion of the program, students receive commissions as officers. Students enrolled in an ROTC program live in the dorms and take classes like their peers, and they sign up for ROTC as an additional activity. Not all colleges and universities host the program, but students at a school that does not offer ROTC can sign up at a program at a nearby institution.

In the classroom, ROTC students are introduced to the customs and traditions of their branch of service, and they study the principles of military operations, tactics, weapons, logistics, leadership, and the role of an officer. The first two years of ROTC are introductory and do not require any commitment from the student. During the summer before their junior year, ROTC students attend a summer basic training course similar to enlisted basic training. Students continuing on with ROTC in their final two years of college commit to serve as commissioned officers, usually active duty, occasionally in the reserve forces. Most, but not all, students in the Advanced Course, as the final two years are called, receive scholarships and stipends. They also attend an advanced training camp in the summer between their junior and senior years. As in the service academies, the students in an ROTC program are organized into units similar to those in the armed forces, and ROTC students use military ranks within their units as a method of leadership training.

Officer Candidate School

The final way to become an officer is to advance from the enlisted ranks. Enlisted personnel who wish to become officers go through a program called OCS (Officer Candidate School), or OTS (Officer Training School) in the Air Force. OCS/OTS lasts for several months and is extremely difficult. Admission is very competitive; fewer than 20 percent of applicants are accepted. Candidates for OCS/OTS must have excellent military records and four-year college degrees. Civilian college graduates who would like to be commissioned officers can enlist, then after basic training go directly to OCS/OTS, but this must be negotiated with the recruiter beforehand and should be part of the service contract. Recruits who do not make it through OCS/OTS must serve their terms as enlisted servicemembers.

There are also schools called COT (Commissioned Officer Training) or DCOC (Direct Commission Officer Course) that train physicians, lawyers, and chaplains for the military. These courses are four or five weeks long, and they introduce military service to professionals who then receive commissions. Generally, professionals receiving direct commissions this way enter with a rank of O-2 or O-3.

A BRIEF HISTORY OF THE PROFESSIONAL OFFICER CORPS

Although wars have been fought throughout human history, for most of that time, those who led men into battle did not need any special training different from that which they received as members of the ruling class. In medieval Europe, there was little distinction between social class and the military occupation; male members of the nobility generally became knights, or mounted warriors. Knights learned their skills through childhood activities like riding, hunting, and jousting, and led men into battle as a matter of course.

In the late fourteenth century, wars began to be fought by mercenary armies commanded by "entrepreneurs" hired or commissioned by a prince or king.[14] Like the knights of the medieval era, these entrepreneurs did not have any formal training in war, but they did take on warfighting and military leadership as a distinct profession. As the European nation-states grew more powerful with advances in technology, production, and trade, rulers fielded larger armies than ever before. These larger armies, made up of conscripted or mercenary soldiers, required commanders who knew how to deploy them on the battlefield. Soldiers armed with muskets needed drill and training to be effective, and support services like that of the quartermaster, the officer who went ahead of a moving army to find space to set up a camp, became essential for armies numbering 20,000 or more.

By the eighteenth century, the science behind military engineering, artillery, and infantry tactics grew increasingly complex, beyond what a commander could learn informally on the job. Rulers responded by creating professional schools for officers. In 1741, George II of Great Britain, for example, established the Royal Military Academy at Woolwich, and in France, the famous Ecole Militaire was founded in 1751.

Even so, European armies were still organized on the basis of social class. Officers, whether formally trained or not, were members of the aristocracy, while peasant conscripts made up the bulk of the common soldiery. All too often officers from important families attained the highest military ranks even if they were incompetent, elderly, or physically disabled. The development of effective leadership and command in European armies was hindered in large part by the limitations of the rigid class structure.

During the French Revolution, the French army, hitherto among the most class-based of European armies, was reorganized to allow promotion to all based on merit. The new revolutionary army allowed talented commoners like Napoleon Bonaparte to rise to positions of high command. Napoleon was a military genius who transformed contemporary ideas of leadership, strategy, and tactics, but most other military forces in Europe, while recognizing the need for professional officers, implemented necessary changes more slowly. As late as World War I, commissions in the German, Russian, and Austrian armies continued to be restricted to members of the upper classes.

In the United States, this long history of military leadership and class privilege gave the founders of the nation pause, even when the federal government accepted the need for trained officers in command of a permanent military force. George Washington, who had experienced firsthand the disadvantages of "amateur" officers in the militias, advocated the creation of an academy to train Army professionals. Nothing came of it until 1801 when Congress finally authorized the establishment of a school for engineers at West Point.[15] The seventeen officers and cadets in the first class began their studies in 1802, but they were a sorry lot. Cadet rebellions and quarrels among the school's leaders marred the early years of the USMA, and the school floundered from crisis to crisis until the arrival of Superintendent Sylvanus Thayer, a graduate of the class of 1808. From his arrival in 1817 until his departure in 1833, Thayer established the methods and philosophy of the military academy, methods still in use today. Modeled after the Ecole Militaire and other French academies, West Point's curriculum was heavily based on engineering and math. In and out of the classroom, cadets were held to strict standards of behavior, ethics, and appearance and adhered to a rigorous daily schedule of classes and study. Thayer created the "General Order of Merit," a regular ranking of the cadets, designed to instill competition among the cadets. The General Order of Merit was used until the late 1970s, and shaped the choices of officers throughout their careers.

Ambitious cadets competed for a place at the top of the hierarchy, but the "Goat," or lowest-ranking cadet of each graduating class, held a special place in the hearts of his peers. Quite often, the Goat was often a cadet who displayed nonconformist tendencies throughout his cadet years; probably the most famous Goat was Cadet (later General) George Custer of the class of 1861.[16]

The need for a school to educate naval officers was, if anything, more pressing, but although President John Quincy Adams recommended the creation of a professional institution in 1825, nothing was done about it for two decades. As it happened, the establishment of the Naval Academy emerged from a tragedy. In 1842, the USS *Somers* set sail with a group of teenage apprentices. The idea was that the experience would provide on-the-job training for future officers, but the novices were poorly prepared for the experience, and a mutiny ensued. Three ringleaders, including a midshipman apprentice, were hanged for their role in the rebellion. In the wake of the *Somers* disaster, the Secretary of the Navy established a school at Annapolis in 1845 with a class of fifty midshipmen and ten instructors. The curriculum of the Naval Academy, like that of West Point, was heavily focused on science and math, and held midshipmen to high standards of conduct and discipline.[17]

In the early years, American military officers came from established upper-class families of the original colonies, especially those in the Northeast. After the Civil War, however, an increasing proportion of cadets and officers came from the southern states and the Midwest. Whether a northeastern WASP or a southern gentleman, an officer's professional success in the nineteenth-century armed forces depended to an unfortunate extent on his social or family connections to members of Congress and other VIPs.[18] Officers pulled strings to get staff assignments in Washington, D.C., where they could spend much of their time cultivating even closer ties with those in power. The unfortunate officers who did not have social connections, or did not use them well, found themselves commanding units of the Indian-fighting Army on the frontier, a tough and thankless task that many found distasteful.

Officers in the post–Civil War armed forces, especially those commanding line units, faced many tribulations. Pay was negligible and prospects for promotion bleak. The Navy established a rudimentary mandatory retirement system, but there was no mandatory retirement in the Army, and promotions were governed strictly by seniority. During the second half of the nineteenth century, a glut of middle-ranking Civil War veterans clogged the promotions ladder. By the 1870s, it was not unusual for captains in their sixties to retain command of frontier companies, elderly and infirm but unable to afford retirement. There was little hope of relief; the only movement came when a fellow officer died. After the tragedy of

Custer's defeat and death at Little Bighorn in 1876, officers first expressed shock and horror, then wondered who was next on the promotion list.

By the turn of the century, the last Civil War officers had retired or passed away, and the career outlook for officers improved. By the eve of America's entry into World War I, the War Department realized that it needed larger numbers of officers than the academies could provide, and it created the first Army (1916), Navy (1926), and Air (1920) ROTC programs.

The concept of ROTC originated in the land-grant colleges established in the mid-nineteenth century. Under the Morrill Land-Grant Act of 1862, eligible states received 30,000 acres of federal land to be used for colleges and universities, large public institutions like Ohio State University or Texas A&M. In return, the schools taught their students military tactics in addition to agricultural and technical subjects. These college graduates formed a pool of reserve officers who could be mobilized in case of war.[19]

ROTC was an outgrowth of this early reserve officer pool. Not only was ROTC a source of additional officers, but its founders expected that it would counter a worrying trend toward an isolated and closed professional officer caste. In the century between the founding of the academies and America's involvement in World War I, the population of the nation had changed dramatically, with immigrants from Ireland and Eastern and Southern Europe making up a larger proportion of the population. The academies, however, remained the province of more established native-born white Protestant families. The advocates of ROTC hoped the program would create a more representative population of citizen officers, balancing the corps of conservative military professionals.

The two world wars brought a huge number of citizen soldiers into the armed forces, and a corresponding increase in citizen-officers. Still, graduates of the academies like Admirals Chester W. Nimitz and Ernest J. King, and Generals Dwight D. Eisenhower, George S. Patton, and Douglas MacArthur conducted the war for the United States. (General George C. Marshall was the exceptional non–West Pointer who made it to the highest ranks.) Until World War II, the officer corps in each branch of service remained small and familial. The senior commanders of World War II knew each other well and had served together for many years. Most of them had spent their careers commanding troops, often overseas, and had little or no experience in administration. They succeeded brilliantly, however, with the help of thousands of citizen-officers.

The global responsibilities of the United States in the years after World War II transformed the officer corps of the American forces. The enormous growth of the armed forces meant that the officer corps was larger and less personal than it had been. The task of coordinating huge standing forces stationed all over the world meant that staff positions became much more numerous and important. The Cold War military developed into a gargantuan support organization providing housing, schools, shopping, recreation, transportation, health care, retirement, and more to its personnel and family members. All this was coordinated by staff officers. The growth in the armed forces swept away the last vestiges of the old officer corps structure and brought in many citizen-officers through ROTC, which until the late 1960s was mandatory at many colleges and universities.

Whether from ROTC or the service academies, the officer corps was overwhelmingly white. During the Civil War, a handful of black officers were commissioned by the state of Louisiana to command all-black militia units, and the state of Massachusetts also commissioned almost a dozen African-American NCOs. After the Civil War, many African-American servicemen received commissions in state National Guard units. They were not accepted, however, in the national services; the Army created all-black cavalry and infantry regiments, which were commanded by white officers. A few black cadets were accepted into the USMA in the late nineteenth century, but only three made it through, in large part because extreme harassment and isolation rendered life for African-American cadets almost unendurable. The Naval Academy did not admit African-American midshipmen until 1936, and cadets in both academies suffered extensive hazing and discrimination.

When the United States entered World War I, only a few black officers were serving in the Army, but by the end of the war in 1918, about 1,400 African-Americans had received commissions. They commanded all-black units, most of whom performed labor or transportation duties. In 1936, Benjamin O. Davis, who later became one of the Army's most distinguished officers, graduated from West Point. For all four years of his studies, white cadets had shunned him. During World War II, larger numbers of African-Americans received commissions, still commanding segregated units. It was only in 1948 that the armed forces began to integrate, and black officers could work their way up the ranks.

The immediate postwar period also saw the beginnings of gender integration of the officer corps. In 1947, Army and Navy nurses received permanent commissioned officer status for the first time since their branches had been established in the first decade of the century, and a year later women were allowed to join all branches of the armed services. It was a marginal victory, however. By law, women could make up only 2 percent of the entire enlisted force, and the number of female officers was limited to one-tenth of the female enlisted population. In most cases women could not command troops, and the number of female officers above the rank of O-3 was severely restricted. During the Korean and Vietnam wars, the vast majority of female officers were nurses.

The needs of the Vietnam era forces and the AVF dictated sweeping changes in the status of and opportunities for female officers. In 1967, official restrictions on promotions of female officers were lifted and by 1971 the Army, Navy, and Air Force had female brigadier generals in active service. In 1978, even the combat-oriented Marine Corps promoted its first female brigadier. By then, a few female officers in other branches had attained their second stars.

Equally important for the future of female officers, in 1972 ROTC was opened to women, and in 1976 the first female cadets and midshipmen began their studies at the service academies. The welcome women received at the service academies and in nontraditional branches of service was far from enthusiastic.[20] The less attractive side of officer culture emerged as male cadets, midshipmen, and officers treated their female peers to extra hazing, harassment, and ostracism. Female cadets and midshipmen endured a staggering amount of sexual harassment and violence, often in silence, as they chose not to bring further harassment on themselves by reporting it. Socially conservative higher-ranking officers failed to provide the strong and unequivocal leadership that would have facilitated gender integration of the officer corps, and female officers, who generally shared male ideals of patriotism, duty, and honor, had to prove themselves again and again. They succeeded; in the mid-1980s, several top graduates at the Air Force, Navy, and Coast Guard Academies were women.

One of the central systemic difficulties for women was their exclusion from combat branches of service. Aside from limiting their chances of promotion, combat exclusions also enabled male officers who opposed gender integration to continue in the belief that women were not capable of serving in combat situations.[21] This handicap faded at the end of the Cold War. Between 1989 and 1994 many restrictions on women serving in combat zones were dropped. Women commanded units in combat zones in Panama and the Gulf War and were assigned to service on combat aircraft and naval vessels. Female officers now serve at the rank of O-8, command Navy warships and military bases on land, and in 1999 a female Air Force officer commanded the space shuttle. Gender integration in the armed forces is far from perfect, but many of the problems that women experienced in the early decades of the AVF have diminished.

Today, officers grapple with a number of complex and demanding tasks. Above all they are commanding units in Iraq and Afghanistan, where leadership skills and combat training are not simply ratings in OERs, but are matters of life and death. Not since Vietnam have so many junior officers experienced leadership in combat. Moreover, their training in complex weapons systems and Cold War-style high-intensity warfare has become somewhat superfluous in a war of counterinsurgency operations and low-level conflict. Today's officer corps is grappling with the substantial gap between traditional military doctrine and the wars that are being fought now.

For another thing, officers are increasingly called upon to work with people and institutions outside their own branch of service. This is not entirely new; during the Cold War, officers worked closely with other military forces, in NATO for example, or with the ARVN (Army of the Republic of Vietnam) during the Vietnam conflict. Today, however, international operations are de rigueur. In addition, officers must work with each other across branches in multiservice operations and with civilian defense contractors providing logistical services and security. And finally, officers today interact with a civilian public that is increasingly unfamiliar with and, in many cases, unsympathetic to the armed forces. Officers today must be not only professional soldiers and leaders but also politically astute and diplomatic, aware that one minor misstep can bring on a storm of controversy.

CHAPTER 4

MILITARY BASES

A decade and a half after the end of the Cold War, the United States continues to maintain almost 1,200 military installations in 39 nations, taking up about 46,880 square miles of land altogether. That's a lot of space, about the size of the state of Mississippi, and it doesn't include the total area of the navy's ships, especially aircraft carriers such as the Nimitz, which has a flight deck of 4.5 acres and can accommodate about 6,000 people. This real estate is home to servicemembers and their families, military equipment, and facilities like airfields, missile silos, and ports. Without bases, the U.S. forces cannot carry out their missions. The urgent negotiations conducted by the U.S. government for the use of military bases in Central Asia and the Middle East in the aftermath of the September 11 bombings underscore the importance of bases for overseas operations.

Even so, the purpose and nature of military bases is changing. In the twentieth century, America's military was a garrison force, living on bases located near the possible threat. Bases in Europe and Asia had a large "footprint," or impact on the societies in which they were located. Today, the armed forces are moving to an expeditionary model, with most troops stationed in the United States and deployed to FOBs or "forward operating bases" when necessary to face an enemy. The footprint is smaller, but the coordination involved in deployment is immense. In addition, military personnel and families in the United States will be concentrated on fewer larger bases, while many small bases will close.

To many civilians, a military base is a mysterious place. Especially overseas, they are surrounded by high walls and topped with loops of concertina wire. From the outside (and even from the inside) they tend to be drab and ugly, predominantly dull brown and olive green in color. At first glance, it's hard to tell one military base from another. Since September 11, access to military facilities of all types has been strictly limited to those holding a military ID card. Most are surrounded by civilian communities of some type, and many bases, have had enormous economic, social, cultural, and political effects on civilians living nearby.

Military bases, especially the larger ones, are self-contained company towns designed to meet virtually every need servicemembers and their families might have. Personnel work on the base, then return home to their base quarters. Their food comes from the commissary, their furniture and clothing from the post exchange. Their children go to base schools, and they worship at military chapels. When they are sick they go to the base clinic or hospital. They relax at base clubs, gymnasiums, movie theaters, and recreation centers.

Of course, not all military personnel live "on base," in military parlance, either by choice or because of housing shortages. And most of those who do live in base quarters like to leave on occasion to shop, travel, and relax. But even with options in the civilian world, a military base is an unusually complete community, whose residents are connected by one thing—their military service. Friends, neighbors, and fellow members of the PTA, church group, or hobby club are all coworkers. As a result, the division between work and private life that is a common part of modern life is blurrier for military personnel than it is for civilians. A military base can be a comforting, stable environment, but it offers little privacy and no anonymity.

THE U.S. BASE SYSTEM, PAST AND PRESENT

Military installations may be large, sprawling cities or tiny, isolated stations with only a few hundred personnel. They may date back to the early nineteenth century, or be just a year or two old. They may be popular and well integrated into the surrounding civilian community, or the target of anti-American attacks. Military bases may contain facilities used in training and missions, such as artillery ranges, airstrips, or refueling stations, or house equipment like tanks and missiles. Not all military installations are large; there are many tiny outposts where a few dozen personnel operate radar stations or other monitoring facilities. Until the 1990s, the U.S. forces held on to thousands of odd pieces of real estate like office buildings, private homes, and athletic fields that had been confiscated from the Germans or Japanese at the end of World War II and never returned. Most bases, even small ones, contain at least a few quarters and a convenience store. Military housing areas, on the other hand, contain only family housing, shopping, and other "quality of life" facilities, while the work of the military is conducted elsewhere.

In the past, permanent installations of the U.S. Army were called forts, posts, or garrisons, and temporary installations were called camps.

"Base" was the term used for naval and Air Force facilities. Today, many Army installations still use "camp" or "fort" in their names, and Army people refer to them as posts, but the general term "base" is used for larger facilities of all branches.

It is extremely difficult to get a precise idea of how many military facilities the DoD holds at any given time. Definitions of what constitutes a U.S. base vary widely—is a small radar station a base? An equipment depot? Some experts count each individual piece of property as a separate facility, while others, including the military itself, group related properties together as "base sites," "base communities," or some other term. Some writers use terms like base, facility, and installation to differentiate between different types of real estate held by the military, but there is no standard definition for any of these words. To make matters more complicated, military base use overseas is governed by a bewildering variety of treaties that the United States has concluded with other nations. The U.S. forces lease most of their bases overseas, but they also have arrangements to use foreign bases under certain circumstances, or they share their bases with allies.

Whatever the definition, the web of U.S. military facilities in the United States and around the world exists because the mission of the American forces requires it. When military doctrine changes, as it does on occasion, to address a new threat or because an old threat has disappeared, the network of military bases no longer serves the mission, and may change to fit new needs. Moreover, when military technology changes—when missiles can be fired accurately from thousands of miles away, for example, or nuclear submarines can traverse the seas for months without stopping for fuel, the military's need for bases may change.[1]

It is only in the past six decades that the United States has maintained a global system of military bases through which American power is projected. Throughout most of American history, there were two main types of military installations, both used by the U.S. Army and built in North America. The first was the string of artillery forts along the Atlantic coast and along inland waterways. These existed to defend U.S. shores from naval attack by foreign powers, mostly Great Britain. Artillery forts are among the oldest in the nation, many dating from the colonial period, although there are some artillery forts on the Pacific Coast as well. The second type of fort was the garrison on the western frontier. From these lines of interior forts running north to south, the U.S. Army protected white settlers as they pushed farther west, while driving Native American tribes into restricted areas and reservations.

Many of the coastal artillery forts had outlived their usefulness by the mid-nineteenth century and were abandoned or taken over for other purposes. The forts of the interior were by their nature temporary; as the

frontier shifted, they followed. Particularly after the Civil War, most frontier posts had short lives. The Army established them to deal with a
specific mission, such as protecting an overland trail or a railroad project,
and when the mission was achieved, they were abandoned.

By the 1890s, after the trans–Mississippi West had been settled by
whites and the Native groups forced onto reservations, the fort system
was no longer needed, and many of the smaller forts closed. But between
1899 and 1911, the U.S. armed forces established its first long-term overseas presence: in Cuba and Puerto Rico, Hawaii, Guam, and the Philippines, all gained from Spain after victory in the Spanish-American War;
in the Panama Canal Zone; and in Tientsin, China, after the collapse of
the Qing dynasty.

Forts and garrisons in the tropics, like those on the frontier, were laid
out in a rectangle, with a row of officers' quarters on one side, the enlisted
men's barracks on another, a headquarters building on a third side, and a
dispensary, stockade, or other buildings on the fourth. All the buildings
faced the parade field in the center. Forts sometimes had stockade walls
or fences, but not always. Stockades took time and resources to build,
and the level of danger did not always warrant them.

The "Old Army" lived its last decades in a network of tropical para-
dises, mostly in Hawaii and the Philippines. The idyllic life ended when
major American installations in the South Pacific were attacked by the
Japanese in December, 1941, bringing the United States into World War
II. During the war, the United States built or borrowed military bases
along the major fronts in Europe, North Africa, and the Pacific. The armed
forces also set up camp in exotic locales like the Arctic and the Caribbean,
where, it was feared, attackers might gain a foothold close to North
America. By 1945, the United States held over 2,000 major basing sites
throughout the world.[2]

After 1945, most of the temporary wartime bases closed down. But in
the 1950s, the Cold War began and the U.S. basing system expanded once
again. The new or reopened bases brought American military power
closer to the borders of the USSR, so that American bombers, fighters,
submarines and aircraft carriers, and ground forces could react if the
Soviet Union threatened another nation.

The basing system was far from perfect. Basing expert James Blaker
notes that most U.S. bases during the Cold War were located in Europe
and Northeast Asia (Japan and South Korea), a legacy of World War II
rather than a rational response to the threat.[3] Moreover, influenced by
their experience in the war, policymakers held certain preconceptions
about U.S. bases overseas, assuming that "overseas base sites are an inherent part of superpower status; that more base sites were better than fewer;
that necessary basing could be created from scratch and did not depend

on an existing infrastructure; and that the proper location and distribution of base sites is a function of existing aircraft technology."[4] They ignored the potential economic, social, and political impact of the bases on civilian communities when they decided on the location of a base and negotiated basing rights with the host nation.

The Cold War system continued with relatively few changes for forty years, when suddenly at the end of 1989, the raison d'etre of many U.S. bases disappeared with the fall of the Berlin Wall. Even before the Wall came down, the Pentagon had been fighting to close unneeded bases to free funds for other more valuable projects; almost immediately planners began thinking about shutting down parts of the Cold War system. Since then, many overseas installations have been closed and returned to the host governments, but bases in the United States have proved remarkably difficult to close because of natural resistance from those who would suffer from a base closure, usually civilians who stand to lose jobs, businesses and real estate value, and their Congressional representatives. In 1990, after much grappling with the issue, Congress passed the BRAC (Base Realignment and Closure Act), which spelled out how bases in the United States were to be evaluated and, if necessary, shut down. The BRAC called for reviews and closures of bases in the non-election years 1991, 1993, and 1995, and required environmental cleanup and job training before returning the bases to the community.

The base-closing process begins with the selection of a BRAC commission. The Pentagon then presents the commission with a list of bases it believes should be closed, and the commission reviews the recommendations. The commission reports to the president, who submits the plan to Congress. Congressional representatives and communities respond, usually to defend "their" bases. Before a base, which is federal land, is actually given up by the military, the Pentagon must offer the land to any other federal agency that might be able to use it. If no other agency needs it, the land is put up for sale to state or local governments or private firms.

The rounds of BRAC during the 1990s succeeded in closing almost 100 major bases in the United States, out of a Cold War total of 500, or about 20 percent of the total. Overseas bases did not fall under the BRAC regulations, so were easier to close. By 1997, the Pentagon had closed about 60 percent of the bases it held overseas.[5]

There was no BRAC activity after the 1995 round of twenty-eight major closings, but Secretary of Defense Donald Rumsfeld began pushing for more streamlining of the base system when he came to office in 2001. At first nothing happened, because of the conflicts in Afghanistan and Iraq, and because Rumsfeld examined base closings as part of a larger transformation of America's armed forces. In 2005, after two and a half years, a new BRAC finally convened. The final list included 25 major base closures and almost 800 realignments or consolidations of smaller installations.[6]

The BRAC is just the most obvious sign that the system of military bases in the United States and around the world is beginning to change. The large garrisons of servicemembers and their families in Western Europe and Asia no longer advance the mission of the U.S. forces. In fact, bases housing large numbers of family members and civilians create security problems that can outweigh any value the base may have.

The solution, Pentagon planners have decided, is a combination of large garrison bases in the United States combined with a web of forward sites overseas. These sites may be equipment depots, inactive installations with facilities like airstrips, bases shared with allies, or more fully equipped FOBs located in combat zones.

In Kosovo, Iraq, and Afghanistan today, the forward site concept is being tested. There are at present at least 100 FOBs scattered throughout Iraq, on which deployed servicemembers and civilians live. It is somewhat risky to generalize about the FOBS, as they range from extensive Cold War-style military towns to remote outposts with only a few hundred troops. Moreover, the conditions at FOBs change almost weekly. But it is safe to say that military leadership envisions FOBs as safe and comfortable refuges from combat. At first, most FOBs were rudimentary camps, where personnel lived in tents and amenities were sparse. Most of them have been upgraded to include either metal trailers for quarters and offices or more durable cinder block structures. Many quarters and offices on FOBs have air conditioning, and there are usually at least some quality of life services. Most FOBs have a dining service run by civilian contractors, an exchange, a gym, and a recreation center where phone and Internet service is available.

FOBs are not home—servicemembers are rotated in and out of forward locations every twelve or eighteen months, they are separated from their families, and, most importantly, they must go outside the FOB to conduct combat operations in a hostile environment. But FOBs, in the words of one report, "have become refuges from danger, places of renewal for physical needs, a respite from the mental stresses of battle, and, finally, a means for soldiers to stay connected with the world outside Iraq...."[7]

MILITARY BASES AND THE CIVILIAN COMMUNITY

The BRAC commissions consider the military utility of bases and installations and determine whether they should stay open or close down. Of course, military bases do not exist in isolation but are surrounded by civilian residents whose lives are dramatically affected by the presence of a military community. Part of the impact of a military base comes from the physical presence of the base itself. Bases take up valuable real estate; create traffic delays; use scarce resources; cause air, noise, or water pollution; and spur inflation. Bases create jobs as well, both directly on the base and in the community. Another part of the impact of a base comes from the military community itself—the people who live and work on the base. Personnel and families purchase local goods and services, act as informal ambassadors to local residents, and participate in charitable and community activities. They can also be a source of tension, misunderstanding, conflict, and even violence in the civilian community.

Throughout history, military establishments, however temporary, have had a huge impact on nearby civilians. In Europe, armies billeted and supplied themselves from local civilian towns, sometimes paying for the goods and services they used, sometimes simply stealing them and leaving civilians destitute. The U.S. Constitution prohibits this kind of exploitation of civilians by armies, and Americans have not been abused by their own armed forces the way members of some other societies have. However, even a tiny post can have a big impact if the surrounding community is small and fragile. Army posts on the Western frontier, for example, garrisoned only a few hundred people at most, but they needed consistent sources of food, fuel, and forage for their livestock in harsh and unforgiving environments. When a post or fort was built, a squalid community of camp-followers would sprout up outside the stockade walls. Small farmers sold their produce at inflated prices; Native Americans peddled blankets, skins, and handicrafts; and, most notoriously, whiskey sellers established "hog ranches" where soldiers drank and pursued "sporting women."[8] Even when the Army created the sutler system, whereby a merchant was authorized to establish an official trading post and sell liquor, soldiers managed to squander their pay in off-post establishments.

In spite of the drawbacks, community leaders saw the posts as a source of economic worth and vied for the opportunity to host a new installation. One of the major benefits of a military post was the road or rail service that would be built to connect the post with others. Civilian communities used these transportation lines as well; in the trans–Mississippi West, the difference between a thriving small city and an incipient ghost town was often the transportation line, built by the Army, that connected or bypassed it.[9]

The numbers of civilians affected by the frontier forts of the nineteenth century was minuscule, but during the two world wars of the twentieth century all that changed. The armed forces created huge camps to train the millions of citizen soldiers needed for the war effort, transforming small towns and rural areas all over the United States. The Army, which handled the largest number of servicemembers, deliberately chose sites that were far from the fleshpots of large cities, so that the men would not be tempted. But enterprising civilians flocked to the outskirts of the training camps to meet the needs of soldiers and make some money.

During World War II, military bases connected innumerable isolated communities to the outside world for the first time. From the Arctic to the island archipelagos in the South Pacific, airstrips and dirt roads brought new money and new customs to traditional societies. The disruption could be intense, though many communities welcomed the lifeline. After the war was over, the bases closed but the roads and airstrips survived, along with the economic, cultural, and social changes ushered in by the U.S. forces.

During the Cold War, millions of people lived in the shadows of U.S. bases both at home and overseas. In the first decade of peace, civilians living near overseas bases were grateful for the opportunity to earn a decent wage and, more important, receive a few hot meals every day. By the 1950s, however, some nations rejected the American presence. The nationalist governments of Morocco and Libya demanded that the U.S. forces vacate the air bases they had built after the war, and the last American personnel left North Africa in 1970. In Panama, anti-American riots caused an international crisis in 1964 after American high-school students raised the Stars and Stripes in the Canal Zone in defiance of presidential orders to show more sensitivity. In the 1960s, opposition to U.S. bases in Japan was so heated that most installations on the mainland were closed and moved to Okinawa, an southern island that today hosts 75 percent of the U.S. personnel in Japan. The disaffection spread to Europe as well; in 1966, French president Charles De Gaulle pulled France out of NATO and demanded that foreign troops leave the country.[10]

U.S. bases continued to feed the economies of smaller towns and villages throughout the world, but their political costs grew in the 1980s and 1990s. In the Philippines, anti-base extremists killed half a dozen Americans, and in West Germany terrorists kidnapped or killed a similar number of military personnel. In 1991, after years of acrimonious debate, the Philippine government and the U.S. forces had finally agreed on a plan to phase out the American presence when a volcano destroyed Clark Airfield, one of the two main installations, in 1991. The remaining bases closed shortly thereafter, ending ninety years of American military presence in the country. In the past decade American bases in Okinawa and South Korea have been the targets of anti-base protests as well. Opposition in both areas had been increasing for years, but public anger boiled over after a gang-rape in Okinawa in 1995 and a fatal traffic accident in South Korea in 2002. Both gruesome incidents involved young girls, making their emotional impact all the more bitter.

Organized opposition to bases is uncommon in the United States, for both social and economic reasons. Military personnel and families are relatively more integrated into American host communities than they are into foreign communities, and there is, obviously, no nationalist resentment of the U.S. military presence. On the contrary, most American host communities are proud of their bases and are very supportive of the military. Economically, however, bases play an ambiguous role. While tens, perhaps, hundreds of thousands of Americans owe their jobs to the military, there is also some evidence that the presence of a military base tends to depress wages on the civilian economy. Large populations of servicemembers tend to exacerbate other scourges, such as increased prostitution, drinking, and violence.[11] Still, Stateside bases rarely spark controversy in their host communities.

The base closings of the 1990s had significant effects on surrounding towns.[12] For many communities overseas, base closures were the long-awaited answers to prayer, but in the United States they seemed to represent at least temporary economic ruin.[13] Under the BRAC legislature passed in 1990, an OEA (Office of Economic Adjustment) was created to help U.S. towns and regions anticipate the effects of base closures: job losses, decreases in school enrollment, loss of real estate value, and changes in infrastructure use.[14] The OEA helps communities create plans to attract new businesses and develop the land that has become available. Planning for a base closure is a long and drawn-out process, but in the end many communities find they have gained more than they have lost.[15]

One of the problems some civilian communities discover when they take over a closed military base is a plethora of environmental problems. From UXO (unexploded ordnance) to massive dumping in landfills to years of toxic runoff from planes or tanks, military bases can leave quite a mess behind. Before a base is declared to be surplus property and sold off, the DoD must clean it up according to environmental laws. The cost of environmental cleanup can be enormous and is really unknowable. Until the 1980s, the military rarely kept records of any dumping or environmental accidents. Artillery ranges did not even document the use and disposal of ordnance, so no one knows how many shells lie underneath the land that the military wants to get rid of. At the former Fort Ord, in Monterey, California, for example, the Army has recovered 8,000 unexploded shells, and 3.2 million pieces of scrap metal. But this progress, as impressive as it seems, has taken ten years—and the Army has only cleared 5 percent of the former range.[16]

The problem at Fort Ord is replicated all over the country. The military has set aside up to $10 billion for cleanup, but if it is to be done properly, the costs will rise much higher and the work will take years. On overseas bases, the military has resisted calls for cleanup, saying that they will abide by the environmental laws of the host nation, which are usually less stringent than those of the United States. As a result, former bases in the

Philippines and other countries have not been cleaned up, leaving enormous messes for nations too poor to do it by themselves.

However, the military is beginning to advance the cause of environmentalism as well. In recent years, as suburban sprawl has pushed up against military installations, civilian residents complain about noise and danger from airfields, artillery ranges, and other facilities. In 2003, the Pentagon began a program called the Readiness and Environmental Protection Initiative, which works with environmental groups to set aside land as a buffer zone between military installations and civilian communities. Some environmentalists are skeptical of the military's motives, but, for better or worse, the buffer zones have helped preserve wildlife habitat and vulnerable ecosystems from development.[17]

LIFE ON A MILITARY BASE

Military bases affect the civilian communities surrounding them, but they also have a life of their own. Some bases boast populations similar to those of medium-sized cities, with a similar range of choices and opportunities for their residents. For example, Camp Lejeune, the 156,000-acre Marine Corps installation in North Carolina, counts about 150,000 servicemembers, family members, civilian employees, and retirees living on or near the base and using base services. It has about 4,450 family housing units, 22 bachelor officers' quarters, and 363 barracks for single enlisted personnel. Shopping facilities include two commissaries (supermarkets); a chain of stores and shops known as the MCX (Marine Corps Exchange), which operates three large department stores and several dozen smaller stores and convenience stores; and numerous barber shops, dry cleaners, florists, banks, service stations, Laundromats, bookstores, opticians, video rental shops, snack bars, garden centers, package stores, thrift shops, and travel agencies. For families, Camp Lejeune has six day care centers, another six elementary schools, a middle school and a high school, and an adult college education program. Camp Lejeunians can worship at any of eleven chapels with their choice of Catholic, Protestant, Jewish, Christian Orthodox, Christian Scientist, Mormon, and Buddhist services. It has a hospital, nine medical clinics, seven dental clinics, a pharmacy, and a veterinarian. The base offers a 32-lane bowling center, five swimming pools, gymnasiums, recreation centers, two golf courses, horse stables, 62 tennis courts, a marina, a fishing pier, and campgrounds. For the less athletic, it offers movie theaters, auto and hobby shops, officers, NCO and enlisted clubs, a youth center, and libraries.[18]

This dizzying array of quality of life services is not at all unusual for the larger bases. Smaller installations will have fewer options, of course.

In terms of their physical size, major bases can be surprisingly expansive: Fort Bliss, outside El Paso, Texas, for example, stretches over 1.1 million acres. Much of this is uninhabited shooting range, but altogether the base is larger than the state of Rhode Island. The population of Fort Bliss is not especially huge: about 21,000 personnel and families, plus about 7,500 civilian employees. This number will grow after the next round of base closings consolidates units at the base.[19] Fort Hood, also in Texas, hosts a population of over 105,000 and about 9,000 civilians,[20] and Fort Bragg, North Carolina, is home to about 166,000, including 47,000 Guard and Reserves and 8,500 civilians.[21] These numbers do not include the extensive retiree communities around those bases. Overseas bases tend to be smaller, although the Ramstein Air Base community in Germany includes about 20,000 personnel and family members and 1,200 civilian employees,[22] while Camp Courtney in Okinawa hosts 25,000 active duty Marines.[23] These and other large bases at home and overseas offer servicemembers and families the same type of extended support services as Camp Lejeune.

The creature comforts on military garrisons were not always so elaborate, of course. In fact, during the nineteenth century, posts on the Western frontier offered every conceivable type of discomfort, from blistering heat and sandstorms to insect infestations to blizzards and ice storms to flash floods. Housing was rudimentary; in newly established forts, officers and men lived in mud dugouts or tents while they built their own quarters.

Officers and their families arriving at a post received quarters if they were available, but, under a somewhat bizarre system of seniority known as "ranking out," an officer arriving at a post could choose quarters occupied by any officer below him in rank. The "ranked out" officer and family would have to move immediately, but they would have the right to "rank out" someone else, and down the hierarchy it would go. This would occur without regard to the family status of the officers. A bachelor officer could "rank out" a man with a wife and five children. As a result, no officer except the post commander could ever really feel secure in his quarters.[24]

On many frontier posts there were not enough quarters to go around, so families shared space. Most housing was of poor quality, made of rough logs, the cracks filled in with mud. Thatch roofs let rain and dust in, and inhabitants slept under sheets stretched over the beds to prevent insects, rodents, and snakes from dropping down on them at night. And these unpleasant dwellings were the officers' quarters. Enlisted men lived in crowded barracks with even greater discomfort and no privacy.

In the desert or on the plains, frontier Army garrisons had to be self-sufficient. The soldiers built the forts themselves under the supervision of the Quartermaster, an officer in charge of planning housing and supplies for the troops. They produced much of their own food, but a sutler, or civilian merchant, ran a general store and tavern on the post grounds. Late nineteenth-century posts also had hospitals or dispensaries, chapels, post and telegraph offices, small libraries, stockades or jails, and cemeteries. Aside from the sutler and the library, there were no facilities for recreation. Corrals and barns for horses took up a large proportion of the space on both cavalry and infantry posts.

In the twentieth century, the facilities on military posts improved. In the United States, most frontier posts closed, but the ones that survived, like Fort Riley, Nebraska, and Fort Leavenworth, Kansas, expanded and their importance increased. Along with the rest of the country, military posts upgraded with electricity, indoor plumbing, telephone service, and central heating. Posts also improved their recreation options. In the 1920s, commanders authorized the construction of movie theaters, a staple by World War II, and, after Prohibition ended in 1933, clubs and outdoor beer gardens as well. The 1920s and 1930s were the golden age of military athletics, with promising enlisted men singled out by officers to represent their posts in sporting contests; all personnel had access to athletic fields and gymnasiums on post.[25]

It was overseas that military bases in the early twentieth century really took on a life of their own. In the Philippines, Hawaii, and Panama, Army, Navy, and Marine Corps posts promised a life of tropical ease to their lucky residents. Post facilities included libraries, movie theaters, and athletic facilities like those back home, plus opulent officers' clubs and somewhat less opulent clubs for enlisted men. Servicemembers and families enjoyed the use of tennis courts and riding stables, golf courses and camping grounds, marinas, and miles of beaches reserved for military personnel (officers and enlisted men each had their own sections). Palm trees and exotic flowers surrounded lush parade grounds, and family quarters were built in tropical style, with high ceilings and wide covered porches to keep the heat out.[26]

After World War II, military bases took on the character of "Little Americas," a term sometimes used for large garrisons overseas. As the numbers of personnel in the armed forces grew, housing and support services expanded to fill their needs. Larger numbers of servicemen forced leadership to pay more attention to morale, discipline, and health; many of the recreation activities, for example, were designed to keep troops busy on base rather than prowling the bars and brothels outside.

A more important change after 1945, however, was the huge number of wives and children who made their lives with the military. Families had always lived on military posts, but they were a minority of the residents of the garrison and the military made no provision for them. The wife of the common soldier and the wife of the commanding general were both "camp followers" in the eyes of the nineteenth-century military and were officially ignored. The status of family members began to change in the twentieth century, and by the Cold War, family members outnumbered personnel. Many of the facilities on "Little Americas," such as schools, shopping, and medical services, were used largely or entirely by family members. During the mostly peaceful years of the Cold War, the major activities in military hospitals, for example, were delivering babies and vaccinating toddlers.

HOUSING ON MILITARY BASES

It is an unfortunate fact that the only truly racially integrated residential areas in the United States are on military bases. Servicemembers are assigned to on-base housing using only two considerations, first, whether they are accompanied by family members or not, and second, their military rank. For unaccompanied personnel, there are barracks or dormitories for junior enlisted personnel and one-bedroom apartments for NCOs and officers. Family housing, usually single-family homes, duplexes, or fourplexes, is separated into areas for junior enlisted families, junior and senior NCOs, company grade officers, field grade officers, and flag officers.

When a single servicemember is assigned to his or her first permanent posting, he or she will be assigned a barracks or dormitory room on base. Single enlisted personnel below the rank of E-5 or E-6 are usually required to live on base, and personnel of the same unit normally live in the same building. The DoD is in the process of implementing a plan to house all enlisted servicemembers in private rooms, with two sharing a kitchenette and bathroom; by 2020, DoD wants to go further and house all enlisted personnel in their own efficiency apartments.[27]

Efficiency apartments may be part of future plans, but today many servicemembers, especially in the Marines and Navy, still live in two-person rooms, with communal bathrooms. Rules on furnishings vary; some bases insist that personnel use only the blocky furniture issued to them, while others allow more individual choice. Servicemembers living in barracks or dormitories eat together at a mess hall or dining facility, similar to those at colleges and universities.

Barracks or dormitories are unlike college housing in many ways, however. The commanding officer and the NCO in charge will inspect the barracks or dorms regularly, for cleanliness and for contraband. Residents pitch in to clean the common areas and showers, and there are rules about who may or may not stay overnight.

Family housing is like civilian housing in some ways. In the United States, base quarters are usually single-family or duplex homes designed much like others in the geographic area. On the sprawling bases in the hot South and West, ranch-style homes prevail. In the Midwest, quarters often have two stories, the older homes constructed with covered wrap-around porches to ward off the summer heat. In more northerly locations in New England, housing can be multistory, with less space around each house. Most family housing overseas is in apartment buildings, known as "stairwells," because they are built around central stairways.

Some military housing is unique. At Fort Myer, for example, outside Washington, D.C., officers' quarters consist of charming brick homes, most with front porches painted white. It is unfortunate that civilians who see this lovely setting may believe all military posts to be as elegant as Fort Myer. In fact, the small post was originally a plantation owned by Martha Washington's son, and later owned by Robert E. Lee. The Union confiscated it from him after the Civil War, and it has been an Army post ever since. Most of the homes on Fort Myer were built between 1895 and 1905 and are historic landmarks.

Family housing areas are quite different from civilian neighborhoods, however. For one thing, as mentioned earlier, housing is segregated by rank, but nothing else. Homes usually have signs on the door or in the yard saying who lives in each house and what rank they hold. Even without the signs, though, a visitor would recognize the difference between junior enlisted duplexes and the stately homes of general officers.

The visitor might also notice that the yards and exteriors of even the most modest homes are neat and well maintained. There will be no clutter of children's toys in the yards, no half-finished barbeque pits, no sagging rain gutters. There will be no oil stains in the driveways, and the grass will be trimmed to regulation length.

The military is strict about its housing areas. The Provost Marshall's office, in charge of the housing areas, sends personnel on weekly checks, and offenders receive a ticket. Families with too many tickets will be evicted from family housing. Along with the stick, there is a carrot: the best-looking yard in each housing area wins an award for Yard of the Quarter.

Inside the homes, the residents have a little more leeway, but they still are bound by rules and regulations. When families receive housing, they are required to attend a briefing or workshop on home maintenance standards. When families move, they must clean the house and have it inspected. The inspection is so strict that most families hire professional teams who specialize in cleaning military homes, rather than risk failing the inspection. In recent years, some base housing offices have begun to supply cleaning teams to families moving out, making the process less costly and fraught with anxiety.

Military housing is a venerable institution, but it may be going the way of electric typewriters and pay phones. Housing on military bases all over the world has long been plagued with problems, from leaky pipes to persistent mold, making "daily activities a trial and lower[ing] morale" according to a 1995 DoD report.[28] Many housing areas were built in the 1950s, when the armed forces were expanding rapidly, and they have, in the opinion of many, outlived their usefulness. A 2003 DoD study concluded that 60 percent of military housing was in such poor repair that it was not worth saving. In 1996 the DoD passed the Military Housing Privatization Initiative, which mandated that all family housing and barracks will be converted to private housing built and owned by private developers. Under the plan, families and servicemembers living in privatized housing will pay rent in the form of BAH, the subsidy received by families living off-base. The initiative was supposed to save the DoD millions, and improve housing within a decade, but it has gotten off to a slow start, as unanticipated problems with bidding and contracts have delayed projects.[29] It remains to be seen whether the privatization plan will solve the military housing problem.

SHOPPING FACILITIES

Shopping facilities on a base offer significant savings for servicemembers and families, a benefit that goes unrecorded on military pay stubs. In most areas, military shoppers can save 30 percent or more by shopping at the commissary and the exchange rather than in civilian supermarkets and department stores. Of course, savings rates depend on the cost of living in the host community; military shoppers in the Washington, D.C., area will save more than those in most parts of Texas. For residents of overseas bases, the commissary and exchange are the only places to buy American products. Only military ID card holders can shop at base facilities, and merchandise is tax-free. The prices in exchanges are the same all over the world.

The commissary is a venerable institution dating back to 1867, when the Army began selling food to officers and men at cost. The practice developed into the modern commissary system, managed by the DeCa (Defense Commissary Agency) and funded, about $1 billion a year, by Congressional appropriations. There are over 300 commissaries throughout the world, run on a nonprofit basis, charging shoppers the wholesale cost of goods cost plus a 5 percent surcharge to cover operations. Commissaries have the same items that are in most civilian supermarkets, as many as 17,000 different items in the largest stores.[30] Commissaries stock brand-name items from the United States, as well as fresh produce, dairy products, and meat from local sources. They try to carry local specialties; in Germany they carry many types of wurst, for example, and in Korea, military shoppers can buy the spicy pickle known as kimchee.

The "exchange" is the military equivalent of a department store. It is called a PX in the Army, BX in the Air Force, NEX in the Navy, and MCX in the Marines. The concept was established in 1895 by the War Department, when garrison commanders were ordered to create post exchanges, or canteens, as they used to be called, to replace the sutler system of informal traders supplying military posts.

There are three separate exchange services, the largest of them known as AAFES (Army and Air Force Exchange Service), which runs 12,000 facilities of varying sizes. The Navy Exchange Service Command manages about 100 NEX stores and 159 Ship Stores on board naval vessels. Finally, the Marine Corps Personal and Family Readiness Division manages the fourteen MCX operations around the world. Exchanges must be profitable to stay in business; they receive only about two percent of their operating costs from Congress. After covering their costs, however, most of their profits are returned to the military community in the form of funding for MWR (Morale, Welfare, and Recreation) activities.

Exchanges are found at bases large and small, on FOBs, and on board ships. At major bases, they may be comparable to large department stores. On small bases, they may be the size of a convenience shop. In addition to the main outlets, most bases of any size have a cluster of smaller shops also run by the exchange service, such as electronics shops, computer stores, furniture outlets, cafes, bookstores, and gas stations. Even the Navy's tiny Ship Support Office in Hong Kong, home to seven active duty Navy personnel and nine civilians, has a small NEX, barber and beauty shops, a furniture store, a bookstore, a video/CD store, an optical store, a post office, a fast food restaurant, and a Laundromat. It also has an oriental carpet store, a Chinaware store, "Arcade shops (with guaranteed genuine items)," and other shops for sailors with money to burn and curious relatives back home.

By law, exchanges in the United States are limited in what items they can sell and in their cost–price ratios, so that civilian businesses near installations won't be unfairly undercut. Still, studies show that the savings from shopping at an exchange can be from 40 to 60 percent, compared to shopping in civilian stores. Overseas, there are no limits on what the exchanges can sell, but some items, such as cigarettes and gasoline, are rationed to prevent black market trading. The exchanges have always offered catalogue sales, and in recent years they have begun offering Internet shopping for people who do not have an exchange nearby.

There are many other facilities on today's military bases; schools, chapels, playgrounds, and recreation centers are similar to facilities found in civilian towns. What makes a military base unusual, however, is that servicemembers and families both live and work in the same physical space. It is a fully formed community in itself, with a specific role in the defense mission.

CHAPTER 5

AT WORK IN THE ARMED FORCES

Work in the military is different from the type of work most civilians do. Soldiers and sailors do not "produce" anything, such as automobiles, computer software, or jewelry, nor do they provide consumer services the way financial planners, hairdressers, or consultants do. Rather, they are like firefighters or police officers, who respond to disaster when it happens, and train and practice when it doesn't. Since 2001, large numbers of active duty and reserve personnel have been deployed to combat zones in Afghanistan and Iraq. When they are not deployed, however, servicemembers spend much of their time preparing for combat missions in exercises, drills, and maneuvers. Training exercises come in as many varieties as there are job specialties, from firing live rounds on an artillery range to treating mock casualties of chemical warfare to loading trucks in under fifteen minutes. The military cannot afford to leave anything to chance.

When they are not deployed or in training, many servicemembers, as well as most civilian employees on military bases, provide support services to military personnel and their families. Health care workers, military police, administrative and finance specialists, and many others spend their workdays keeping the military community running smoothly. Even though civilian contractors are taking over more and more jobs formerly done by servicemembers, there is still an important role for military personnel in supporting the community.

The Army, Navy, Air Force, and Marine Corps are unusual workplaces not only because of the work they do but also because of their strict hierarchy and culture of obedience. Only in the armed services are subordinates required to greet their superiors with a salute, and only in the armed services can an employee be arrested and jailed for not showing up for work. The rigid rank structure has some drawbacks. The flow of information and ideas between higher and lower ranks may be more constrained than in some other work environments, for example, and the habit of unquestioning obedience can be abused by superiors. On the battlefield, though, the hierarchical culture of the military is not a hindrance, but a necessity.

The military's emphasis on obedience is beneficial in another way: it can deal strictly and forcefully with organization-wide social or cultural problems, such as sexual harassment and racial discrimination. When orders come down from the top, things really do change. As one study of women and African-Americans in the military observes: "The military is the only large organization in which large units (comprised mostly of men) are led by women, and large units (comprised largely of whites) are led by minorities."[1] While the military is not a perfectly integrated or gender-neutral organization, it is much more integrated than any civilian organization of any type.

TOOTH OR TAIL?

Like employees of other large organizations such as corporations or universities, members of the military either perform the task of the organization—in the case of the military, fighting—or support those who perform the task. In military slang, combat and support troops are known as "tooth and tail," respectively. The types, or branches, of combat arms include armor, infantry, combat engineering, aviation, Special Operations, air defense artillery, and field artillery. Personnel in CS or "Combat Support" branches such as Intelligence, Signal (communications), Military Police, Engineering, or Civil Affairs directly support combat operations. Another type of support known as CSS or "Combat Service Support" keeps the military organization running in peace and war. The CSS arm includes jobs in administration, transportation, supply, and medical care.

The role of support is changing rapidly. In the past five years or so, training for all personnel, whatever their job specialty, has included more practice in combat skills than ever before. Moreover, the ongoing transformation of the military under the Bush administration aims to decrease the "tooth to tail" ratio by turning over many CSS jobs to civilians so that military personnel can fight rather than file papers or do laundry. During the Cold War, the tooth to tail ratio was, according to some reports, as high as 1 to 11—one combat troop was supported by eleven CS/CSS troops. Today, it is closer to 50/50, and may decrease further as more CSS jobs are turned over to civilians.

Even as higher percentages of troops participate in combat operations, the skills and training of combat troops have changed and will continue to change dramatically. Historically, the military, especially the Army, used large numbers of young men for ground combat during periods of conflict, but "dogfaces" were citizen soldiers, not highly trained professionals. In the course of the twentieth century, mechanized forces such as armor and aviation became increasingly important in warfare, and this technology required better-trained troops. In recent decades, computer technology has further transformed warfare, and there is less of a need for warm bodies to act as cannon fodder on the battlefield. Currently, light infantry makes up only 10 percent of the Army, "and even these units have become highly specialized," according to one expert.[2]

So, if servicemembers in the modern armed forces, whether in the combat or support arms, are more than simply "boots on the ground," what kinds of work do they do? In large part, troops operate and maintain high-tech equipment. Today's weapons systems are very sophisticated, and there are a lot of them, from the traditional-sounding field artillery cannon to the ICBMs (intercontinental ballistic missiles) that use rockets for propulsion. The Army's description of the Patriot, an air-defense system, for example, tells us that the missile is

> equipped with a track-via-missile (TVM) guidance system....The target acquisition system in the missile acquires the target in the terminal phase of flight and transmits the data using the TVM downlink via the ground radar to the Engagement Control Station for final course correction calculations. The course correction commands are transmitted to the missile via the Missile Track Command Uplink.[3]

It goes without saying that the Patriot's guidance and tracking systems are extremely complex and require highly trained personnel to operate them if there is to be any chance that they will work the way they should. Many servicemembers attend advanced training schools to learn how to maintain and repair a specific weapons system or type of weapon, like the Army's Bradley Fighting Vehicle System Maintainers, for example, or the Marine Corps' Avenger System Repairers and Towed Artillery Systems Technicians.

Equally important are the surveillance and communications systems that track enemy movements and equipment. ELINT (Electronics Intelligence) specialists use radio frequency systems to monitor, detect, and jam signals coming from enemy communications equipment. Communications specialists operate computer, radio, telecommunications, satellite, and microwave systems. All the branches of the military train a large number of specialists in aviation and avionics (the electronic instruments and systems on aircraft), and all branches also train specialists in cartography, geodetics, and meteorology.

Of course, not all jobs in the military involve science-fiction technology. The Army, for example, needs many vehicle mechanics, and the Navy's Machinist Mates "operate, maintain and repair steam turbines used for ship's propulsion and auxiliary equipment." Hull Maintenance Technicians earn their pay repairing damage to ships, while Explosive Ordnance Disposal Technicians get rid of bombs.

There are many other jobs in the military, from chaplain's assistants to journalists to band members, that civilians probably don't imagine when they think of military service. These personnel help to maintain the quality of life for troops and families in the military, as do military police, finance and legal specialists, and many others.

TRAINING

When they are not deployed in an area of conflict, military personnel spend a good deal of their time training and practicing for when they will be mobilized. Training achieves several purposes. First of all, whether they drive tanks or install communications centers, servicemembers must refresh their skills periodically. Some personnel are able to do this by using their training in daily life; medical personnel, for example, spend their days caring for patients, military police patrol the base, and administrative specialists work in offices. But others, like Multiple Rocket Launch System Crewmembers, do not have a chance to fire their weapons outside of an exercise or a visit to a special training center.

Training benefits not just the individual but the entire group. Exercises reveal how well units, from platoons to divisions, will operate when deployed or when facing a crisis. The military conducts exercises and maneuvers to test new procedures, to coordinate operations across branches, and to practice working with allies. Some exercises are enormous. NATO's annual Reforger (or Return of Forces to Germany) exercise, held each year from 1969 to 1993, involved airlifting thousands of American troops from the United States and bringing them to West Germany, where they connected with other American and allied forces and trained using equipment that had been stockpiled in Europe. Another large exercise, Cobra Gold, held in Thailand each year since 1981, involves thousands of troops from the United States and Thailand, and sometimes other Asian nations. Some exercises require troops, aircraft, and ships to be deployed overseas, but others focus on leadership and coordination without actually moving the troops and war materiel. In command post exercises like NATO's Allied Warrior, or the more prosaically named RSOI (Receiving, Staging, Onward-movement and Integration), held annually in South Korea, personnel practice organizing major troop movements in and out of the country.

In some cases, exercises are used to conduct experiments. In September 2000, for example, the Army began a series of exercises to see whether infantry troops could become lighter and more flexible without losing lethality.[4] In Sharp Focus, a 2005 exercise in Germany, American forces worked from a script that imagined an African nation disintegrating into chaos. U.S. forces arrived to help out, testing methods and procedures.

"The essence of Sharp Focus 05," according to the *Stars and Stripes*, ". . . was to weigh diplomatic, economic, cultural and regional factors before directing troops on the ground."[5] In these and other exercises, the goal was to see what worked and what didn't, rather than to practice an already established technique.

And, of course, units practice and drill to prepare for combat. In 2003, Army combat units getting ready for the war in Iraq rehearsed aircraft takeoffs and landings in desert sand and dust, fired live rounds at targets, and practiced communicating with each other and with other branches. As the war has continued, the military has incorporated recent combat experiences into drills and training. Units carry out mock cordon-and-search missions, deal with ambushes of convoys and exploding IEDs (improvised explosive devices), and practice capturing HVTs—high value targets—such as terrorist leaders.[6]

Exercises take place all over the world. In recent years, U.S. forces have trained in many nations from Israel and Egypt, to Thailand and the Philippines, to Niger and Mongolia. In many of these exercises, U.S. service-members train military forces from the host nation. Such international exercises have been stepped up in recent years as the United States tries to help other nations defeat terrorists and insurgencies. Despite public concerns in many host nations about the U.S. troop presence on their soil, the American forces have tried very hard to "minimize the amount of soldiers' boots that are on the ground," in the words of one Army colonel involved in operations in Africa. "We're not trying to create a huge footprint."[7] Wherever they go, U.S. forces offer goodwill humanitarian aid, setting up temporary medical clinics, delivering supplies, or building roads and bridges. A major who organized a series of clinics in Thailand summed up the goal of the Army's humanitarian efforts, noting that when a civilian receives help at an Army medical clinic, "he remembers the Americans did that."[8]

Some drills and maneuvers require firing ranges, fields, and tracks that are specially designed for exercises. The Army has three major combat training centers: the NTC (National Training Center) at Fort Irwin, California; the JRTC (Joint Readiness Training Center) at Fort Polk, Louisiana; and the CMTC (Combat Maneuver Training Center) in Hohenfels, Germany. These training centers have huge firing ranges, but they offer much more than target practice. In the past several years, the units operating the centers have created elaborate "sets" to give the troops on maneuver the feeling that they are actually in Kosovo, Afghanistan, or Iraq. The sets include fake villages with shops, restaurants and homes, and populations of "citizens" who are hired to act the part. "Civilians on the battlefield" or COBs, as the amateur actors are called, dress authentically, act the way civilians in the country would, and sometimes cause trouble the way real civilians might. The cast may include "'pregnant' women, men with heart conditions, confused civilians yelling in foreign languages"—the types of people the troops will encounter when they are deployed for real.[9] Residents from towns near the training centers play the roles, earning up to $80 a day.[10]

COBs can act the part of civilians, but they cannot pretend to be enemy combatants. For this role, each of the training centers is home to an "Op For" or opposing force, an infantry unit whose purpose is to play the part of an enemy force for units training at the center. Using laser weapons, the Op For harasses the visiting unit with ambushes, roadside bombs, snipers, and other attacks. When a troop from either side is "hit," sensors record a casualty. Troop movements are electronically monitored, and the entire event is recorded and analyzed. According to a senate staffer who visited the training centers in the United States, the visiting units are "typically pretty thoroughly whipped by the very highly skilled—virtually elite" Op Fors.[11]

The training centers also operate simulators of various types. Using this arcade game-like equipment, servicemembers can train at a fraction of the cost of real equipment, and the simulators enable them to train in different types of conditions. Shortly after the NTC was established, one battalion commander said that with its new and extensive simulators, it was "one of the greatest things that ever happened to the Army."[12]

The variety of exercises the military conducts is astounding. Some are obvious: for example, after practicing on simulators, tank crews maneuver their M1 tanks into battle position and fire live rounds at plywood targets, which move along on tracks far in the distance.[13] Infantry teams spend weeks in the jungle conducting ambush and reconnaissance patrols and attacking the "enemy."[14] Army helicopter pilots fire Hellfire missiles at targets on the ground while communicating with tank crews, to "replicate the combined arms fight."[15] Air Force pilots and crews practice "surges" working at an exhausting pace for a week or more as they will do in war.[16]

Other exercises test the skills and readiness of support troops. The annual Combined Endeavor exercise, held in Europe for two weeks each spring, brings troops from forty-one nations together to test their communications equipment, much of which is incompatible.[17] In another annual exercise, the Air Force uses its C-130 aircraft in mock airlifts, moving Army troops and equipment from one place to another.[18] There are exercises for the security forces who guard military bases, giving them practice in what to do if a vehicle crashes through the gate or tries to carry a bomb onto the base,[19] simulated emergencies to test medical personnel, and even drills for public affairs officers, in which they face hostile questioning from "reporters" and "the public" in the wake of (mock) incidents like civilian riots or terrorist attacks.[20]

It may sound strange to civilians, but for most servicemembers, exercises are among the high points of life in the military. On one hand, they take personnel away from their families to work long hours, sometimes in uncomfortable conditions. But exercises are where the troops do what they are trained to do in the job specialities they have chosen. And they know the value of practice and drill. After a month-long exercise in clearing mines and other obstacles, one private in a combat engineering battalion noted: "That was a lot of fun...It was a long exercise, but you can never do too much training."[21]

Unfortunately, the unexpected duration and intensity of the wars in Iraq and Afghanistan has put a serious dent in military training. Active duty units in the Army and Marines have only twelve months, or even less, to retrain after returning from the combat zone before they are deployed overseas once again. They simply do not have time to plan and conduct the exercises that are necessary to keep their skills sharp. Moreover, their equipment is being damaged and degraded by harsh use in Iraq, and so even when they have the time, they do not always have the vehicles, weapons, and gear they need to train with. In the beginning of 2007, the new Democratic Congress began holding hearings on the U.S. forces. Dire warnings came from commanders that the pace of deployment and the lack of equipment would lead to a crisis in readiness.[22] Some of this concern was politically driven by members of Congress who opposed a troop "surge" in Iraq, but the problems faced by overstretched combat units are not imaginary.

An additional, and perhaps more worrisome problem is emerging from the battlegrounds in Iraq and Afghanistan: American troops are fighting a different war than the one they trained for. Since World War I, America's armed forces have been trained and equipped to conduct high-intensity, mechanized warfare using sophisticated aircraft, tanks, and weapons systems. The enemy they expected to face (and which they did face in four twentieth-century wars) was a nation-state with relatively well-equipped and trained military forces, such as Germany and Japan, the Soviet Union, North Korea, Iraq under Saddam Hussein, or Iran. Indeed, the American military twice proved its prowess in high-intensity combat against Saddam Hussein's forces. But today it is fighting a low-level counterinsurgency carried out by a shadowy coalition of guerillas and terrorists from all sides of a very complicated conflict. It is, of course, a good thing that lifesaving counterinsurgency skills are being incorporated into exercises and maneuvers. But this training is eroding the warfighting skills that would be needed should the United States go to war with Iran or North Korea. Military leaders are struggling to find a balance between the war they are fighting and the war they might be called upon to fight in the future.

RESERVE AND NATIONAL GUARD FORCES

Reserve and National Guard troops play a more important role than ever in today's national defense. Taken together, 850,000 servicemembers in the seven branches of the reserve forces make up about 40 percent of the total strength of the U.S. military. The 1997 Quadrennial Defense Review states: "Reserve forces are part of all war plans. No major operation can be successful without them."[23]

Reliance on the reserve forces has been official policy since the switch to the All-Volunteer Force in 1973, but during the Cold War the part-time forces were thought of as a "strategic reserve," available in case of serious national emergency where a conflict went on for an unexpectedly long time. Meanwhile Reserve and National Guard units regularly coped with a variety of short-term emergencies, such as wildfires, floods, and other natural disasters. Since the end of the Cold War, and especially since 2001, the reserve forces have become a major part of the operational forces available to defense planners; that is, they are routinely deployed along with active duty forces in Iraq, Afghanistan, and around the world. No longer is the Reserve or National Guard a matter of one weekend a month, two weeks a year. "When a guy gets in the Guard nowadays," says the commander of the Alabama Army National Guard, "he can figure that he's going to be deployed somewhere."[24]

National Guard troops from New York were mobilized within hours of the attacks on the World Trade Center on September 11, and since then, Guard and Reserve units from all fifty states, especially military police and civil affairs units, have been deployed along with active duty forces. Over 60 percent of the Army's support forces are Reserves or National Guard,[25] so when active duty Army units began to be sent to Afghanistan and Iraq, the reserves stepped in to guard bases, perform maintenance and construction, drive trucks, gather intelligence, and deal with the public as civil affairs specialists. For the past five years they have been an important presence on military bases in Europe and Asia. In fact, reserve engineer battalions built many of the mock villages and urban areas at the Army's training centers.[26]

Reserve forces make up about 40 percent of the 130,000 troops in Iraq and the 20,000 in Afghanistan. The deployment of reserves in the past few years is the largest since World War II. The normal tour of duty in Iraq for both active duty and reserve personnel is twelve months, but many reserve units stay even longer, up to two years. It is not especially uncommon for reserve units to serve in Iraq, return home, and within 18 months be sent to Kosovo, Afghanistan or even to another tour in Iraq.

The mobilization of reservists in today's hot spots has not come without costs. For one thing, many reserve units, especially early in the war, were poorly equipped with outdated surplus weapons and vehicles. When the war in Iraq began, the Pentagon took some of the modern equipment that the reserves did have and gave it to active duty units.[27] Another problem has been the integration of reserve forces into the combat units in Iraq and Afghanistan. According to a 2003 survey by the *Stars and Stripes,* many reserve troops have felt that they are treated like second-class soldiers. Although many or most of them have had prior active duty experience, they perceived a lack of respect from the full-timers and felt that they received more than their fair share of the less desirable duties.[28] Lately, this problem seems to have been resolved, but in the first months of the Iraq conflict, reserve troops were much more likely to suffer from low morale than active duty personnel.

On the home front, the reliance on reserve forces has caused stresses and strains as well. Families of reservists, living in the civilian world, do not have access to the same support networks that active duty families do. They don't always live near a military base where they can shop and socialize with other military families. They may suffer financially as well; when reserve troops leave their civilian jobs to serve overseas, they often take significant pay cuts. Reserve troops must fight a war in another country while worrying that their families are struggling and their careers damaged by their absence.

The deployment of reserves is taking its toll on communities as well. Many people in the reserves hold civilian jobs as firefighters, police officers, sheriffs, prison guards, and other security and emergency personnel. When they deploy, they are sorely missed. In one Arkansas town, the mayor and the police chief were both sent to Iraq at the same time, leaving the 79-year-old town treasurer to step in. The mobilization of reserve forces has left states worried about their ability to respond to natural disasters.[29] Most tragically, when a reserve unit is hit in an attack or roadside bombing, the casualties are likely to be from the same or neighboring towns, creating a sudden, devastating cluster of losses.[30]

CIVILIAN EMPLOYEES

In May 2005, a unit of U.S. marines in Iraq arrested sixteen civilian contractors and held them in the military brig for three days. The Marines claimed that the civilians, who were working as armed escorts, had fired on them and on Iraqi civilians. According to the American civilians, however, the Marines abused them during the arrest and later in detention. "When I was put face down on the ground to be cuffed," one contractor told a reporter, "I heard one Marine ask me, 'How's it feel to make that contractor's money now?'"[31] Unsurprisingly, the Marines denied the allegations. Reports indicate that all of the contractors, who worked for a company called Zapata Engineering, were former military personnel, and half of them had been in the Marine Corps.

Whatever the truth of the Zapata story, it illustrates the complex and sometimes tense relationship between the armed forces and the civilian employees working with them. The 16 men arrested by the Marines in 2005 were just a few of the estimated 130,000 civilians employed by private contracting firms hired by U.S. organizations in Iraq.[32] About 10,000–15,000 of these are American citizens; according to Peter Singer, an expert on the privatization of the military, there is one civilian contract employee for every ten military personnel in Iraq.[33]

There are several reasons for the large number of civilian contractors. For one thing, the U.S. and Iraqi governments have hired many civilian companies to do reconstruction work in Iraq, rebuilding the damaged infrastructure and the oil-based economy. There are also civilian guards providing security for the civilian reconstruction companies as well as for U.S. agencies like the State Department.[34] Most importantly, since the 1990s, the military has hired increasing numbers of private firms to do tasks that the military itself used to do, as a way of cutting costs and enabling military personnel to focus on its core capability, that is, combat. Privatizing government services, from airlines and telephone companies to banks, has been a trend in the United States and around the world for several decades, so the privatization of some military work should come as no surprise.

The civilians who work for these companies are from other nations as well as the United States. Some have military experience, or specialized skills of some sort, while others do not. But whatever their particular circumstances, most are attracted by the hefty pay offered by the private firms, up to $1000 a day in some cases. It is not uncommon for American civilian contractors to make six-figure salaries as drivers or guards in Iraq.

The civilians have taken on a number of tasks. According to a 2005 *Frontline* report, some 50,000 civilians in Iraq alone, mostly Filipino, work for Kellogg, Brown and Root and other companies that provide logistical services to the armed forces. KBR, which holds DoD contracts in Afghanistan, Bosnia, and Kosovo, has earned enormous sums providing food, fuel, laundry services, recreation, cleaning, and maintenance for the troops living in camps and bases in those areas.[35] Another 20,000 provide security services of various types. They are bodyguards for VIPs and guards for military bases and civilian sites where the threat of attack is high. Some of these employees are former military personnel from the United States and other nations, and they train and supervise larger numbers of Iraqi guards.[36] Other companies, like Zapata Engineering, dispose of bombs and explosive materials. There are also companies that provide military training and advice to local forces. Most of the employees in this second group are former military personnel, who command high salaries for their experience and skills.[37] A final group of 40,000–70,000 engineers and construction experts have been hired to help rebuild Iraq.[38]

The main reason for using civilian contractors is that they cost less than military personnel. They are paid more, it is true, but military personnel receive costly training and benefits for themselves and their families. The contractors, on the other hand, are paid as long as they are needed, and then let go. The government is not responsible for their pensions, health care, or housing. All experts agree that this is the most commonly cited justification for using civilian contractors, but they disagree on whether civilians actually do cost less, or whether civilians are worth the money they are paid. Some see graft and corruption built into the system. KBR, for example, has been accused of overbilling the government to the tune of billions. For-profit firms, unlike government agencies, have every reason to charge the government as much as they can, while skimping on services if they can get away with it.[39]

Cost is just one reason why many critics are concerned about the increasing use of civilian contractors by the armed forces. Another worry is that civilians are not under the military's control, and in a dangerous environment where people are either friends or foes, but never neutral, poor coordination between civilians and military can put lives at risk. Civilians can unintentionally interfere with military operations, or appear to pose a threat to edgy troops by being in the wrong place at the wrong time.[40] A third problem with civilians' ambiguous status is their lack of accountability. They operate in a gray zone where they are immune from prosecution if they commit crimes. In 2002, for example, civilian contractors working for DynCorp, a security and equipment maintenance firm, were accused of keeping a ring of young women and girls as sex slaves in Bosnia. There was no investigation; instead, the alleged perpetrators were simply fired and sent home.[41] Several civilians were implicated in the 2004 Abu Ghraib prisoner abuse scandal in Iraq, but, unlike military personnel, they could not be court-martialed.[42] Critics have accused the government of relying on civilian contractors to get around Congressional restrictions on troop use and avoid public outcry against shady operations. Even if civilian operations avoid attention in the United States, however, abuses by individuals acting in the name of the U.S. military can bring worldwide wrath down on the United States, undoing American friendship efforts and endangering deployed troops.

A final problem with contractors is that they are not bound by an oath of allegiance as military personnel are. If individuals or corporations decide it is too dangerous to stay in an area, they can leave. This does not seem to have happened yet, but if it does, the military forces relying on contractors may be left dangerously vulnerable.

Civilians worked alongside military forces long before the current conflicts began, of course. The military has long hired private firms to provide specific services for military personnel. The advertising firms hired to recruit young people, described in Chapter 1, are civilian contractors for the military, for example. Civilian contractors handle much of the quotidian work done on military bases and especially in housing areas. Civilian construction firms build and maintain the facilities on bases. Most large bases have fast-food restaurants and shops in their exchanges that employ civilians, and since the late 1940s, colleges and universities have held contracts with the military to provide higher education to military personnel and family members.

Another type of civilian worker is under the administration of the DoD. Civilian DoD employment on base is funded by either AF (appropriated funds) or NAF (nonappropriated funds). The AF positions, more commonly known as GS, are funded by Congress and regulated by the civil service. The DoD employs about 616,000 GS civilians around the world, and they receive the same benefits and salaries that employees of federal agencies everywhere do.[43] GS employees on military bases usually work in offices like payroll, housing, and public relations. NAF positions are funded by the proceeds from MWR activities and may include work in base clubs, commissary cashiers, child-care workers, and other work related to the support operations of the base. They are regulated by the DoD, not the federal civil service, and funding fluctuates depending on the amount of revenue the MWR takes in. Many GS and NAF employees are former military personnel; the federal government gives preference to veterans in its hiring. Others are family members, who find it easier to move from job to job in government service than to start fresh in private firms every time they relocate.

ON DUTY IN THE MILITARY, PAST AND PRESENT

Today's servicemembers work extremely hard, but they devote less time than ever to the boring and strenuous labor that filled the days of soldiers and sailors in earlier decades. Until the recent move toward privatizing noncombat related work, military personnel even during wartime spent many hours each day performing cleaning, maintenance, and guard chores. In the nineteenth-century Army, soldiers and officers living in frontier garrisons labored to make their living spaces habitable. They built their forts themselves, and grew, raised or hunted most of their food. Soldiers who enlisted in the Army to get away from lives of hard labor on farms or in cities found themselves doing the very work they had joined the military to escape—caring for livestock, tending vegetable gardens, collecting

firewood, and building stockades and barracks. Enlisted men also operated bakeries, milled their own lumber, and collected firewood and water.
Work on board naval vessels was even worse, consisting of hundreds
of maintenance chores that had to be performed each day in order to
keep the harsh wind and sea from picking apart the wooden vessels or
their rigging.

Through most of the nineteenth century, the U.S. armed forces acted as
constabularies or police forces, patrolling the seas or protecting white
settlers from Native American fighters. Later, the Army and Navy did similar work in the Philippines, Panama, and other areas of American
influence outside the United States. In those days, rebellions and unrest
would flare up regularly, and regiments would receive sudden orders to
move to a new area to quell a rebellion. Soldiers looked forward to setting
out on the campaign trail. It usually meant miles of hard marching every
day, camping outdoors, and subsisting on rations and whatever fish and
game was available, but it was always a welcome break from the tedium
of garrison life.

One additional job that some soldiers took on was that of "striker," or
servant to an officer's family. Strikers cooked, cleaned, even ironed and
took care of children. Soldiers earned extra money as strikers and temporarily escaped the restrictive barracks life. Other soldiers took extra work
teaching in elementary schools for children on military posts. But for most
soldiers, life on frontier garrisons was monotonous and isolated, and it is
no surprise that desertion on the frontier was a constant problem, especially when soldiers had been in garrison for extended periods.

Soldiers were not averse to lives of ease, of course, and in the period
between the two world wars, when the armed forces had no imminent
threat to prepare for, garrison life was relatively easy. After spending
three years suppressing the Philippine insurrection (1899–1902), the
Army occupied the country for another four decades. When they moved
into a new area, they built their quarters and barracks from wood they
had brought in and laid down new roads. In some more dangerous areas,
the threat of violence never disappeared, so soldiers continued to be on
the alert, called to arms when insurrectionists attacked. In more peaceable
regions, the routine was relatively easy. The day began early: soldiers rose
at reveille at 5 or 6, ate breakfast, cleaned their barracks and equipment,
and performed drill until lunchtime. Work broke after lunch to avoid
the heat, and afternoons were mostly quiet, with classes and inspections
taking up a few hours. The workday ended at around 5 P.M., although soldiers took turns guarding the posts day and night. Cavalrymen cared for
their horses, infantrymen practiced close-order drill, and company clerks
always had paperwork to finish.[44] But, by and large, it was an easy life.
Officers had an even easier time of it. "This post is like a big country

club," wrote Lt. Col. William Lassiter in 1915. "A little work in the morning. Golf, polo, tennis, riding in the hills in the afternoon. The Club at sunset. Dinner in the evenings. A lazy man's paradise."[45] Life was even better for the 2nd and 3rd battalions of the 15th Infantry Regiment who were stationed at Tientsin, China, and the Marine Corps stationed in Beijing and Shanghai during the decades before World War II broke out. Sent to China to protect American interests during the tumult of the civil war period, the American personnel in China led a notoriously comfortable existence. Chinese servants did almost all the work for officers and men, and life consisted of parades, inspections, and the very occasional response to an outbreak of violence. Many men enlisted in the Army with the sole intention of going to China with the 15th, and those who were there tried to stay. The Army left Tientsin in 1938. The Marines in Beijing and Shanghai were not so lucky—several hundred were captured by the Japanese and spent the war years as POWs.

RACE

It is a common observation that African-Americans are overrepresented in the armed forces today. While this overrepresentation is not spread equally across the different branches of the military or among the ranks, it is true that the proportion of African-Americans in the armed forces—about 25 percent—is more than twice as high as the proportion of African-Americans in society as a whole.

There is some irony in this, because the military in the United States has been strongly discriminatory against African-Americans for far longer than it has welcomed them in. In colonial America, African-Americans were not allowed to serve in the armed forces, for fear that they would use their weapons and fighting skills to support slave revolts. They joined on both sides in the Revolutionary War, hoping for better treatment when it was over, but afterwards they were again barred from service. They fought in large numbers for the Union during the Civil War; at the close of hostilities there were 166 black regiments.[46] For the next eighty years, African-Americans served in segregated units, mostly in transportation and labor support units. There were all-black infantry and cavalry regiments in the frontier Army, but they were led by white officers. African-Americans volunteered and were drafted to fight in World War II, and about 1.8 million black soldiers, sailors, airmen, and Marines served in the armed forces during the war. [47] The wartime forces were segregated and most African-Americans served in support units, but at times black troops fought alongside whites.

The war, and especially the occupation of Germany and Japan, highlighted the absurdity and unfairness of segregation. Germans noticed that they were being taught lessons in democracy and equality by white military government personnel who would not eat in the same restaurant as their African-American comrades. African-Americans hoped that their military service would earn them more respect and equal opportunity.

The military was officially desegregated on July 26, 1948, by order of President Harry S. Truman, but several years later, in the early days of the Korean War, the historic all-black 24th Infantry Regiment was deployed as a segregated unit. In time, however, the needs of that conflict put an end to unofficial segregation.

During the 1950s, when large numbers of troops were stationed overseas in countries with no history of antiblack discrimination, African-American troops experienced for the first time the sense that race was not the most important characteristic that defined them. The military itself was integrated in terms of housing and jobs, and in relations with local civilians, black troops experienced relatively little discrimination compared to what they put up with the United States. African-American servicemembers married European, Japanese, Filipina, and Korean women, and often requested extended tours or stayed overseas when they got out of the military.

However, in the United States, black troops still could not find suitable housing off-base, they could not eat in restaurants with white friends and they found themselves in danger if they appeared in public with their white wives. As the civil rights movement dovetailed with the Vietnam War, issues of discrimination in the military resurfaced. Critics pointed out that although the military was officially desegregated, in fact it was quite unbalanced racially. African-Americans were more likely to get drafted because fewer of them were in college, and because of lower average test scores, they were less likely to be allowed to train for skilled occupations. They were overrepresented in the combat arms branches where they suffered disproportionate numbers of casualties. The injustice went even further; many African-Americans were not accepted into the military because of low test scores or criminal records, so the black troops who did make it in were in fact among the most educated and the most able young men in their communities.[48]

The upheaval of the Vietnam War and the civil rights movement further disrupted race relations in the military as angry black soldiers demanded an end to informal, subtle discrimination such as a lack of black hair and skin care products in the PX or the jukeboxes in base clubs that played only country music. Between 1968 and 1973, serious racial unrest and riots embittered the atmosphere on bases in the United States and overseas.

In spite of racial tensions in the armed forces, however, African-Americans continued to join the ranks. When the draft was abolished in 1973, black participation in the military rose dramatically. By 1981, 19.8 percent of the armed forces were African-American. In the Army today, African-Americans make up 33.2 percent of the enlisted force, and African-American women make up about half of the Army's enlisted women.[49]

Some critics have charged that overrepresentation of African-Americans in the military is in effect exploiting the most vulnerable members of society, those with the fewest choices in life. It has been said that African-Americans in the military are an "underclass," disposable men and women used as cannon fodder, and that recruiters target them deliberately. It is certainly true that the overrepresentation of African-Americans in the military is a troubling sign of societal imbalance, but the facts are somewhat more nuanced, if no less of a matter of concern. The critical interpretation assumes that military service is a burden unfairly borne by underprivileged African-American youth. Not everyone sees it that way, however. Many African-Americans look at military service for what it can offer: steady employment, health and retirement benefits, education and training, and a chance to start a new life. African-Americans in the military are better educated, have more stable and better-educated families, and make more money than their peers in civilian life.[50] For many African-Americans, military service is an attractive career path for the most upwardly mobile members of black communities. African-Americans are more likely to finish their first enlistment periods successfully, and they choose the military as a career much more frequently than whites do.[51] A study conducted in the early 1990s showed that 69 percent of black veterans wished they had chosen the Army as a career, opposed to 37 percent of white veterans. The overrepresentation of African-Americans in the armed forces is not so much a sign of exploitation as it is a reflection of lack of opportunity in the civilian world.

Certainly there are racial problems in the military. One concern is the structure of military careers and leadership. The proportion of African-American officers in all branches is less than their representation in civilian society, although over 11 percent of Army officers are black,[52] and 35 percent of the NCOs in the Army are African-American. African-Americans are less likely to sign up for special operations training such as Navy Seals or Army Rangers, even though such elite training can be a boon to a military career,[53] and some occupational specialties, such as fighter aircraft pilots, still seem to be "white men's clubs." On the other hand, African-American servicemembers are more likely to pursue a college education than their civilian counterparts. The statistics paint a confused picture, and clearly there is work to be done. But more progress toward racial equality has occurred in the military than in any other organization in American society.

GENDER IN THE MILITARY

Women have served with the armed forces since the Army and Navy were established in the 1790s, although usually not in officially recognized ways. Military wives traveled with their husbands to isolated posts, sharing the hardships, dangers, and excitement of frontier life. In the nineteenth century, the Army authorized women to work as laundresses, four to a company. They were the only women in garrison who received pay and rations; many of these women were married to enlisted men, while others lived in squalid conditions in "soapsuds row" on the edge of the post. Occasionally, women got closer to the action. Calamity Jane, the famous frontierswoman, served in Gen. George Armstrong Custer's Seventh Cavalry Regiment as a scout, and possibly as an enlisted soldier.

During World War I, at a time when American women did not have the right to vote, about 33,000 served the nation as part of the armed forces. The Army and Navy Nurse Corps accounted for about 20,000 of these women, and the rest enlisted in the Navy and Marine Corps as regular active duty personnel, performing clerical and administrative tasks and earning the same pay as men.

Shortly after the Japanese attack on Pearl Harbor, Congress created the WAAC (Women's Army Auxiliary Corps), which later became part of the regular Army as the WAC (Women's Army Corps). Members of the WAC and their naval counterparts, the WAVES, served in support positions, "freeing up the men to fight," and about 350,000 women served in World War II. Most women left military service after the war, but the WAC continued as a permanent corps until the 1970s.

In 1948, Congress capped the percentage of women allowed to serve at 2 percent, but with the creation of the AVF, the cap was lifted and more and more women joined. By the late 1970s, about 7 percent of the enlisted force was female.

Toward the close of the Cold War, women served in military operations in Grenada, Panama, and the Persian Gulf, many in combat, which was officially against the rules. In the 1990s, many of the restrictions on women serving were lifted, including most combat exclusion laws and the risk rule, which prohibited women from serving in areas where they faced a "risk of exposure to direct combat, hostile fire, or capture."[54] Basic training was integrated in all branches but the Marines, and today, women are eligible for 95 percent of the job categories in the military, restricted only from direct ground combat. They make up about 15 percent of the armed forces, and are more likely than their white male coworkers to make the military a career.

But that is not the end of the story. In the years directly following the expansion of women in the military, a spate of sex scandals heated up the debate about whether and in what circumstances women should serve. The most notorious of these include the story of the "Love Boat," the Navy ship Arcadia, on which 10 percent of the 360 women serving became pregnant while serving in the 1991 Gulf War; the Tailhook debacle of the same year; the Aberdeen Proving Ground scandal of 1996 that ended with several drill sergeants sent to prison for raping or harassing female trainees; and the 1997 resignation of B-52 pilot Kelly Flinn, who left the Air Force after facing a court-martial for having an affair with a married man.

It is little wonder that many in and out of the military called for a reassessment of the role of women in the armed forces. Some critics saw a "fatal feminization" of the military, as standards eroded and toughness went out.[55] Others asserted that the presence of women in military units hurt morale and *esprit de corps*, and introduced sexual tensions that were not present in single-sex units. "A higher percentage of women was associated with lower cohesion," according to a 1999 study published in *Armed Forces and Society*.[56] Still others cited concerns about the ability of women to "pull their weight"—to perform physically demanding tasks, cope with mental and emotional pressures, and if necessary show the same ruthlessness as men.[57] Finally, some opponents of women in the military charged that female servicemembers deliberately became pregnant to receive special treatment or to avoid deployment, and accused men of sexual harassment when challenged.

Countering these arguments, defenders of women in the military pointed to studies showing that women did their jobs as well as men and had lower rates of indiscipline than their male counterparts. They claimed that gender stereotypes among both males and females[58] and a pervasive "masculinist culture" in the armed forces denigrated women and denied them equal rights.[59] Women who had served in the military complained of a hostile environment, and research backed this up.[60]

Experts were divided on whether the military should change its inclusive policies, but many recommended that the military combat harassment and discrimination by "controlling overt sexual commentary and public behavior"[61] first of all, and deal with underlying attitudes next. The military responded energetically, rejecting the idea of cutting the number of women in the armed forces and creating new policies on sexual harassment. Other subtle changes improved the climate for women. Military-related media outlets, for example, like the *Army Times* and the *Stars and Stripes,* have taken great pains to include the voices of women in stories about military matters of all types. Above all, women have played an important role in Afghanistan and Iraq, where everyone faces the risk of combat. As of the end of 2006, 155,000 women were deployed to the war zone, 68 women died there, and 430 have been wounded.

To be sure, some may see this as a dubious achievement, but it is proof that women's contributions to the war effort are wide-ranging and valuable.[62]

GAYS IN THE MILITARY

The issue of gay soldiers has been a contentious one since 1993 when President Bill Clinton tried to do away with the ban on homosexuals serving in the military. In response to the uproar in and out of the armed forces, the policy was amended to prohibit recruiters from asking questions about a recruit's sexual orientation, while officially gay men and women were still not allowed to serve. The "don't ask, don't tell" policy proved to be an awkward compromise that satisfied no one.

As early as 1978, some law schools banned military recruiters from their campuses because the military discriminated against homosexuals. Since then, a number of school districts and state universities have followed suit, but in the mid-1990s, Congress retaliated with the Solomon Amendment, denying federal funds to schools that prohibit military recruiting on their campuses. In 2003, under pressure from the DoD, many colleges and universities made exceptions to their nondiscrimination policies, allowing recruiters on campus. A recent Supreme Court decision sided with the DoD, but said that schools did not have to welcome the recruiters on campus with open arms, suggesting that schools voice their opposition by organizing protests against the presence of the military.

Critics of the ban on homosexuals in the armed forces charged that the rule was simply unfair and because of simple prejudice denied qualified individuals the right to serve their country. Those advocating the ban said that the presence of gay soldiers hurt unit morale and cohesion, and that the military was not the place to carry out social experiments. Whatever the merits of the arguments, the "don't ask, don't tell" policy failed to please anyone. Between 1994 and 2003, 9,500 military personnel were discharged from the service for homosexuality, costing the government over $360 million in lost training and recruiting replacements. Moreover, gay servicemembers, studies show, tend to have more advanced training than others, as linguists, medical specialists, and intelligence experts. As many as fifty-five Arabic and Farsi linguists were discharged from the military for homosexuality between 1998 and 2004, according to a 2005 report.[63]

The DoD says that only about 10 percent of the involuntary separations in the military involve homosexuality, far lower than the rates of discharge for drug abuse, pregnancy, weight, and behavior problems.[64] Like the assimilation of African-Americans and women into the armed forces, the gradual acceptance of gay soldiers, already begun on the small unit level, will probably seep up into the higher ranks until the policy is changed.

CHAPTER 6

OFF DUTY IN THE ARMED FORCES

Today's servicemembers work longer hours than ever before. But whether they are stationed at an FOB in Iraq or at a large base in the United States, they do occasionally go off duty, and, like anyone else, they want to relax and have fun in their free time. Unfortunately, soldiers and sailors are all too often celebrated as they are sent off to war but shunned when they return to the garrison and to the civilian world.

Civilian neighbors, both in the past and today, often worry about what will happen when troops leave their bases and interact with residents of the local community. And there's a lot of common sense in this concern. Soldiers are young, usually single, male, and tend to socialize in groups. They are far from home and free from the cultural and social pressures that might put brakes on their behavior. They have money in their pockets and, if they are lucky, few bills to pay.

Such a profile would give anyone pause. In every society, young men comprise the vast majority of those accused and convicted in crimes and antisocial behavior. Moreover, some critics of the armed forces contend that the culture of the military exacerbates aggression and even criminal behavior on the part of military personnel. Soldiers, some argue, have been acculturated to violence through their combat training; the cultural norms of the armed forces include tolerance of aggression toward women; and military commanders turn a blind eye to the shenanigans of their soldiers off base, excusing them as normal "boys will be boys" behavior.

In the past there was a great deal of truth to these charges, and older attitudes may not have disappeared entirely. But military leadership at all levels devotes a great deal of time to thinking about how to keep soldiers and sailors occupied while they are not working or training. Base commanders make sure that facilities like movie theaters, bowling alleys, gymnasiums, and libraries are attractive and available. The military has an extensive sports program, college education opportunities, and civilian experts on base to help soldiers plan trips and vacations.

Commanders also monitor the off-base establishments frequented by soldiers, using military police patrols and off-limits designations to try to keep everyone safe and happy. It doesn't always work, but there is less reason than ever before to mistrust today's servicemembers.

ON-BASE RECREATION

Military personnel have available to them a wide variety of entertainment and recreation options on base. Most of these are organized by personnel at Morale, Welfare, and Recreation offices, which exist on almost all bases, large and small. From organized sports to hobby clubs, the MWR tries to give troops and their families a choice of things to do when they get out of work.

Although the MWR office plays an important role on a military base, the activities it offers vary from base to base and from year to year because since the mid-1980s they have been funded with NAF revenues rather than through annual Congressional appropriations. That means that the taxpayer doesn't pay for most MWR activities; the military itself must come up with the money (libraries and gymnasiums are the exception). Part of the funding for MWR comes from user fees and rentals, and part comes from the slot machines that are ubiquitous on military bases overseas. The slot machines, mostly run by the Army, bring in about $75 million a year, and fund programs and construction of MWR facilities throughout the world.[1]

There are some MWR programs and facilities that are fairly standard on military bases, such as recreation centers, where personnel can buy tickets to local shows, arrange vacations, and take classes. Others, like hobby and auto shops, bowling alleys, swimming pools, and community theaters, are found only at larger bases. MWR programs vary according to locale; servicemembers can ski, scuba dive, play golf, climb mountains, or bicycle across Europe, depending on where they are stationed.

MWR also operates Armed Forces Recreation Centers in Hawaii, South Korea, and Germany. These are resorts where military personnel and families can vacation at a fraction of the cost of civilian resorts. They are booked well in advance, but are well worth the effort necessary to plan a visit. Another well-known MWR facility is the military club system. In the old days, MWR operated separate clubs for junior enlisted personnel, NCOs, officers, and even civilians, but today the club system has consolidated. On most bases, there are no longer separate clubs for NCOs and lower enlisted personnel, but rather an "all grades" club for all enlisted ranks and an officers' club. They offer dining rooms, bars and game rooms, and sometimes golf courses, swimming pools, and tennis courts.

Morale is one of the great intangibles of an organization, and nowhere is it more important than in the military, where troops live and work together in close proximity. Serious disaffection can spread through a base community like a disease, rendering units almost nonfunctioning. Commanders have long known this, and good leaders keep a close eye on morale. Starting at the end of the nineteenth century, the Army and Navy began operating libraries, sports clubs, and troop canteens for the troops. In World War I, morale activities expanded, and in 1920, the Army Motion Picture Service began showing films to soldiers. By the 1930s, most wartime morale programs had disappeared, but in 1940, the Army established the Morale Division, which later became Army MWR; other branches established their own MWR organizations. From the end of World War II until the mid-1980s, morale programs were run by active duty personnel; One of the Army's MOS options was "recreation specialist," highlighting the importance the Army placed on MWR activities. Today these positions are filled by civilian employees, but the MWR continues to add to the plethora of military support services available.

MWR activities have assumed greater importance in recent years for several reasons. The first is a simple matter of recruitment and retention—troops who are bored and dissatisfied with off-duty life will leave the service, no matter how much they may enjoy their jobs.[2] In today's AVF, the military cannot afford to lose large numbers of expensively trained troops simply because they have nothing to do after work.

A second reason that, with so many troops deployed to Iraq and Afghanistan, commanders want to make sure that those left behind, whether active duty personnel or family members, do not have a reason to "sit on base and mope," as one Outdoor Recreation center director in Germany put it.[3] Recreation specialists organize shopping and sightseeing trips off base for spouses and various family-friendly activities to ward off the worry and loneliness of separation.

Perhaps the most important reason that commanders are expanding the MWR programs on their installations is because they want to keep the troops on base. Troops with nothing to do after work will leave to spend their money and time in nearby civilian towns, where they all too often make adversaries rather than friends. Off-duty carousing results in lost productivity, health problems, and crime; in addition, commanders do not want their soldiers preyed upon by unscrupulous civilian merchants. Moreover, commanders are increasingly aware of the importance of the public reputation of the U.S. armed forces, especially overseas. In many strategically vital regions of the world, such as Okinawa, the Philippines, and South Korea, the behavior of American soldiers has led to calls for their removal. Today, when a soldier commits a crime against a civilian, it often becomes a rallying cry for opponents of military bases. Sensitivity has only heightened since September 11; at the beginning of the Iraq war in 2003, many bases established curfews for troops going off base or put specific establishments off-limits to troops to avoid clashes with civilians over American involvement in the Middle East.

For these reasons, MWR has been ramping up its activities for single soldiers, offering more activities with them in mind. It isn't easy. In 2004, Army MWR in South Korea conducted an extensive survey of soldiers' off-duty preferences. Significantly, the survey was called "Stop Human Trafficking and Prostitution"; MWR came up with the idea in response to news stories about women who were being forced into prostitution in the bars and brothels around military posts.[4] According to the survey, paintball and go-carts topped the list of requests, but soldiers still preferred to leave base after work. "We cannot compete with the Ville [Tongdu-cheon's red-light district] as far as being a nightclub and providing a male–female social environment," explained the commander of a garrison in South Korea. "I'm never going to get 50 percent of the patrons in here [at Mitchell's, the base club] to be women."[5]

The Navy has also been paying more attention to young, single soldiers. After a string of brutal sex crimes devastated military–civilian relations in Okinawa in the late 1990s, the Navy MWR on the island began offering a program of classes called REAL, or Recreational Education and Leisure, for single soldiers. Soldiers who take the classes learn about on-base recreation options, and they bring the knowledge back to the rest of their unit. "I've been here [Okinawa] for four months, and a lot of the stuff that we've done I didn't even know existed on base," said one sailor.[6] The point of the REAL program is to "keep troops from mischief," according to the *Stars and Stripes,* and it is based on the insight that many younger soldiers do not actually know what is available for them.[7] At sea, MWR is also getting more serious, with "cappuccino machines, aerobics classes, weight rooms, [and] salad bars" added in recent years to improve the quality of life for sailors on board ships.[8]

MWR also provides recreation and entertainment for troops deployed in Iraq and Afghanistan, showing films, operating fitness centers, and distributing books donated by civilians. While MWR offerings in forward areas are more limited than those on bases in Europe, Asia, and the United States, they are appreciated all the more by patrons who are separated from their families.

The USO (United Service Organization) and the American Red Cross are private organizations that provide morale services to troops. According to its Web site, the USO operates 120 centers around the United States and in Germany, Italy, the United Arab Emirates, Iceland, Japan, Qatar, Korea, Afghanistan, Guam, and Kuwait. During World War II, the USO was famous for organizing dances, canteens, and reading rooms for troops on leave or in transit. From its beginnings in 1940 until today, the USO has brought celebrities from Bob Hope to Jessica Simpson to entertain to the troops overseas. One of the goals of the USO has been to provide a "little bit of home" to lonely servicemembers. In 1974, the DoD examined the role of the USO and concluded that it served a valuable purpose, because "isolation of the military from civilian influences is not...in the interest of this nation." The USO also helps troops and their families at home, operating eighty-four family centers near bases. Finally, volunteers at thirty-one USO centers in major airports help servicemembers while they are traveling.[9]

The Red Cross, founded during the Civil War by Clara Barton, is perhaps best known for its blood drives and disaster relief services. But it also provides troops and families with support centers where they can contact home, receive care packages, and see a friendly face. In addition, the Red Cross helps relatives contact servicemembers in case of family emergency.[10]

EDUCATIONAL OPPORTUNITIES ON BASE

One of the most popular off-duty activities for enlisted personnel is working toward a college degree. Many people join the military because of the money offered for higher education, which they put to use when they return to civilian life. Besides Montgomery GI bill benefits from the VA, however, active duty personnel can take courses for free at colleges and universities that offer classes on navy ships and on military bases in forty-eight countries. The largest school serving the military is the UMUC (University of Maryland University College), which has one of the oldest and largest continuing education programs in the country.[11] It won its first military contract in 1949 and has expanded its programs to include masters' degrees as well as four-year bachelors' and two-year associates' degrees. Students at the University of Maryland, Central Texas College, the University of Oklahoma, and Embry-Riddle Aeronautical University can study business, vocational-technical subjects, computer science and information technology, liberal arts, and the natural sciences. Courses are offered at night and on weekends, and degree programs are designed for adult students. They accept course credit from other institutions, and they give students credit for passing subject examinations like the CLEP (College-Level Examination Program) and the DANTES (Defense Activity for Non-Traditional Education Support).

As flexible as the continuing education programs are, however, there are many troops who cannot fit three-hour classes two times a week into their work schedules. For them, the Army created eArmyU, an Internet hub offering online classes from twenty-nine colleges and universities to troops all over the world.[12] Students who are eligible for the program (not everyone is) receive a laptop computer to work with and can connect to the Internet in their barracks or recreation centers to take the free courses.[13]

Since the 1980s, higher education has become one of the more important support services the military provides. The eArmyU project, which has been very successful since it became available to all Army personnel recently, was initially designed as a recruitment incentive, but now has become a reenlistment benefit. A four-year degree is now virtually mandatory for servicemembers who want to make the military a career. And even for those who do not plan to stay in for twenty years, higher education benefits the individual and the organization. According to former Secretary of the Army Thomas E. White, "An educated soldier clearly gives the Army a tremendous return on investment."[14] The military wants to see its troops studying, not carousing, in their free time.

GOING OFF BASE

During the Cold War, soldiers and their families, especially those overseas, were encouraged to go off base and explore the culture and communities in which they were living. As "goodwill ambassadors," they would, it was thought, show residents of their host societies that Americans were friendly, open, and likeable. Equally important, by getting to know the civilian community around them, Americans would have a better appreciation for the people for whom they might have to put their lives on the line.

In the early decades of the Cold War, American troops overseas generated a lot of curiosity and attention from civilians, much of it positive. Intercultural friendship clubs sprang up, enabling Americans to get to know their neighbors and learn about their host culture. Marriages between Americans and host nationals, as civilians living near military bases overseas are called, were very common. Americans participated in festivals and public activities in their host communities, and sponsored their own friendship events throughout the year.

Relations between American military communities and their hosts soured during and after the Vietnam War, however, when U.S. troops earned a reputation for bad behavior such as drug use, alcohol abuse, and crime. As more local nationals objected to the presence of the U.S. forces on their soil, both because of the social problems troops brought and for reasons of national pride, close and friendly contact between military personnel and their hosts grew less frequent. In the 1970s and 1980s, many of the traditional friendship activities withered and disappeared. Americans still left the bases to shop and travel, but their interaction with their hosts was likely to be infrequent and superficial. In the major base locations in Europe and East Asia, many civilians came to oppose the U.S. bases and pressured their governments to expel the Americans.

At the same time, during the 1990s the DoD closed many installations and withdrew over 60 percent of the U.S. military personnel stationed overseas. Americans who had once taken apartments in towns and villages now moved into cheaper base housing, and more Americans spent their free time in base clubs and shops. From their extremely visible (and sometimes annoying) presence in the 1940s and 1950s, they became virtually invisible to their neighbors by the 1990s.

In recent years, base commanders and other individuals have tried to reverse this trend. In South Korea, for example, the 2nd Infantry Division tries to teach its new soldiers more about Korean culture and history in its orientation classes.[15] Public affairs officers in Germany try to interest Americans in German–American contact groups. MWR offices sponsor trips and tours of nearby museums, churches, shopping areas, and restaurants. But it appears that most American servicemembers and families have relatively little interest in or time for interaction with their neighbors.

ALCOHOL AND DRUGS

Unfortunately, much of the off-base activity that troops engage in revolves around alcohol. Military personnel from all nations, not just Americans, have always been known for their love of intoxicating drink. In wartime, the physical and mental rigors of battle produce what many describe as an insatiable craving for alcohol, and even in peacetime the crudeness of barracks life makes inebriation less of a social taboo than it might otherwise be. Most troops are very young and inexperienced, and their drinking behavior, while not attractive, may not be so different from that of college students of the same age.

Alcohol abuse has long been tolerated in the military, and in the past, both officers and men thought of it as a traditional part of military culture. In the first decades of their existence, both the Army and Navy distributed daily rations of whiskey mixed with water, known as grog, to the enlisted men. The grog ration was abolished by the beginning of the Civil War, but throughout the nineteenth and early twentieth centuries, alcohol abuse and alcoholism were endemic in both services. Officers could be court-martialed for alcohol-related behavior problems, but generally they received a fine or restriction to post for a specified period. Enlisted men who drank to excess generally were not punished unless they caused trouble, and even then they would, at most, lose a stripe or two and spend a night in the brig. Prohibition in the 1920s caused the rates of alcohol abuse in the military to decline, but, like their civilian counterparts, the troops managed to find alcohol somehow, and what they drank was all the more lethal for its illegality. Commanders and friends protected officers and NCOs suffering from severe alcoholism until they could retire and collect their pensions. In the aftermath of the world wars, GIs coming to Europe from conservative small towns found a paradise of wine, beer, and hard liquor. In both the 1920s and the 1940s, American soldiers overseas quickly earned a reputation for their enthusiastic drinking.

During the Cold War, alcohol use was a normal and accepted part of life on military bases. Base clubs held happy hours after work with half-price drinks and free snacks, and the officers' parties known as "Hail and Farewells" given for officers arriving at and leaving a unit always involved alcohol. In the old days, drinking in the armed forces was almost *de rigeur*.

Drug abuse is a different story. Among military personnel it was never a significant problem until the late 1960s when drug use rose dramatically, mirroring patterns in the civilian population. Easy access to drugs like marijuana and heroin in Vietnam led to widespread drug use among the troops, and some of them, though not all, brought back their habits when they returned to the United States. The problem became especially acute in Europe, because veterans returning from their yearlong tours in Vietnam were sent to bases in Germany to complete their enlistment periods. Having spent twelve months in a chaotic war zone, they were in no mood to tolerate military discipline and behavior standards, including prohibitions on drug use. By the early 1970s, drug use among military personnel and family members in Europe had soared.

As early as 1967, the DoD had began studying the issue of substance abuse among service members, and as the problem became more acute the Pentagon hurried to establish a policy to deal with it. In the 1970s, the DoD's approach to drug use emphasized treatment and rehabilitation and returning the servicemember to work. Treatment centers were established on bases throughout the world. Only if a servicemember were unable or unwilling to be rehabilitated was he or she separated from service.

In 1980, the Pentagon's policy on drug abuse began to change, moving away from rehabilitation and toward prevention, detection, and punishment. The first challenge was to assess the extent of the problem. To this end, DoD began conducting a series of surveys of personnel around the world, asking them about their drug and alcohol use and the impact that it had on their work life. The first survey, in 1980, revealed that while 20.7 percent had abused alcohol within the past thirty days, a stunning 27.6 percent of personnel had used drugs.[16]

A year later, a jet crash on the aircraft carrier *Nimitz* brought the problem home: almost half the sailors killed in the crash, including the pilot, showed evidence of drug use.[17] Responding to the crisis, the military began random urine testing of the troops and increased the number of police investigations of drug-dealing servicemembers. It also developed a series of prevention programs, because the 1980 survey, which showed such high rates of drug use, also suggested that most users were experimenters rather than addicts. While treatment and rehabilitation did not disappear, the penalties for drug use increased. Officers and career NCOs were separated from the service on their first offense, although junior enlisted personnel sometimes received a second chance. The strict policies put in place in the 1980s sharply reduced drug use in the military. By 1988, the rate of drug use reported in the surveys had gone from 27.6 to 4.8 percent,[18] quite low compared with rates among the civilian population.

Success was not quite so marked in the area of alcohol abuse reduction. While the percentage of heavy alcohol users in the military decreased from 20.7 to 17.0 percent during the 1980s, it could not be called a dramatic reduction; levels of alcohol use among military personnel remained higher than among comparable civilians.[19] Still, the improvement in the quality of military recruits beginning in the 1980s, and the policies and programs implemented at the same time, led to a general decline in substance abuse and, with it, declines in substance abuse-related behavior problems.

Today, rates of alcohol and drug abuse in the military are fairly low, and the military has maintained its strict policies against substance abuse. But, especially for young enlisted personnel, military life involves unique strains and stresses, including long working hours, living away from home, and lack of privacy. Substance abuse continues to be a problem among some servicemembers. In Europe, the use of "club" drugs like Ecstasy and methamphetamine increased in the late 1990s, but in recent years seems to have leveled off. Marijuana continues to be the most popular illegal drug among military personnel.[20]

Alcohol abuse, and the misconduct that often results, has become more problematic in the politically sensitive and security conscious atmosphere of today's military. Especially in areas like Japan, where there is widespread opposition to the presence of the U.S. forces, commanders are forced to punish everyone for the crimes of a few. "Whether you wear a uniform, teach in a DODDS [[Department of Defense Dependents Schools] school or bag groceries on base," says a Navy spokesman, "everyone here under the auspices of the Department of Defense is an ambassador," and military leaders try to send a strong message that abuse of any type is unacceptable.[21] In August 2002, for example, six sailors from the USS *Kitty Hawk* were arrested in two separate incidents, one a carjacking and the other the robbery and beating of an elderly Japanese man.[22] In both crimes, alcohol was involved, and the commander of the Kitty Hawk Battle Group ordered a midnight curfew for all sailors E4 and below. It was unpopular, but the policy had some success. "Look what's happened since those rules were started," one career NCO pointed out. "You haven't heard about nearly as many incidents. So, I guess they were right."[23]

Another tragedy occurred in January 2006 when a drunk sailor from the *Kitty Hawk* beat a Japanese woman to death. In response, the Navy mandated that there would be no public drinking by American service-members or civilians, on or off base, after midnight. "Alcohol abuse in particular," the commander of Naval Forces, Japan, acknowledged, "continues to be a root cause of nearly all incidents of inappropriate conduct. We must change this fact."[24]

South Korea is another place where alcohol abuse continues to be a problem. In some units, it is three times the Army average.[25] Korea has long been known as an assignment where hard drinking is tolerated, and certain customs reinforce this perception. Thunder Run, for example, a "pub crawl" where new soldiers try to drink at every club in the nearby town, and kettle drinking, a game in which everyone pours their favorite drink into a kettle then drinks the resulting mess, are typical drinking "traditions" in Korea.[26] Substance abuse counselors say that the worst times for troops are immediately after they arrive in Korea, and in the month or two before they leave. "Those last 60 days, they just go crazy as hell," notes a counselor at Yongsan.[27]

To combat these problems, all the branches of the armed forces are instituting zero tolerance rules. They are less likely to give second chances for abuse, instead separating servicemembers who get caught using drugs or abusing alcohol,[28] and they are stepping up their already strict screening programs to test young enlisted troops more frequently than they did before.[29] In the clubs and bars around military bases, "courtesy patrols," an informal supplement to the military police presence, keep an eye out for boisterous behavior.

Alcohol and drug abuse incidents continue to be a problem. Military police record frequent alcohol-related altercations off base, and the military has seen a slight increase in drug use among its personnel after a 20-year decline beginning in 1980. The increase must be seen in context; in 2002 only 1.5 percent of troops tested positive for drug use, while among civilians of the same age, the rate was 16 percent.[30] However, military officials note that alcohol and drug abuse is increasingly common among troops in Iraq and Afghanistan. Civilian contractors smuggle "hajji juice," bathtub liquor made in Iraq, onto bases and sell it, and troops themselves smuggle liquor in mouthwash bottles. The high incidence of post-traumatic stress syndrome (see Chapter 9) is spurring substance abuse, some military psychiatrists say, and illegal alcohol and drugs play a role in much of the crime perpetrated by soldiers in the war zones, including assaults, rapes, and murders.[31] In the next few years, rates of alcohol and drug abuse are likely to go up among troops returning from the combat zones as troubled soldiers try to cope with the mental and physical effects of battle.

LET THE GOOD TIMES ROLL

If troops are notorious for their off-duty imbibing, they are even more famous for their attention to women. Young, unattached soldiers far from home have always been preoccupied with sex, and American servicemembers are no different. Young women, for that matter, are often fascinated by soldiers, and when a new unit comes to town it doesn't take long for women and (male) military personnel to find each other.

Sometimes interaction between soldiers and women is thoughtful and romantic. In World War II, carefully supervised dances run by the USO brought soldiers together with women who were screened and chaperoned. Tens of thousands of soldiers met their future wives at USO dances and other respectable venues. On the other hand, however, prostitution flourishes wherever soldiers are found. The extent to which the sex industry develops around a military base depends a great deal on the economic strength of the civilian economy. In more affluent areas, where women have more employment options, they will avoid prostitution. In underdeveloped regions, they may have little or no choice.

The "world's oldest profession" is not always precisely professional, at least when it comes to soldiers, sailors, airmen, and Marines. Particularly in poor or war-ravaged areas, women who congregate to meet soldiers often do so hoping to meet a boyfriend or husband who will provide for them and their children. In postwar Europe, for example, women and girls looked for GI boyfriends who would be steady sources of staples like food, soap, and clothing. Most of these women were not professional prostitutes and in fact thousands of marriages resulted from such relationships. Nevertheless, women were compelled by economic deprivation to look for men who could provide for them and their families.

During the Cold War period, the same economic pressure was responsible for the seedy camptowns that sprouted up around military bases in Panama, the Philippines, Okinawa, and South Korea. During the Vietnam War, the military organized R&R (Rest and Recreation) breaks for the troops, flying them for several days at a time to cities and towns in Thailand, the Philippines, Japan, Hong Kong, Malaysia, and other Southeast Asian nations. The soldiers called the breaks "I&I," or intoxication and intercourse, a more accurate description. Large numbers of U.S. troops in Asia on R&R spurred the growth of the sex industry in many countries. A famous example is Pattaya Beach in Thailand, one of the largest red-light districts in the world; it was a fishing village until the 1960s when the Air Force built bases in Thailand, and additional thousands of troops from Vietnam showed up for R&R. Today, Pattaya Beach hosts more European and Japanese tourists than Americans, but the heart of its economy remains sex tourism. Prostitution in South Vietnam flourished during the war as well. When the last Americans flew out of Vietnam in 1973, they left an estimated 700,000 prostituted women behind.

Prostitution serving the U.S. armed forces in Asia predates the Vietnam War, of course. From the time Americans arrived in the Philippines at the turn of the century, the country was heavily dependent on American military customers of the sex industry. When the bases closed in the early 1990s, bar and club workers protested the loss of their livelihood, but today prostitution continues to thrive in the impoverished nation. South Korea, too, has a long history of tolerating clubs, bars, and brothels around U.S. bases on its soil.

Whether in Vietnam, Thailand, the Philippines, or South Korea, the routine in these clubs and bars is the same. As a foreigner wanders down the street in an Asian red-light district, touts standing on the sidewalks call out, listing the varieties of sex shows to be seen in their establishments. Inside, young women mingle with customers, chatting with them and trying to get them to buy them "ladies' drinks," usually small cups of diluted fruit juice or tea, for ten or twenty dollars apiece, while other women dance on stage or perform sexual acts. Some of the "drinkie girls" simply work the bars in this way, splitting the profits from the drinks with the owner, but most owners expect their employees to have sex with customers. If a customer wants to spend more time with a woman, whether a dancer, a "drinkie girl," or one of the waitresses, he pays the owner a "bar fine" to allow the woman to leave the club for a short time or overnight. "You go in the bars, the girls sit with you and talk with you, and you just buy the drinks," according to a sailor from Okinawa. "The house gets a cut, and after you talk to the person in charge, you pay more—whatever the house prescribes. Then she can leave with you."[32] Depending on the country, the woman's bar fine may be separate from the price of sexual services, which are negotiated between the woman and the customer.

Prostitution is ubiquitous in the towns around military bases, but in recent years the military has been trying to crack down on it. For one thing, it arouses resentment and disgust against Americans and blackens the reputation of the U.S. armed forces. For another, it repels many servicemembers, male and female, who do not want to be associated with it. In spite of its legions of bars and clubs, South Korea has for years been considered an undesirable assignment, and retention rates are lower among troops coming from a year-long tour there. While many are fascinated by the Wild West atmosphere at first, it soon becomes depressing and degrading for all involved.

The most important reason for the military's crackdown on prostitution is its association with human trafficking. In 2002, the Bush administration began focusing considerable attention on the problem of women and children trafficked from impoverished nations to brothels in Asian and European nations as well as in the United States. In March 2002, Fox News reported that military courtesy patrols monitoring bars and clubs in South Korea were aware that women working in the establishments had been victims of sex trafficking. One courtesy patrol officer told Fox reporter Tom Merriman that the women, who came from Central Asia, Russia, and the Philippines, "get off the plane and the Korean nationals that work at the airport take their visa and their passport away, put them in a line on the side, and they go to auction. All these clubowners buy these girls at auctions." [33] Agents entice women and girls in impoverished countries, telling them that they will be working as dancers, singers, or waitresses. They go deeply in debt before they arrive, then they are told they must perform sexual services to pay back their creditors. They are forced to live in cramped rooms above or behind the club with other trafficked women, and they are not allowed to leave. Experts in the trafficking problem consider the "penalty" system, where women must pay the owner a "penalty" if they do not return to their rooms at the club at the end of their shifts, to be sexual slavery, because the women do not have freedom of movement. Of course, if women do not return, it is usually because they are with customers, and a common arrangement is for the customer to pay the "penalty," similar to paying a bar fine, as well as a fee for services.[34]

In the wake of the uproar caused by the report, military officials in South Korea and elsewhere began cracking down on prostitution. They raised the off-base drinking age to twenty-one, established a curfew, and put most clubs and bars off-limits. They held briefings for club owners and workers informing them of the conditions they had to meet if they wanted to do business with military personnel—no trafficking, no holding employees' passports, no prostitution. In 2006, the DoD passed a law making it a crime for a servicemember to hire a prostitute anywhere in the world. "Our policy is based on an abolitionist approach to trafficking in persons," DoD spokeswoman Lt. Col. Ellen Krenke told reporters.[35] Penalties could include up to a year in prison, forfeiture of pay, and a dishonorable discharge.

The law was not without controversy in the military. Some in Europe questioned its fairness, because prostitution is legal and regulated in most European nations, and many felt that the issues of trafficking did not apply there. Others pointed to the implausibility of stamping out prostitution altogether, or the unfairness of ruining a long-time soldier's career for what previously had before been a minor crime.

But others disagreed. Some female servicemembers hoped that a ban on prostitution would help increase respect for women in the armed forces.[36] And there are a few signs that attitudes about prostitution are beginning to change. A Marine taking part in a two-week exercise in the Philippines told a reporter that his friends had met women working in a bar but were startled by the "fear they saw in the women's eyes." He said that "Some of the girls started crying...They [the servicemen] felt bad, and gave them more money and walked away."[37] Another recalled: "It was interesting to see the look on the girls' faces....You could tell some of the women's self-confidence and self-worth was down. They didn't feel good about what they were doing."[38]

CRIME

The problem of crime committed by or against servicemembers is closely related to the prevalence of substance abuse and prostitution. Most crimes committed by off-base, off-duty troops are minor infractions like larceny, public drunkenness, and fighting. Military personnel, however, are governed by a complex and very different code of justice than their civilian counterparts, and even petty crimes can have a devastating effect on a servicemember's career.

Military personnel are subject to the UCMJ (Uniform Code of Military Justice), a code of law created in 1951 for personnel in all branches of service. Family members and civilian employees of the military, whether American or not, are not subject to the UCMJ. In some ways, the UCMJ is similar to civilian law. Crimes against property and against persons are defined in similar ways in both systems. The UCMJ, however, also criminalizes a variety of other behaviors that would not be considered crimes under civilian law. These include being AWOL (Absent Without Leave), failure to obey a lawful order, fraternization (intimate contact) between an officer and an enlisted person, and other behaviors that are offenses against the good order and discipline of the armed forces. In addition, the UCMJ addresses crimes that are committed while a servicemember is on duty, from fatal traffic accidents in which a military vehicle is involved to abuse of civilians or prisoners of war.

In fact, troops who commit crimes are not always subject only to the UCMJ. If an off-duty servicemember commits a serious crime against a civilian, such as rape or murder, while off base in a foreign country, he or she may be turned over to the civilian authorities of that country. Each nation that hosts U.S. bases or personnel has a slightly different agreement with the United States on this matter, and in each case the rules of jurisdiction are spelled out in a SOFA (Status of Forces Agreement), a treaty signed by the host nation and the United States.

The UCMJ defines several types of punishment, the most common being courts-martial and a lesser punishment known as the "Article 15."

There are three types of court-martial: summary, special, and general. The summary court-martial is for misdemeanors punishable by thirty days of confinement or less; the special court-martial deals with more serious crimes involving punishment of up to a year in prison; and at the general court-martial, reserved for the most serious crimes, the court, made up of five officers, can sentence a defendant to life in prison or even the death penalty.

Much more common, however, is punishment under Article 15 of the UCMJ, officially known as nonjudicial punishment. Usually handed down for military crimes like going AWOL, an Article 15 is a less-serious but usually career-ending reprimand, a restriction to base, or a reduction in rank that comes from the commanding officer. Under the terms of Article 15, a commander can also sentence an offender to "confinement on bread and water or diminished rations for not more than three consecutive days," but today this punishment, presumably, is rarely carried out.

The question of military crime, especially crime against civilians in other nations, has been a hot issue for a number of years. Even more than alcohol abuse and participation in the sex industry, violent crimes committed by military personnel against host nation civilians have sparked opposition to the U.S. military presence overseas. Perhaps the most notorious and far-reaching of these incidents was a 1995 rape in Okinawa committed by two sailors and a Marine. According to court documents, the three men did not have enough money to hire a prostitute, so they decided to kidnap and rape a young woman or girl. They purchased duct tape and other items for the kidnapping, then cruised the streets of the town looking for a victim. They came across a 12-year-old girl who was walking home after buying a school notebook, and they dragged her into their car, bound her, and raped her. They dumped her by the side of a deserted road; she made her way to a nearby home, whose residents alerted the police.

The gruesome brutality of the crime appalled Japanese and Americans, and the already simmering anti-base opposition movement in Okinawa exploded. Since then, military commanders on Okinawa, especially those of the Marine Corps, which had earned the worst reputation, have taken strict measures to control their troops, including curfews, courtesy patrols, and harsh punishments for transgressors. But as many Americans and Japanese leaders point out, "Every time a servicemember commits a crime or is involved in an accident, the resentment to the presence of the troops grows."[39] The rate of crime committed by the American troops in Okinawa is, in fact, lower than the rate of crime committed by Japanese or other foreign residents, but sensitivity to American behavior is more profound. One commander says that "Anything that happens off base is twice as bad," because of the repercussions for everyone.[40]

In areas where the armed forces have established a presence only in the past few years, leaders are trying to prevent the growth of camp towns around the bases. In Bosnia and Kosovo, for example, troops have not been allowed off base at all, although recently a program has been established where troops may leave for carefully supervised outings. Islamic nations are especially sensitive to the presence of U.S. troops and insist that they be isolated from the civilian community. In Saudi Arabia in the 1990s, soldiers did not leave the base to wander the local area. Female soldiers going off base for any reason had to wear an abaya, the long black garment worn by Saudi women, although unlike Saudi women, they could drive.

Of course, servicemembers in conflict-torn areas like Iraq and Afghanistan do not leave their camps and bases to spend their free time in civilian establishments. But sexual relations between male and female troops (or, for that matter, between troops of the same gender) is more common than many would like to admit. Female troops are also the victims of sexual assault, ranging from sexual harassment to rape. It is difficult to tell whether sexual assault of female troops is on the rise, but a notorious incident in 2003, where several female soldiers in Iraq died of dehydration, not drinking water because they were afraid to use the latrines at night, illustrates the severity of the problem. Many of the female veterans receiving services at Veterans Administration hospitals are being treated for sexual trauma.

FINANCES

For many young men and women, military pay is the first substantial and regular income they have earned in their lives. It may seem to them that one paycheck will last forever because many of their needs, such as food and housing, are taken care of by the military. They probably have more cash at their disposal than ever before, and if they do not have families to care for, they can enjoy themselves and splurge a little. They are good credit risks; they are unlikely to get fired, their paychecks arrive regularly, and if they fall behind in paying their creditors, their commanders will intervene.

It is unfortunate but not surprising, therefore, that young servicemembers often find themselves drowning in bills. There are many temptations for the servicemember away from home for the first time: outings to restaurants, clubs and bars, travel, and expensive hobbies. Outside most military bases there is a strip of car dealerships, stereo and electronic equipment emporiums, and furniture warehouses offering financing for large purchases. Even the most junior enlisted personnel are barraged with offers of high-rate credit and charge cards. They are tempted by seemingly inexpensive adjustable rate mortgages and time share deals that look too good to be true (and usually are).

Servicemembers are also targets of shady salespeople hawking financial products, and unfortunately those who want to do the best for themselves and their families are most vulnerable. Although they usually sign up for SGLI, the inexpensive term life insurance offered to them in basic training, civilian insurance agents pressure them to buy even more expensive and unnecessary life insurance policies that offer small payouts and minimal cash values far in the future, at ten or fifteen times the cost of SGLI. "Financial advisors" push them to sign up for mutual fund programs, known as contractual plans, in which half of their contributions during the first year go into fees, "a deal," the *New York Times* reported, "considered so expensive that such funds all but disappeared from the civilian market almost 20 years ago."[41]

When they need extra money to tide them over, "payday lenders" loan them quick cash at exorbitant rates, and pawn shops outside the gates of every military base in the world will take their belongings as collateral for a small loan. Worst of all, servicemembers are easy victims of fraud and identity theft. Their social security numbers are printed on their military ID cards, and they move around frequently, switching banks and addresses so often that they may not receive their mail regularly. Since the increase in deployment after September 11, the problem of identity theft has become more serious. "The opportunities have certainly increased," says a JAG Marine officer who deals with fraud, "and criminals have taken the opportunity."[42]

Sometimes the military itself is to blame. Financial services companies targeting servicemembers hire retired military personnel as agents, and although DoD regulations prevent anyone from selling products on bases, the regulations have been poorly enforced. Agents pitch insurance and mutual funds under the guise of command-sponsored financial planning seminars. "It's an environment where you do what you're told," explained one commander, and few young servicemembers know what questions to ask. They are pressured to sign papers, including allotment forms allowing their paychecks to be docked, but they do not have a clear understanding of what they are buying and what the alternatives might be. Even officers and NCOs can be pressured into buying expensive financial products when they hear recommendations from commanders and from groups like the AUSA (Association of the United States Army) or the NCOA (Non-Commissioned Officers Association).

The Pentagon has known about these problems for years, but industry pressure has prevented them from instituting stricter rules against such abuses. In December 2004, however, First Command, a mutual fund company marketing to military personnel, agreed to settle complaints by the SEC (Securities and Exchange Commission) and the NASD for $12 million. The SEC and the NASD charged that First Command used improper marketing tactics and gave out misleading information in its sales pitches, defrauding thousands of servicemembers. In September 2006, in the wake of reports that many servicemembers had lost security clearances because of out-of-control debt, Congress passed a bill prohibiting sales of certain mutual funds and life insurance policies on military bases, and many bases have been cracking down on payday lenders.[43]

When personnel get into financial trouble, they can get help from financial management experts at the Community Services Center or the Family Support Center on base. Some go for help voluntarily, while others are referred to the center by their first sergeants or commanders. They can learn how to create a budget or refinance expensive credit card debt. Recently, the military has begun a series of financial management program to inform personnel about scams that target them.[44] Unfortunately, too many young troops learn the hard way that temptation lurks around every corner.

CHAPTER 7

MILITARY FAMILIES

Military families seem to be receiving more notice these days, as the ongoing conflicts around the world draw attention to the nation's armed forces. Newspapers and television news shows run feature stories on family life during deployment, columnists urge more funding for family support, and journalistic accounts show military life from the spouse or child's view. Inside the community, military leadership at all levels pledges support for military families and claims to recognize their importance to the institution and the mission. Throughout the 1990s and particularly since September 11, the DoD has initiated a blizzard of new policies and programs aimed at improving the quality of life for military spouses and children, from more job placement help and better housing to a reinvigorated zero-tolerance program on domestic violence.

Nevertheless, many inside and outside the military community charge that the military does not really take the needs of families seriously. Some critics focus on specific programs, like the relatively new FSB (Family Support Battalion) structure, a command-sponsored support system that appears to some family members to be just a glorified telephone chain. Others attack more broadly, saying that support programs for military families are window dressing to disguise a fundamental lack of concern.

It is quite easy to be skeptical of the military's commitment to families. The military is, in sociologist Mady Wechsler Segal's memorable phrase, a "greedy institution," which demands time, energy, and commitment far beyond the hours of the traditional workday. When the needs of the family, another "greedy institution," clash with the demands of the military, the family usually loses.[1] Some scholars, such as Cynthia Enloe, have written extensively on the military's uses and abuses of women. Enloe suggests that exploitation of women sits at the heart of the military institution, vital to its articulation of masculinity.[2] Other observers, pointing to numerous sexual harassment scandals and high levels of domestic violence, say that the military tolerates or even condones aggression and violence against women, and has been lackluster in its response to wide-spread problems. In the 1970s, a decade during which the military had a particularly bad public image, one scholar posited a "military family syndrome" of domineering fathers, submissive mothers, and out-of-control children;[3] others have written about an "authoritarian personality" most likely to be attracted to military service.

Nevertheless, it is probably unfair to doubt the military's genuine concern for families. After all, most decision makers in the armed forces have families themselves and are sympathetic to the sacrifices and hardships military families endure. And it does not negate this sincerity to point out that much of the military's attention about families has been prompted by studies showing that concerns about the quality of family support are one of the largest factors influencing reenlistment. While their efforts are not always successful, the armed forces are responding to family issues at a level that would have astounded families 100 or even 50 years ago.

THE UNIQUENESS OF MILITARY FAMILIES

Military families face special challenges unfamiliar to many civilians today. Perhaps the most noticeable is the instability of military life. Serv-icemembers receive sudden orders to move to new and unknown places, are given only a short period of adjustment, and finally, when life has settled down, they receive new orders to go somewhere else. About 33 percent of military families move each year; only about 5 percent of civilian families do.[4] It is quite common for long-time military families to have moved twenty or thirty times during their servicemember's career, and children rarely attend the same school for more than two or three years. This is hard enough on spouses, who must leave jobs or interrupt education to do the lion's share of the packing and unpacking, setting up the new home, registering children in new schools, and so on. It can be harder on children, who must switch schools and make new friends each time orders come through.

The peculiar "greediness" of the military institution is another challenge facing families. Its all-encompassing nature, blurring of work and private life, and strict hierarchy affect families as well as servicemembers, or "sponsors," as they are often called. Military wives and husbands learn that the military comes first, the family second. For spouses who grew up in military families, and there are many of them, this may seem normal, but for a spouse with civilian roots it can take some getting used to. The demands of the military are, perhaps, not entirely unlike the expectations a corporation holds for its top executives, who put in long hours and are transferred regularly. Military spouses, and servicemembers themselves, however, often come from tight-knit working- or middle-class communities where work and family life are balanced somewhat differently. In any case, military personnel are not compensated at the same levels as corporate executives, so the sacrifice takes on an entirely different meaning.

The military truly is not just a job, but rather a constant commitment to a finicky and unpredictable institution. Extra-long shifts are normal, and servicemembers must be ready to mobilize at a moment's notice; they can be called for extra duty at any time, during holiday celebrations, anniversaries, or birthdays. Until recently it was a relatively rare occurrence, but today most military families have experienced such interruptions. Maneuvers and exercises last beyond their expected durations, with little or no advance warning. Perhaps the most difficult situation arises when a servicemember deployed overseas is prevented from returning home at the last minute, leaving spouse and children to fold up the "welcome home" banners, eat the specially decorated cake by themselves, and wait for another few weeks or months.

Families living in on-base housing have little privacy and must conform to the rules of the base command and the housing office with regard to the upkeep of their property. Families may choose to live off base to get away from the close atmosphere, but it will likely be more expensive and inconvenient. On or off base, there is great pressure to conform to common standards of behavior, from home decorating styles to dress to recreational activities. When a family problem arises, it is more than likely that those in the chain of command will get to know of it. Unruly teenagers and unhappy marriages have destroyed more than a few military careers.

Military society, especially for officers, has changed a great deal since the white-glove days, but officers' spouses, mostly wives, are still expected to provide leadership for junior wives and enlisted families. This can include mandatory social events, checking in on enlisted wives, and acting as a conduit between the command and families. This work is all unpaid, but wives feel pressure to participate even if they hold jobs and have children. To decline these responsibilities, many wives worry, might harm a husband's career. Although the military specifically forbids taking a spouse's support activities into account when evaluating a servicemember, many wives still feel the need to conform for the sake of the sponsor's career.

A final note on the nature of the greedy institution: the job of a soldier, sailor, or airman or Marine doesn't just require long hours at modest pay and a great deal of sacrifice from families. It also brings with it the possibility of injury or death in combat. Military families tend to place this reality firmly in the back of their minds, but, as events of the early twenty-first century have shown, it is a reality of military life.

A third challenge to military families is the unavoidable stress of young adulthood, stress that single military personnel and civilians of the same age face as well. Young military families deal with maturity issues and inexperience along with modest incomes and living far away from home and familiar social structures. Junior enlisted personnel are more likely to be married and to be caring for children than their civilian peers; almost 20 percent of 18-year-old Army personnel are married, compared to less than 5 percent of 18-year-old civilians; about one-third of all junior enlisted personnel are married.[5] These families are only beginning to learn how to cope with the military bureaucracy, manage tight budgets, and be good parents to small children. Young families everywhere struggle with the challenges of adulthood, but in civilian society they are more likely to have support from family and friends, while military families usually do not have the same kind of support.

To make matters even more complicated, military families, like their civilian counterparts, have been changing rapidly in recent decades. Increasing numbers of military families are two-career couples, with both parents on active duty. Such a commitment to military life takes special planning, because both parents must be ready to deploy at any time. Also, military wives, who in former times stayed home with children, are likely to be pursuing careers or higher education, and they are less than overjoyed about being uprooted every year or two. And although military children are more likely than civilian children to live in two-parent homes, there are increasing numbers of single parents and blended families in the military today, bringing additional challenges for parents and children. Finally, military families include a large number of intercultural and interracial marriages, which are prone to additional stress, as will be discussed below.

That is one version of military family life, and a grim one it is. But military families can point to special advantages as well. For one thing, military life provides them the chance to travel and to live in new places, even foreign countries. Military spouses and children tend to become flexible and broad-minded in the course of their wanderings. Some, though not all, attain fluency in one or more foreign languages, and most are comfortable with foreign customs. Military families accumulate experiences and adventures that most civilians can only dream of.

On average, military families are closer and more stable than their civilian peers. Studies have shown that children in military families enjoy unusually high levels of support from their parents and that family separations, while stressful, do not usually have severe or long-term negative consequences. Members of military families themselves note that they are extremely close with other family members, and the bonds between mother and children in particular are strengthened by the frequent moves and separations. In fact, studies have shown that military children have higher median IQs, do better in school, and are less likely to have behavior problems than civilian children. In contrast to the depressing image of the "military family syndrome," military children actually show high rates of functioning and adaptation, whether because of or in spite of the rigors of military life.

Like all communities, the military communities in which families live have their positive as well as negative characteristics. For every uninspiring Burger Bar or PX on base there is a free or inexpensive tennis court, swimming pool, or movie theater. Support organizations like MWR offer a wide variety of classes, clubs, and special events for families and personnel. There is almost certain to be a mountain, beach, forest, or desert nearby to explore. And even within its instability, military life offers a certain kind of steadiness. With experience, many military families learn to adjust to the hardships and take advantage of the benefits. A lot depends on individual attitudes and choices.

THE HISTORY OF MILITARY FAMILIES

It is ironic, in a way, that the military is giving so much attention to the needs of family members now, because for most of its history the military did not officially acknowledge the existence of family members at all. In the nineteenth century, as the U.S. Army was pushing the American frontier across the trans–Mississippi West to colonies in the South Pacific Ocean and Indian Ocean, there were no provisions made for military wives and children. If an officer or soldier wanted to bring his family with him, he paid for their transportation himself. Some wives remained with their parents, seeing their husbands briefly every few years. Most, however, accompanied their husbands to one isolated post after another, enduring blizzards, baking desert heat, flash floods, earthquakes (San Francisco was the major military center in California at the time of the 1906 catastrophe), insect infestations, and monsoons, all the while in various stages of pregnancy or with small children in tow.

Children of officers and enlisted personnel lived strange but eventful lives on western posts. Formal schooling was almost nonexistent, and older children were sent to boarding schools or to live with family back East, but until that sorry time, children grew up with all the adventures of a life on the frontier. They rode horses and learned to hunt and shoot, and occasionally would have the opportunity to participate in a skirmish or battle with the men. One officer took his six-year-old son with him to the Modoc War in 1873; the boy rode with the men and tended the sick and injured.[6]

Toward the end of the century, a few early signs of the recognition of military wives and children began to appear. Women formed wives' organizations of various types, and posts founded schools for Army children. In 1891, Congress conducted a review of Army families on the frontier, but there was no concerted effort taken to improve conditions. Families of enlisted men began to receive rations and benefits in 1896, but those of officers did not. As late as 1913, the Army officially discouraged marriage for soldiers, saying that it had a negative effect on service.

After World War I, as the military shrank back to the size it had been before the war, Regular Army personnel and families got on as best they could. The prewar bases in the United States and overseas, especially in the Philippines, continued to house most military families, but military life had indeed changed. The tough conditions of the frontier had disappeared and military families benefited from higher standards of living and official recognition of their existence. In the 1920s, more elaborate social customs replaced the simple ad-hoc entertaining of the nineteenth-century frontier. Wives of officers enjoyed, or endured, glittering rounds of dinners, parties, and balls, as well as tennis, golf, riding, sailing, and swimming on post facilities. Bridge was ubiquitous on military posts, and formal calls were exchanged among wives according to a complex protocol. Enlisted families lived much more simply, but housing for NCO families was built on many posts in the 1920s, and in the 1930s the first overseas schools for military children were established.[7]

The world of military wives and children seemed strange and exotic to most civilians. It was only after World War II, as the size of the armed forces increased, that military families moved into the mainstream of American culture. Since 1946, when the first military families joined the occupation forces in Europe and Asia, millions of wives and children have participated in America's huge global military presence.

In the months after the end of the war, morale among the millions of soldiers in Europe and Asia collapsed, and military leaders confronted a potentially explosive situation. Soldiers were shipped home as quickly as possible, but in the days before airline travel, demobilization was slow. A partial solution to the problem of soldier indiscipline was to bring wives and children to Europe and Asia, where, it was hoped, they would exert some positive influence on the men, or, at the very least, shame the men into better behavior.

The first wives and children arrived in Europe in April 1946, and in Japan a short time later. They lived in homes requisitioned from the civilian population, cordoned off with barbed wire and guarded by local national employees. They shopped at makeshift commissaries, choosing among limited offerings of institutional-size canned goods and military surplus. In time, the PXs began selling a few items for women and children.

The arrival of family members did seem to humanize overseas bases somewhat, but it also exacerbated some problems. First, additional homes and schools were requisitioned for the use of American families, which aggravated already severe housing shortages. Second, military families required additional services, such as medical care, schooling, shopping, and recreation, and these needs placed a burden on the demobilizing military of the late 1940s. Even so, wives helped create a "normal" atmosphere during the occupation. As soon as they arrived in Europe and Asia, military wives organized charitable efforts for local families and children, established friendship clubs with European and Asian women, and began to assume volunteer duties on posts and bases.

In the first few years after 1945, it was widely expected that almost all the U.S. forces would return home, leaving small occupation forces in Germany and Japan to monitor the progress of democratization. By the early 1950s, however, all such ideas had been scrapped, and the U.S. forces overseas and at home were rapidly built up once again. Along with the huge increase in active-duty personnel came a corresponding increase in family members. Moreover, military couples, like civilians back home, were anxious to start families, and a military baby boom soon overwhelmed the limited facilities on bases. In 1952, a DoD study found that the lack of basic services for families was a major problem. Military communities built family housing, commissaries, shopping centers, and recreation facilities as quickly as they could hire construction teams. By 1960, family members outnumbered military personnel, and in the mid-1960s support programs like the Family Services Program (1962) and the ACS (Army Community Service) Program (1965) came into being. In 1962, the DoDDS school system was set up overseas for the large numbers of military children entering school. Military bases took on the appearance of "typical" American towns, the look that they still maintain today.

As the United States became more and more involved in the Vietnam War, however, the good life for military families came to an end. Base housing grew shabbier and more unpleasant while personnel and funding shortages made life more inconvenient in a hundred different ways. Medical personnel were stretched to the limit, so wives and children waited for months for appointments. Shoppers could wait for several hours in commissary lines, library hours were cut back, shuttle bus routes eliminated, and recreation options curtailed. Individually, such changes may have appeared petty, but altogether they added up to a diminished quality of life for military families.

A NEW COMMITMENT TO MILITARY FAMILIES

The coming of the AVF forced a major change in the way families were treated by the military. During the draft era, a large proportion of service-members were young and single, and had no intention of staying in the service beyond their first tour of duty. As the military moved away from conscription toward the creation of an older, more career-oriented force, the percentage of the military population with spouses and children also rose. The services were spending more and more to recruit and train personnel, but they didn't get their money's worth if servicemembers left after a few years. Research showed that the biggest reason for leaving before retirement was the poor quality of life for families, so for the AVF, family satisfaction became a retention issue.

The DoD became aware of the role that family quality of life played in retention and readiness at the same time that civilian society was beginning to confront issues of gender inequality. In the 1970s, the divorce rate in both civilian and military society skyrocketed, more women were pursuing jobs and careers, and the public was beginning to take note of problems like domestic violence. Congress and the DoD responded to these concerns in typical fashion, with programs and mandates. In 1975, new legislation required that servicemembers' wages be garnished for payment of child support and alimony. A year later the DoD created the FAP (Family Advocacy Program), which addressed the problem of domestic violence. In 1979, the Quality of Life Program was established, an early attempt to improve family services. From these beginnings, the DoD organized the first Family Symposium in 1980. In 1981, a second symposium was held and the DoD established a Family Liaison Office to coordinate programs and services.

These initial efforts to address the needs of military families revealed something that everyone in the military community already knew: servicemembers and their families were unhappy with the quality of life in military communities. Surveys confirmed this, and in 1983 the Army, the branch with the biggest problem, committed itself to change in an official report. General John A. Wickham, the Army Chief of Staff, promised that the Army would build a "strong partnership" with its families, and called for more research into their needs.[8]

In 1985, Congress passed the Military Family Act, which established an Office of Family Policy, a subbranch of the DoD's Force Management and Personnel office. The organizational hierarchy is illuminating; the DoD viewed family issues as an issue of "force management," an acknowledgment that family needs and working conditions for the servicemember cannot be considered separately. The office conducted service-wide surveys to learn more about what personnel and families wanted, then began to develop programs to fill those needs.

In 1988, the DoD allocated $8 billion for family programs and issued its Instructions for Family Policy. The list of needs, as determined by surveys, included:

> premobilization and deployment support, relocation assistance, special needs support, elder care, family advocacy, foster care, family life education, dependents' education, substance abuse prevention, family health and

fitness, spiritual growth and development, emergency services, counseling, support and services for off-base families (outreach), consumer affairs and financial planning assistance, volunteer training and management, separation and retirement planning, family centers, and community development.[9]

It was a good start, and Congress helped by passing legislation like the MCCA (Military Child Care Act) of 1989, which mandated the creation of child care facilities on base, organized and overseen by the military. Research at the end of the 1980s suggested that overall the family support programs, while not perfect, did help to improve morale and readiness among servicemembers by helping their families.[10]

The post–Cold War drawdown put a crimp in the family support programs, as budgets were slashed and bases closed. At the same time, the drawdown increased stress on families; servicemembers who once assumed they would have stable 20-year careers in the military faced the possibility of being let go with no retirement benefits and few civilian job prospects. The Gulf War deployment of 1990–1991 came at a terrible time for military families, who were already reeling from the unexpected change in plans. Bases lost support personnel like physicians and medics, who had until that point had spent most of their time caring for family members. Families were forced to seek medical care and other help off-base, in environments they did not understand and among civilians who did not understand them.

Civilian communities in the United States did, however, step in to help military families with everything from special discounts in stores to free tax advice. Families stationed in Europe and Asia had a tougher time. They remained overseas as their sponsors were deployed to the Gulf, but at the end of hostilities, many units never returned to their original stations. Instead, they were downsized back to the United States or even deactivated altogether, and families were left to pack up and move back to their next assignments by themselves. At the same time, servicemembers everywhere worked longer hours and were deployed more frequently. The deterioration of the quality of life in the military caused no end of resentment, and as the economy boomed in the middle of the decade, many servicemembers decided that the civilian world offered a more appealing future. By the end of the 1990s, recruitment and retention had emerged as problems, and leadership began refocusing its attention on the military family as a way to keep expensive and talented personnel in the ranks.

CHALLENGES FOR TODAY'S MILITARY FAMILIES

September 11 and the conflicts in Afghanistan and Iraq put additional pressure on military leadership to improve not only family support programs but to untangle the web of rules and restrictions that made military life a never-ending aggravation for families. In the past five years, the DoD has been trying to lighten the load on military families in many ways. All too often, however, "transformation" efforts, such as stepped-up deployments and privatization of services, clash with efforts to make life better for military families. The balance seems almost impossible to achieve.

Nevertheless, each branch of the armed services has developed a large number of support services for families. On most bases, programs are coordinated by umbrella organizations: the ACS, the Fleet and Family Support Center (Navy), the Marine Corps Community Services, and the Air Force Family Support Centers. Whatever the name of the center, it will offer a wide variety of programs designed to address the needs of families. In fact, there are so many programs that it can take careful study to distinguish the services they offer. They often have cheerful, similar-sounding names that give no hint of their function. Moreover, the family support programs on bases are mostly run by volunteers, so there is a great deal of variation in their quality and durability.

One of the first programs most families moving to a new base will use is Relocation Assistance. The office assigns new families to sponsors who are living on the base. Sponsors help newcomers adjust to the area and learn what is available on and off base. The sponsorship program kicks in even before a family arrives; active sponsors will contact a family while they are still at their old base. Support centers also hold newcomer's orientations, usually mandatory for lower enlisted personnel and families, and many base support centers offer families extensive orientation programs lasting several days. Experienced families also arrive with information about their new base gathered from the support center at their old base, from the Internet, or from friends.

Sponsors and orientations will alert new families to programs like Lending Closets, where families can borrow household goods while they wait for their own belongings to arrive, and the Housing Office, where families hoping to get housing on base will have to register. The Housing Office may also help families find off-base housing. Spouses who plan to get a part- or full-time job may want to visit the civilian Employment Office, which will provide help with resume-writing, interviewing, and other skills. The centers also offer career counseling and, most importantly, job listings for the base. If they decide to continue an interrupted college education, or to begin work on a college degree, they can sign up for classes at the Education Center.

With the help of welcome packets, a sponsor, and an orientation briefing, most military families can adjust to life on a new base without many problems, especially if they have been through the process before.

They will find the exchange and the commissary, learn their way around the housing area, locate appropriate schools and religious services, and get medical care when they need it. Support services are more or less the same on every base, and military families know how to negotiate them, so they may not need the support center on their base beyond initial orientations.

Support centers do not want to be known simply as places where troubled families go for help, but the fact is that many of the programs they offer are indeed for families with problems. In the military, all kinds of crises can surface, so most military families will probably need the help of their support center at some point in their lives. Programs like the AER (Army Emergency Relief), for example, offer interest-free loans to service-members and families during temporary cash crunches, for emergency travel, or when there is a delay in a servicemember's pay (which happens distressingly often). Financial services programs help families set up budgets, consolidate debt, or deal with consumer issues. The Exceptional Family Members Program helps families coordinate care for a family member with special physical or mental health needs.

Many programs have expanded beyond their original purpose, to offer a variety of classes and help. For example the Army's Family Advocacy Program was originally established to deal with domestic abuse, focusing on treating victims and punishing perpetrators. It now offers home visitors for expectant mothers, classes for new parents, play groups to help young parents learn skills, child safety courses, and stress and anger management help, in addition to responding to domestic violence and sexual assault.

The FAP is only one program that is turning its attention toward pre-vention of problems, rather than responding to them after they have occurred. The Army, Marine Corps, and Coast Guard have developed "Family Team Building" programs that teach spouses how to adjust to life in the military. With classes in interpersonal communication skills, conflict management, and dealing with stress, as well as basic military information, the team building programs "promote self-reliant military families." The programs focus on giving family members the training and confidence to survive and thrive when their sponsors are deployed, and to help others in the community.

Another program, the AFAP (Army Family Action Plan) is an attempt to get families involved in issues that affect them. The AFAP holds con-ferences every year at which delegates, including spouses, children, retirees, active-duty personnel, and others, discuss the major issues facing families. The Navy and Coast Guard have created similar programs with ombudsmen, usually family members, who act as liaisons between families and command.

One of the most commonly utilized programs for families is the FSG (Family Support Group), a unit-based organization which, in a sense, takes the place of the wives' clubs of old. Wives' (or Spouses') clubs do still exist, but the FSGs are officially sponsored groups for all ranks that work with the command to provide information families need, especially when sponsors are deployed. Members of the FSG also help other families with problems and act as a social and support group. FSG leaders are usually, but not always, senior spouses, but anyone may volunteer to lead an FSG. The job can be surprisingly involved. The wars in Iraq and Afghanistan have pushed many marriages to the breaking point, and FSG leaders can find themselves dealing with very grave situations. Marriage and family crises such as infidelity, financial problems, alcoholism, mental illness, and domestic violence have become more frequent as troops deploy repeatedly.[11] Divorce rates in the military have been rising since the beginning of the conflict.

In spite of the sometimes serious nature of family problems, a common characteristic of all these programs is the emphasis on self-help and problem prevention. The military realizes it needs satisfied family members to function, and it is trying to provide the tools families can use to make the most out of military life.

Research suggests that the programs are reasonably successful, but many who have experience with them say that they vary in quality because they are staffed for the most part by volunteers. Moreover, they are not able to offer transportation or free child care during meetings and classes, so young families with small children, who may need the programs most of all, often are not able to take advantage of them.

SPOUSES AND EMPLOYMENT

It is now normal for women, even those with small children, to work outside the home, and many military wives have high levels of education and career expectations. It can be tough, however, to achieve those goals when PCS (permanent change of station) moves happen every year or two. When spouses are called away on field training, TDY (temporary duty) or deployment, juggling parenthood with a demanding career seems impossible. But according to DoD surveys, a higher percentage of military wives (65 percent) work than women in the general population (57 percent).[12] This is contrary to the image of stay-at-home military wives who spend their days attending club activities and socializing, but it should not surprise anyone. Military wives are better educated than the general population; only 5 percent of junior enlisted wives have less than a high-school education, compared with 20 percent of the general population, and more wives have college degrees than their civilian counterparts. In addition, the isolation of military life and the fact that military pay hardly puts military families in the top tax bracket drive many family members to find work as soon as they arrive in a new station.

Many spouses choose careers that are transportable, such as nursing and teaching, for example, although licensing regulations vary according to state, and not all teachers can obtain new jobs without going through additional certification processes. Overseas, certified teachers can work for DoDDS in the base schools, where credentials from all states are recognized.

Spouses also earn money through direct sales work for companies such as Amway, Avon, or Tupperware. These jobs, which involve selling products at parties, can be quite lucrative and can help women get to know others in the community. Many women operate small businesses out of their homes, such as catering, sewing, crafts, tutoring, and other services. Government regulations now allow spouses to operate such businesses out of their base quarters. For parents of small children, a popular option is to become a certified Family Child Care provider and operate a home day care center.

Some spouses work in nearby civilian communities. There is a widespread belief in military communities that civilian employers are reluctant to hire military spouses, because they know that they will not be available permanently. But the average time at the same job for civilians in the United States is less than four years, and most employers know that the mobility of military spouses is not unusual. Spouses can turn their mobility into an asset when they emphasize their wide range of skills to potential employers. The military is currently investigating new programs whereby large corporations like Wal-mart and Home Depot hire military spouses for customer-service jobs that can be done anywhere. The Navy and Marine Corps have a partnership with Adecco, a Swiss personnel agency, to help military spouses find work throughout the world. When they move they keep their seniority and benefits.[13]

It is very common for military spouses to work for the government in some capacity, either as contracted civilians or GS/NAF employees. The 1985 Military Family Act included a Spouse Hiring Preference law (Public Law 99-661), which gives preference to qualified military spouses for many government jobs. It is not a sure thing but makes finding a government job easier than it used to be.

Unfortunately, military spouses earn much less on average than their civilian peers—up to 60 percent less. A large part of this is due to lost seniority because of PCS moves. Another factor is that more military spouses have small children, and work part-time. Furthermore, many large bases in the United States are located in rural areas where the average wage is below national norms. And finally, military spouses overseas are not eligible for many better-paying jobs on-base. Employment on military bases overseas is regulated by SOFAs, which generally give preference to local civilians over military family members for most jobs.

MILITARY CHILDREN

Almost everyone has heard the term "military brat," meaning a child brought up in the nomadic lifestyle of the military. Far from being "brats," in the negative sense of the world, children who have grown up in the military tend to be very flexible and adaptable. They fit into new social situations easily, blending in and quickly intuiting social conventions. But they also may feel like eternal outsiders among people with roots in one community. They tend to be somewhat reticent in discussing their childhoods, which is unfortunate, given the many unusual experiences they are likely to have had. Military children are more likely than civilians to join the military and make it a career or to marry a military servicemember. The military life is familiar to them, so they find it easier to adjust to its peculiarities.

Military children, like military spouses, are above all transient. When asked where they were born, they may give Texas, North Dakota, or Japan as an answer, but they probably haven't lived in their birthplaces for more than a year or two. They switch schools frequently, and the types of schools they have attended vary in size and character, from large civilian public schools to smaller schools on base, to international boarding schools or private schools.

In recent years, the services have established "stabilization" options for career personnel with children in high school. Servicemembers can choose to stay at one base until a child graduates, usually in exchange for extending their service commitments. This has been one of the most popular reenlistment bonuses; as one expert notes, "when you move as a soldier, you take your rank and you take your title and your status and you take it to the next installation. As a child, you could have been the All-Star on a soccer team or done really well on a baseball team, but you take nothing with you."

The transient life of military children today may not be easy, but there are many more options for them than there were in the past. In the nineteenth century, schools for military children were informal or nonexistent. Well-educated soldiers would sometimes be called upon to teach reading and math to the dozen or so children on post, and older children were sent to boarding schools back East, but unless a post was in a well-populated area, there wasn't much choice for parents. More formal base school systems for the children of officers and enlisted men in the Philippines, Hawaii, and Panama started developing in the twentieth century. After World War II, schools were established on bases in Europe and Asia.

By 1962, however, there were so many children of military parents living overseas that Congress ordered the DoD to reform and improve the schools, and the DoDDS (Department of Defense Dependents Schools) was born. The schools on U.S. bases were run by a separate organization, the DDESS (Domestic Dependent Elementary and Secondary Schools), but most military children in the United States attended civilian schools in nearby towns. Since 1994, base schools overseas and in the United States have been administered by one organization, the DoDEA (Department of Defense Education Activity). Children of military and civilian personnel are eligible to go to DoDEA schools, but about 85 percent of the approximately 102,600 children attending are children of enlisted military personnel. There are currently 222 public DoDEA schools in 13 countries (Bahrain, Belgium, Cuba, England, Germany, Iceland, Italy, Japan, South Korea, The Netherlands, Portugal, Spain, and Turkey), 7 states (Alabama, Georgia, Kentucky, New York, North Carolina, South Carolina, and Virginia), as well as Guam and Puerto Rico.[14]

In order to go to a DoDEA school in the United States, families must live on base; if they live off base they must attend the civilian school. Children living on smaller bases in the United States also go to local civilian schools. There are only a few base high schools in the United States: at Fort Campbell, Camp Lejuene, and Quantico. There are a number of high schools overseas, but not all children live close enough to attend them. The NDSP (Non-DoD Schools Program) gives financial support for such children, whose private school tuition is paid for by the NDSP. NDSP also pays tuition for students with special needs when there is no DoDEA school available. DoDEA runs a boarding school in London, and children of military and civilian DoD employees from all over Europe attend it; everything is paid for, including round trip transportation to and from home during school breaks. Civilian employees of other governmental organizations, contracted civilians working for DoD, and military retirees can send their children to the school, but they must pay tuition.

There are currently about 8,785 civilian DoDEA teachers. Like other civilian employees, they are ID-card holders and part of the military community. DoDEA accepts teacher accreditation from all states, so that teachers who are married to military personnel don't have to go through reaccreditation every time they are transferred to a different state.

Schools for military children are important on overseas bases, where children would have difficulty adjusting to the local education system. But even stateside, base schools serve a valuable purpose. For one thing, children of military families are extremely mobile, often going to a different school almost every year. DoDEA schools are better equipped to deal with the problems associated with frequent moves than civilian schools are. They have a standardized curriculum so that students can transfer without much interruption of their education. In addition, DoDEA schools are ready to address any adjustment problems that military children have, whether because of moving or because of a parent's deployment. When all the children in a school are facing common challenges, as during a large-scale deployment like Iraq, it is much easier for military children to be together than with civilian children who have roots in the community and don't understand the military way of life. DoDEA schools also help minimize the burden that large numbers of military children place on the local school system. Military families who use civilian schools usually do not own homes or pay property taxes. The military partly compensates local schools for accepting military children, but districts scramble to make up the difference. When the numbers of military families at a base fluctuate, the problem is magnified.

DoDEA schools are often of higher quality than local schools. On the standardized Terra Nova Achievement Test, DoDEA students score above the national average in every subject, at every level. On NAEP (National Assessment of Educational Progress) tests, taken by students across the country, DoDEA student scores are always at the top of the scale. DoDEA schools also show a smaller achievement gap in races than civilian schools. A study by Vanderbilt University researchers in 1999 showed that DoDEA schools were so excellent that in some ways they could serve as a model for U.S. public schools. The study suggested that the schools' outstanding characteristics included small size, high expectations, strong community, high spending and high teacher salaries, advanced teaching methods, and parents' accountability to commanders for their children's behavior.[15]

JUNIOR ENLISTED SPOUSES

Much of the research and writing on military families has focused on the needs of families in general, but the spouses and families of junior enlisted personnel face special problems that are not always adequately addressed by new policies and programs. Junior enlisted families endure a poisonous combination of all the worst that the military lifestyle has to offer, and it can be very difficult for them to overcome and adjust to military life.

Most recruits are young and single, but increasing numbers of them already have spouses and children when they enlist. If they do, their families are eligible for ID cards and health care, and receive BAH almost immediately. While their sponsors are in training, they remain at home in familiar surroundings, but once training has ended, families usually join their sponsors at their first permanent assignments. Because of their low rank, however, they are not immediately eligible for on-base quarters, so they must rent a home or apartment off base. They still receive BAH, but the allotment is modest, and most junior enlisted families live far from the base, often in substandard dwellings.

The distance from home to the base is often a serious problem. Most junior enlisted families have only one car, used by the servicemember to get to and from work. This leaves the spouse at home, unable to get to the base to shop or to work. Because the spouse is in a new, unfamiliar place, possibly for the first time in her life, she has no support network, no friends or family to help out.

Although the servicemember's paycheck is steady, it doesn't stretch very far. Young families often are inexperienced in money management, and, as noted earlier, they receive a barrage of credit-card offers, quick loans, and attractive-sounding installment plans for purchasing furniture and home appliances. If they are overseas, they may not understand the prices of utilities such as phone service or electricity, which can cost much more than they are used to. As they try to create a comfortable home for themselves, they all too easily run up unmanageable debts. According to one study, over a third of junior enlisted personnel have trouble paying their bills on a regular basis.[16] When servicemembers get into serious financial difficulty, their careers can be adversely affected, so families may try to hide their problems. Sometimes family members end up going to emergency relief programs for extra cash to pay for food and other essentials.

Many or most of the assistance programs on base are designed with the junior enlisted spouse in mind, but it is difficult for young spouses to take advantage of them. They cannot get to the base without their sponsors, and even if they do have a car or some other kind of transportation, they are unfamiliar with the military support system. Their sponsors are their only link to the base, and young husbands, who work long hours and are grappling with maturity issues themselves, often do not relay information about orientations, FSG meetings, or other activities for spouses. Too many young spouses believe, incorrectly, that the FSGs or spouses clubs are for the older officers' family members, and they feel uncomfortable attending.

To make matters even worse, many young wives have small children at home. It is easy for the outside observer to fault young families for making their situation more stressful by adding more mouths to feed, but a young wife with no friends and no job naively hopes that a baby will enrich her life, not add stress. Of course, a young woman with no car, little money, and a toddler or two has even less opportunity to participate in base activities. FSG leaders say that one of their biggest priorities is finding funds to pay for babysitting or day care for the small children of junior enlisted families, so that wives can connect with each other through the group.

Interestingly, although the spouses of officers and senior NCOs are no longer officially required to participate in unit activities, the FSG system, as well as current demographic patterns in the military, has placed an ever-greater burden on them. There are more junior enlisted wives today than there were during the draft era. Although senior spouses may not do quite as much socializing among themselves, they spend more time dealing with the problems of very young and needy women as volunteer leaders in the FSG. In most cases they have no special training for what amounts to social work, and the job can be stressful and exhausting. Although many experts have suggested that the military pay professionals for the support work that senior spouses currently do, particularly with junior enlisted families, studies also show that the hours FSG leaders work, even valued at minimum wage, amount to millions of dollars a year per base, and there does not seem to be any available funding for such an initiative.[17]

INTERNATIONAL MARRIAGES

Another group of spouses that brings special needs and challenges is women from other nations who met their husbands while the men were stationed overseas. Since the 1940s, there have been hundreds of thousands of marriages between servicemembers and women from the countries where the United State maintains bases.

At the beginning of the twentieth century, American servicemembers married or lived with women in the Philippines, Hawaii, and other overseas posts, but the first real wave of "war brides" came during and after World War II. American servicemembers began marrying women from Great Britain and Australia even before the war was over, and as many as 160,000 marriages took place by the time hostilities ended.[18] These women had relatively little difficulty adjusting to American life; the language and culture were similar, although not identical, to what they knew. After the war, American GIs fell in love with German, French, Italian, and other European women, and the question of marriage arose. By 1948, regulations forbidding marriage with women from the former enemy nations were relaxed, and by the mid-1950s, 15 percent or more of the marriages around large U.S. bases in Germany took place between German women and American servicemembers. While language barriers presented problems, these women, like English-speaking British and

Australian women, had relatively little trouble adjusting to life in the United States.

It has been somewhat different for the Asian wives of servicemembers. There have been well over half a million Asian-American marriages since the end of World War II, the largest numbers of wives coming from Japan and South Korea, with smaller but still significant numbers of women from the Philippines, Vietnam, and Thailand. Most of these marriages took place during and after the wars that America fought in Asia, during times of economic hardship as well as social and psychological upheaval.[19]

While many Asian-American marriages are happy and successful, others are much more troubled. One reason is the motivation for the marriage itself. Both partners may come to the marriage with cultural and economic preconceptions about the other partner, and may to a certain extent be attracted to a stereotype rather than a real individual. Psychologists and researchers working with Asian wives of servicemembers suggest that some American men who marry Asian women do so because they have had trouble establishing healthy relationships with American women. They may want a wife who is docile and obedient, and they believe, perhaps based on their experiences with the sex industry in Asia, that Asian women are just such wives. As one Korean wife says, "often Western men are attracted to Oriental girls because they like power and control."[20] If they are combat veterans, and many are, they may suffer from post-traumatic stress disorder, substance abuse, or other emotional problems. Asian women, for their part, create romantic images of their American paramours and idealistically believe that they will enjoy lives of ease and affluence when they reach the United States. Their only understanding of American culture comes from television programs. Unfortunately, neither partner's expectations are likely to be met.

Another problem is language and culture. Even in the healthiest relationships, the language barrier between American servicemembers and Asian women is often more intractable than it is between Americans and Europeans, whose languages are at least somewhat similar. It is much harder for Korean or Japanese speakers to learn English than many Americans realize, and most servicemen do not succeed in becoming fluent in their wives' native languages. When problems emerge, the couple cannot discuss them.[21] The cultures from which most wives come are quite different from American culture, in everything from food to religion and attitudes toward family. This is often not a serious obstacle as long as the couple remains in Asia, but when they are reassigned to the United States, the wife leaves her culture behind.

To make matters even worse, many Asian women who marry servicemembers do so against the will of their families. In some nations, this is due to xenophobia and racism, while in others it is because women who marry American servicemembers are assumed to be prostitutes. The thousands of Korean women who have married American GIs are ignored by the Korean diaspora community, which prefers to imagine Koreans in America as college students or professionals.[22] In the United States, Asian wives have trouble fitting in because of American stereotypes about them. Some Americans assume Asian wives are former prostitutes, or that they do not want to learn American ways.[23]

As Asian wives try to adapt to life in the United States, they find themselves entirely dependent on their husbands, a shocking difference from their earlier lives in Asia, when the servicemember depended on his Asian wife to handle matters in the civilian community. Wives experience debilitating homesickness, made worse because they cannot express it.[24] As they begin to adjust, they also become more independent, an unwelcome change from the point of view of some husbands, who see their Asian wives becoming more like the American women they don't like. They find support groups of Asian wives, or establish new ones, they learn English and take jobs. They begin to push back.

Given all the challenges, it is no wonder that up to 80 percent of Asian-American marriages fail. In recent years, however, on-base organizations like the USO and MWR have established classes and support groups for Asian wives. With the help of energetic and committed veteran wives, they teach new brides about American customs, cooking, interviewing for jobs, banking, and other practical necessities.[25]

DOMESTIC VIOLENCE IN THE MILITARY

In the spring of 2002, four servicemembers stationed at Fort Bragg, North Carolina, murdered their wives in separate incidents of domestic abuse. In the wake of the shocking tragedies, the issue of family violence among military personnel hit the news. Commentators noted that three of the four servicemembers had been involved in special operations in Afghanistan, one a member of Delta Force, and many wondered if the events presaged a wave of violence from veterans traumatized by their experiences in Central Asia.[26]

Fortunately, the wave of violence many feared has not come to pass, so far. The DoD has stepped up its domestic violence prevention programs, created new marriage and family support programs, and taught commanders how to debrief servicemembers and spot signs of stress as they leave the combat zone. But the problem of domestic violence in the military may not be so easy to solve. The factors that add stress in military life—being away from home, long work hours, frequent deployments, financial troubles, lack of privacy, family responsibilities, youth and immaturity—create circumstances in which domestic violence is much more likely to occur.

According to most studies, rates of domestic violence are higher in the military than in comparable civilian populations. One study of the late 1990s suggested that military rates were as much as five times the civilian rates.[27] A study commissioned by the Army showed that during the early years of the drawdown, a period of great insecurity about the future, as many as one out of every three families had experienced some kind of domestic abuse, "considerably higher than anticipated," according to the report.[28] The study revealed some common characteristics of domestic violence in the military. Perpetrators are most likely to be mid-level NCOs—servicemembers with spouses and children, but who make less than $20,000 a year in base pay. They also have both a great deal of responsibility at work and little autonomy, so they bring their stress and anger home. Domestic violence, according to the Army study, escalates at bases that are going to close; whether this is because of insecurity about the future or because the effort required to close a base is exhausting is not clear from the research.[29] Servicemembers are not the only ones acting out violently against family members, either. Young, overwhelmed spouses are the majority of perpetrators of child abuse and neglect. Studies show spouses exhibit more morale problems and more stress, because they have even less control than servicemembers do over their lives in the military.[30] Child abuse is all too often the result.

There may also be some exacerbating factors related to military training and socialization. In the wake of the Fort Bragg killings, many observers suggested that men who are trained in violence have trouble separating their work from their personal life. "The military members who are committing these attacks are, in fact, trained to be this violent," says a former Air Force officer involved in military domestic violence prevention.[31] It is a controversial viewpoint, but there is some evidence of its validity. According to a study of child abuse in the Air Force, servicemembers trained in combat occupations were more likely to batter their children than noncombat personnel.[32] Others, however, are not convinced. "I think the difference might be that when the military knows about abusive behavior, intervention at even relatively low levels of abuse tends to be much more swift and complete," says one civilian expert who studied the problem in the military.[33] In contrast, intervention among civilians may be less consistent, accounting for some of the differences between military and civilian levels of violence.

The structure of military family life makes domestic violence a particularly difficult problem to solve. Spouses are reluctant to report incidents of abuse because they know that a complaint will ruin their sponsor's career and hurt the entire family. If a servicemember is found to be an abuser, he or she will be separated from the military, and the family will not only lose its income but also be ineligible for support services and help. To make matters worse, in the old days, a spouse who complained about abuse would often be received with skepticism or unconcern by a commander who was more interested in maintaining the job performance of a functioning member of the unit. Commanders sometimes believed that wives made up stories to retaliate against their husbands. Because the military did not provide an outside channel for complaints, the issue would have to go through the command.[34] Many spouses chose to keep quiet.

The military began to pay attention to domestic violence in the 1970s, around the same time that civilian society began to realize the extent of the problem. The FAP was the DoD's first organized attempt to deal with family abuse. The FAP provided services for victims, and treatment for abusers, but like civilian programs, in the early years it tended to focus on what to do after abuse had already occurred. In the mid-1990s, the FAP began to put more resources into prevention and awareness. Today, much of its efforts target community education and prevention.

In recent years, the DoD has focused more intensely on the problem. In 1993, it created the Transitional Compensation Program, giving financial support for up to three years to families of active-duty personnel who were separated from the service because of domestic violence. In 2000 and 2001, a task force created by the DoD reexamined the military's response to abuse and suggested dozens of improvements, including a "zero tolerance" policy similar to the military's drug and alcohol abuse policies. In early 2006, the DoD changed its policy on reporting domestic abuse, allowing victims to choose either to allow complaints to be investigated or to receive help without triggering an investigation.

CHAPTER 8

THE MILITARY AS A CAREER

It is probably fair to say that most people join the armed forces with short-term goals in mind: earning money for a college education, learning marketable skills, developing discipline and self-confidence, seeing the world, and serving the country. First-term enlistees and junior officers can "try on" military life without thinking beyond the three or four years of their initial commitment. A significant percentage of those beginning their first tours of duty, however, will be considering military service as a career, perhaps because they were always interested in the military life, or their parents or other family members enjoyed fulfilling military careers, or because of the appeal of the benefits package and long-term stability.

Regardless of whether military personnel join with the intention of serving only one term, or whether they intend to try for a career, at the end of their first commitment period, all servicemembers must decide whether to sign up for another tour or get out and rejoin the civilian world. And if they do stay in for another term, and then another, at some point they have to decide if they want to commit to a military career. After twenty or more years of service, they will retire with a pension and veterans' benefits. However, if they do not stay in for the full twenty, they may serve ten, twelve, or fifteen years and leave the service with no retirement benefits or health insurance.

As many servicemembers will attest, the decision to stay in or get out can be difficult, especially for those with no tradition of military service in their families. Twenty years away from home can seem like a lifetime to those with close networks of family and friends. A military career means that spouse and children will be forced into a nomadic life that they may not want. Moreover, a military career isn't as stable as it used to be. A strict "up-or-out" promotion policy, especially for officers, can push servicemembers out after a number of years of military service but before retirement kicks in. A servicemember may not get a desired assignment, or the military may freeze promotions in an occupational specialty that is overstaffed. Any mistake, such as alcohol or drug abuse, sexual impropriety, or questionable leadership behavior, will kill a career, no matter how much the servicemember wants to serve. Finally, in recent years, the pace of military work has increased dramatically, as units are deployed to conduct humanitarian missions and fight the wars in Iraq and Afghanistan, and this pace can exhaust even the most enthusiastic careerist.

Many of the basic circumstances of military life do not change over the course of a military career. Moves will always be frequent and unpredictable; the organizational structure will remain the same, even when an individual's place in it changes; the military support system will not change significantly. But other aspects of life will be very different at the higher ranks. Senior officers and enlisted servicemembers make a good deal more money than junior personnel, live in better housing, and receive more respect from their peers and subordinates. On the other hand, they undertake more responsibility, and in most cases work even longer hours than they did earlier in their careers. Their spouses may be pressured to take on more visible roles as unofficial community leaders. They are expected to complete both military and civilian higher education. Most of all, they will have to survive the promotions system, which becomes increasingly daunting at the higher ranks.

PERSONNEL MANAGEMENT 101

Every year, in the Defense Authorization Act, Congress fixes the number of personnel the armed services are allowed to employ. The DoD and the individual services spend a lot of time and effort trying to create military forces with the best mix of personnel at different grades, job specialties, and skill levels, and at the levels authorized by Congress. Personnel management experts take into account factors like rates of enlistment, re-enlistment, promotion, and retirement, as well as the services' mission requirements, and try to project personnel needs years into the future. Experts also try to predict the types of training and experience that the senior leaders of tomorrow will need today, and they try to create career path models that make those predictions a reality. The goal is not only to have a balanced force now but also to maintain the balance in five or ten or even twenty years, when some of today's recruits will be senior level NCOs and officers. Moreover, personnel experts must try to maintain this balance at the lowest possible cost.[1]

Creating a smooth personnel management system for the 2.7 million or so active duty and reserve troops in the U.S. armed services is a challenging task. Many factors affect a servicemember's decision to remain in the service, and those factors are in turn shaped by decisions and policies of the individual services, the DoD, Congress, and even the courts.

A seemingly small reduction in benefits, for example, can persuade a larger than expected number of personnel to leave the service for civilian life. The shortfall might be remedied by greater recruitment efforts, but these efforts would probably cost more money and take funds away from other programs. Reductions in other programs might affect individual decisions to stay or leave, creating a vicious cycle. Conversely, DoD or Congress could decide that enlistment bonuses or retirement benefits are the keys to better recruitment and spend millions on them, only to learn later that some other factor was more important in influencing recruitment. As can be imagined, these dynamics are extremely complicated. The new promotion requirement, for example, that flag officers have "joint" or interservice command experience, has forced many officers to choose between fulfilling this new demand and spending command time with their own troops in mentoring relationships that can influence the way younger servicemembers view the service and can impact their career decisions. Obviously, maintaining a steady and stable pipeline of military personnel is almost indescribably complex.

The idea of personnel management in the military is, in fact, relatively new. To the extent that it existed before World War II, personnel management systems dealt primarily with officers. As far as managing the enlisted forces went, the services simply recruited or drafted large numbers of citizens when they needed to fight a war, then let them go when the war was finished. Relatively few enlisted servicemembers made the military a career until after World War II.

In the old days, the services grappled with issues of pay, promotion, and retirement individually, fighting with each other as well as with parsimonious civilian leadership for funding. When the services faced shortages of officers, they sometimes convinced Congress to increase the number of cadets or midshipmen at the academies, but it was a crude tool, and there remained no provision for eliminating incompetent officers short of court-martial.

At the beginning of the twentieth century, the Navy began experimenting with "plucking boards," which selected officers with marginal service records for mandatory retirement, so that more competent officers could move up through the ranks. But the boards were unpopular, and in practice, most officers continued to be promoted by seniority. The Army, meanwhile, stuck to its traditional seniority system for promotions. This ensured a rough equality among peers, but it also had several unintended consequences. First, it drove away many intelligent and ambitious men, who left the services to find better opportunities in civilian life. Second, it allowed marginally competent officers to remain in the service and rise through the ranks, while preventing truly talented individuals from moving forward. By World War II, the senior ranks were full of "deadwood" mixed in with the many brilliant officers and senior enlisted personnel who led the United States and its allies to victory.

The first significant changes in the traditional system came after the war. In 1947, Congress created the OPA (Officer Personnel Act), which set consistent rules for all the services. The OPA replaced seniority with an "up-or-out" policy, which continues to be in use today; officers (and NCOs) must be promoted at specific points in their careers, or they cannot stay. Up-or-out was intended to "keep the officer corps young and vigorous" and weed out the mediocre.[2] "High Year Tenure," adopted at the same time, is the military's expression for the maximum number of years an individual may serve in a given rank without being promoted. Each service sets its own High Year Tenure rules for each rank; in all cases they are fairly generous.

By the 1950s, these personnel management policies had helped to get rid of many incompetents in the military, and rewarded the talented and ambitious. In addition, the services could entice capable servicemembers with generous benefits and a secure retirement system, and new recruits were always available through the draft. In fact, the military became a victim of its own success. Less than a decade after the end of World War II, the percentage of senior officers and NCOs in all the services was higher than it needed to be. In 1954, the OGLA (Officer Grade Limitation Act) set limits on the number of officers that could serve in each pay grade, forcing some to leave or retire.

Still, the problem of top-heaviness continued, and during the Vietnam conflict, the imbalance became increasingly severe. The services faced shortages of junior officers, mostly due to high casualty rates among squad and platoon leaders in Southeast Asia. At the same time, over 70 percent of the enlisted force had reached the rank of E-4 or higher, at a time when the military needed junior enlisted personnel.[3] The Army depended more and more on the draft, but when it ended in 1973, crisis loomed.

In 1974, the DoD ordered the services to come up with personnel management plans so that shortages and bottlenecks in the system could be evened out. It took years, but by the early 1980s, new plans were in place, along with new bureaucracies and research institutions. The EPMS (Enlisted Personnel Management System) and the DOPMA (Defense Officers Personnel Management Act) of 1981 establish the number of authorized personnel at each rank, and planners try to calculate how many recruits in each job specialty will be needed if numbers are to be maintained in the future.

Above all, planners must wrestle with the always-changing pipeline of enlisted personnel, many of whom will leave the service after their first or second enlistment. Planners do not expect all or even most junior enlisted personnel to choose the military as a career, but they would surely be grateful if attrition patterns were stable. Unfortunately, they are not. Retention varies among job specialties, and other considerations, both military and civilian, can change the retention rate from one year to the next. Forecasting retention rates for NCOs with ten or more years in the service is easier because most have made the decision to stay in the military until retirement, but predicting the decisions of junior servicemembers and "midcareer" personnel, those in their second re-enlistment with less than ten years service, is always a headache.

There are many ways the services address shortages caused by unexpected attrition and bottlenecks. Sometimes the services allow "conditional" promotions, where servicemembers who are not yet officially eligible for promotion to a specific rank, but are otherwise qualified, can serve at that rank until they complete training required for promotion. Accelerated promotion is another method of filling positions. In 2005, for example, the Army placed 19,000 E-4s on the E-5 promotion list, even though their commanders had not yet recommended them.

Conditional and accelerated promotions are used relatively sparingly. Normally, cash payments are the most common motivators used to increase retention. Each service is authorized to hand out SRBs (Selective Re-enlistment Bonuses) to servicemembers in understaffed job specialties. In setting SRB levels, the services take into account personnel shortages, the unattractiveness of the job, and the cost of replacing trained personnel, and, during wartime, whether the job is critical to the war effort.[4] A few extremely hard-to-fill jobs, such as Arabic translators, may merit an SRB of up to $60,000, but payments are usually less than $20,000. The bonuses come and go; they may be available one year, but cancelled the following year, having fulfilled their purpose.

Another type of re-enlistment bonus is targeted at personnel assigned to certain regions of the world. In 2003, for example, the Army announced it would pay bonuses of $5,000 to soldiers stationed in Iraq, Kuwait, Afghanistan, and South Korea if they re-enlisted for three years, regardless of their job specialties.[5] Programs like this target personnel who may be more likely to leave the service after a tour of duty in a less-desirable location.

In addition, there are many nonmonetary incentives the services use to induce personnel to reenlist. Personnel serving overseas, especially in less-desirable locations, sometimes have the chance to choose their next stateside posting under the "CONUS Station of Choice" program. Or, they might be eligible for training in a new field. Some incentives benefit family members. The "current station stabilization re-enlistment," whereby personnel reenlist and stay at their current post, is an option that is especially attractive to parents with teenagers who would like their children to stay in the same high school until graduation. An experimental program begun by the Army in 2005 allows spouses to use their sponsors' Montgomery GI Bill benefits if the sponsor re-enlists.[6]

On the other hand, when the services are overstaffed in a certain rank or job specialty, they do their best to reduce the numbers. Too many personnel at a specific rank may spur "retention moderation" rules that make it more difficult for individuals to get promoted to that rank. In 2003, for example, the Army announced that it had a glut of midcareer NCOs, and standards were changed so that NCOs would not be allowed to re-enlist if they had even the tiniest blemish on their records, such as alcohol abuse, weight problems, or financial difficulties.[7]

The Air Force uses a tactic known as "rebalancing the force;" personnel in overstaffed job specialties must retrain for another job. Personnel managers call for volunteers first, then they begin "Involuntary Classification," assigning servicemembers to another specialty (usually, it must be said, one closely related to their original specialty).

A third way to reduce overstaffing is to tighten the "High Year Tenure" standards. If the limit is lowered, personnel approaching the High Year Tenure must be promoted or get out sooner than they may have expected. This tactic is used infrequently, however, and most NCOs with reasonable records are able to stay in the military for twenty years, even if they fall behind their peers in promotion. Because enlisted personnel serve under a series of short-term contracts, they are not eligible for separation pay if they are not allowed to reenlist, so officers and civilian managers are reluctant to force an NCO out of the military after eighteen or nineteen years simply because he or she is in an overstaffed job specialty.

Of course, planners must use care with these types of programs. Whether aimed at keeping servicemembers in or encouraging them to leave, tweaking programs can—and very often do—have unintended consequences on morale, and thus, on retention. If a bonus program is widely available for a number of years, for example, it can come to be seen as an entitlement, and its elimination can cause personnel to leave the service in frustration. Likewise, plans that cause long-time personnel to worry about the stability of their careers may scare talented servicemembers into the civilian world.

ENLISTED PROMOTIONS

Servicemembers may have every intention of making the military a career, but they must survive the promotions process all along the way. Personnel management systems try to make the promotion process as simple and clear as possible, but even so, most career servicemembers consider it anxiety-producing and stressful. When a servicemember earns an important promotion, it is an achievement well worth celebrating.

In the beginning, promotions of enlisted personnel and officers are more or less automatic, as long as the servicemember has not gotten into any trouble and has performed reasonably well. The schedule of "automatic" promotions for enlisted personnel varies with levels of higher education, prior service experience, and other factors, but generally promotions at the lower ranks depend on TIS (Time in Service) and TIG (Time in Grade). Promotion to E-2 comes after six months of active duty (in the Navy, nine months), and promotion to E-3 after a year of active duty. Promotion to E-4 varies with the service, but averages a little more than two years. In the Navy and Marine Corps, promotion to E-4 is not automatic, while in the Army and Air Force, automatic advancements end with promotion to E-5.

Enlisted personnel at and above the rank of E-3 or E-4, depending on the branch of service, must compete with their peers for promotion. The process is complicated and takes place in several steps. The first step is to become officially eligible for promotion. Second, a servicemember must be recommended or selected for promotion, and third, he or she must actually receive the additional stripe. The servicemember has some control over the process, but much of it depends on how many positions happen to be open at each rank and in each job specialty, and also on the quality of the competition. Thus, the chance for promotion can swing widely from year to year. The uncertainty causes much frustration among career-minded personnel.

To become eligible for promotion, servicemembers must be "in the zone," that is, have appropriate TIG and TIS, neither too long nor too short. There are exceptions, but the vast majority of promotions, even competitive ones, occur "in the zone," to insure that NCOs have the occupational and management experience suitable for their rank. Promotion to certain ranks also requires that servicemembers complete specific training courses or other military education.

Next, servicemembers must be selected for promotion. As noted above, the likelihood of selection depends in part on the number of personnel needed at each rank and job specialty. There are also a wide variety of qualifications, educational credentials, and awards that enlisted personnel can accumulate to bolster their chances for promotion. To make a reasonably objective comparison of personnel records possible, each branch of the service has a promotion points system. Servicemembers accrue promotion points for every type of education, training, and work experience they receive. In each service, there is a theoretical maximum number of points a servicemember can earn for promotion to each rank, but the minimum score fluctuates depending on the needs of the service. All branches except the Air Force promote different numbers of people depending on their job specialties. In the Army, Navy, and Marine Corps, the minimum number of points can be relatively low for a job specialty experiencing shortages, and conversely, if a job specialty is overfilled, the minimum will be quite high. The Air Force does things differently; it calculates how many personnel it will need at a given rank, then distributes them equally across specialties. If a particular job specialty ends up overstaffed, the Air Force requires that some of those personnel retrain for another job.

Servicemembers earn promotion points for TIS and TIG, commander's evaluation reports, PT test scores, hardship tours or combat duty, attending military courses and schools, civilian college credit, awards and decorations, evaluation of skills particular to a job specialty (in the Navy they are called PARs (Personnel Advancement Requirements), in the Air Force, skill levels), promotion examinations, and interviews by a promotions board. Once a servicemember has accumulated sufficient promotion points, he or she may "put in" or apply for promotion. In the Army, a board of officers and senior NCOs from the company or battalion meets to review records, interview candidates, and select those who will be promoted. Other branches make the process more impersonal. A recommendation or selection for promotion does not mean that the servicemember can sew his or her new stripe on just yet. Everyone on the promotions list receives a "line number," determined by TIS and TIG, and each month the DoD announces which set of line numbers will be promoted that month. The process ensures a steady stream of newly promoted NCOs, and makes financing promotions easier and more predictable.

At the higher ranks, service-wide centralized boards select candidates for promotion. In some branches of service, the candidates go before the boards in person, while in others, the board scrutinizes candidates' records only. The boards meet annually, and their size ranges from half a dozen members to 70 or 80. They review records of candidates from across the service, not just from one particular unit. Before the members of promotions boards convene, the DoD informs them of the number of promotions they are authorized to recommend. When the recommendations have been made, those selected get a line number and wait their turn.

Some factors, such as TIS and TIG, are out of the servicemember's control, but the ambitious servicemember will do everything he or she can to earn extra points by working hard, staying fit, taking classes, and preparing for exams and board appearances. Every service hosts a Web site that explains exactly what is needed for promotion and how to best negotiate the process. The Marine Corps, for example, has created a set of detailed "MOS Roadmaps," 25-page documents explaining exactly what kinds of training, education, and experience the ambitious Marine should accumulate in order to be promoted to each rank.

The best general advice for servicemembers who want to move ahead is to pay close attention and remain active. Servicemembers should

check their personnel files regularly to make sure that all necessary paperwork and records are up to date; learn what schools and activities are
available to them and take advantage of opportunities; and prepare for
interviews and examinations as carefully as possible. The Army Web
site advises: "you must have the necessary desire to become an NCO.
You must prepare for your board appearance through diligent study,
practice of board procedures, mock boards, and using your NCO Support
Channel. You need to remember that you are not appearing before the
board to impress your supervisor, your First Sergeant, or your peers.
You are doing this for yourself. You are preparing to become an NCO
and a leader."[8]

OFFICER PROMOTIONS

In its most basic outlines, promotion within the officer corps is similar
to that of enlisted personnel. The first promotions are more or less automatic. For junior officers, the "pin-on" time, or the number of months
between one promotion and another, is set by personnel experts in each
branch, but usually for O-1s it is eighteen months, and for O-2s it is
around forty-six months. The services adjust pin-on time as necessary to
manage the career pipeline. In the late 1990s, for example, the Army
began scaling back pin-on time for O-2s because O-3s, Army captains,
were leaving in large numbers. By 2002, O-2s were receiving their captains' bars as early as thirty-six months after they were commissioned.[9]

After officers reach O-3, promotions become more competitive. Most
reach O-4 with about ten years in service, and approximately 80 percent
are promoted. O-5 takes about sixteen years, and 70 percent reach this
level. After twenty-two years, 50 percent of these will reach O-6. Of
course, many qualified officers prefer to retire after twenty years, so the
number of O-5s who are "involuntarily separated"— fired—is much
smaller than 50 percent.

Officers are recommended for promotion by their commanders, and
their records are reviewed by a promotions board, usually made up of
about 20 high-ranking officers. The members of the board, like those of
the NCO board, know in advance how many officers they will be allowed
to recommend. Officers with the most promising records are selected for
promotion and given line numbers based on seniority. They will receive
their promotions when their line numbers come up.

Promotions boards review an officer's entire record, but there are two
elements of that record that matter most of all. Probably the most important consideration is the performance evaluation or report. The report is
written each year by an officer's commander, and details what kinds of
work the officer did and how he or she performed. Officers are rated in

comparison with their peers, and the raters are then rated, an attempt to avoid "grade inflation," in which everyone is given a top rating.

Performance reports are a valuable tool, but some critics complain that too much emphasis is placed on them. All too many officers focus excessively on their evaluations, avoiding innovation and creative decisions that might threaten their ratings. Moreover, evaluation writing is an art that not all commanders take the time to master. Evaluations are not usually written in plain and honest language, and a clever commander who wants to criticize a subordinate praises the subordinate in a slightly lackluster fashion, using words and phrases that have specific implications to the promotions boards. The problem is that a genuinely positive evaluation written by a careless or overworked superior officer might include language that a board will interpret as a subtle rebuke. The difference between "brilliant" and "outstanding" might not seem evident to an outsider, but to a promotions board, words matter.

The other important factor in promotion is the officer's career path. Ambitious officers plan their assignments carefully, making sure to gain experience in a variety of positions. An officer may have a series of stellar evaluations, but if he or she does not accumulate substantial command time, promotion is less certain. Moreover, an officer with any blemish on his or her record, whether duty-related or personal, has virtually no chance of getting promoted. A mishap in an exercise or maneuver, an alcohol-related driving accident, a sexual impropriety, even an ongoing family problem can end an officer's career.

The obstacles to promotion in the officer corps seem almost insurmountable, but in fact, in recent years the military, especially the Army, has struggled to keep junior and mid-level officers in the ranks. Since 2004, the Army has lost up to 8 percent of its lieutenants and captains each year, a figure that should have been around 5 percent. Since 2006, it has increased scholarships for graduate school and offered new officers incentives to extend their service commitments. New programs have helped stem the losses, but the Army's problems are not over. The conflicts in Iraq and Afghanistan require more, smaller units to carry out counterinsurgency activities, and the recent proposed increase in Army and Marine Corps personnel has meant that the officer corps must be expanded further. The Army has been accelerating promotions and promoting a higher percentage of officers than in past years, a trend that critics say could lower the quality of the officer corps.

CAREER PROGRESSION IN THE MILITARY

In today's military, it is no longer enough for career servicemembers to work hard and stay out of trouble. Officers and enlisted personnel alike must plan their careers carefully, making sure that they accumulate the proper mix of military training, education, and work experience to impress the promotions board. Emphasis on proper career planning developed along with the up-or-out promotion policy after World War II, and got a huge boost with the switch to the AVF. After the drawdown, and especially since the beginning of transformation in the past five years, attention to career progression for both officers and enlisted personnel has become mandatory. Successful careers include a mix of command experience, work in staff or administrative positions, training for specific military skills and tasks, broad military leadership education at academies and war colleges, and civilian education.

Every branch of service has a personnel office or department that coordinates assignments for all personnel. These huge departments within each branch include the AFPC (Air Force Personnel Center), the Army HRC (Human Resources Command), the Bureau of Naval Personnel/Navy Personnel Command, known as BUPERS, and the USMC's Personnel Management Division. Their role is to coordinate the needs of the service with the desires of the servicemember regarding assignments and promotions. They take several factors into account in their decisions: what the servicemember has requested, the needs of the service, what special experience and skills the servicemember has, what experience or training the servicemember needs, and where the servicemember is currently assigned. Personnel offices have staffs of career counselors who help servicemembers choose the best next step, and they are trying, with varying records of success, to make more information available online. The personnel experts do their best to play fair and make sure that everyone gets what they want, but of course this is not possible at all times.

Servicemembers usually have some choice in their assignments. They can indicate what base they would like to go to or they can apply to a school or training program. They will not necessarily receive the assignment they are hoping for, but if they continue to work with career counselors, they can often make the best of a less-desirable assignment. Lower and mid-level personnel with good records and commander's recommendations can usually get the assignments they want, if not at the base they hope for. Some assignments, such as command of a vessel or a spot at a war college, can be very competitive, of course, and the assignment that is perhaps most important in a servicemember's career—serving in combat—is a matter of good (or bad) luck.

Throughout their careers, military personnel today must continue their training and education. Some training is simple, organized at the company or battalion level or through distance education. In the Marine Corps, for example, an E-2 Artillery Fire Controller should complete something called a "Gray Belt Qualification" course with his unit, as well as distance education courses such as, for example, "Iraqi Training Reference Materials" and "The Use of Flex Cuffs." Such training courses, which may be only a few hours in duration, include everything from military skills and procedures for specific job specialties to instruction on health, personal finance, and professional demeanor.

Other courses are more involved. Training like Airborne School or SERE requires several weeks or more of temporary duty at a specific base. Each job specialty requires increasingly advanced training that personnel must complete before moving ahead. At the higher ranks, there are general leadership education programs for officers and NCOs that can last a year or more. The continual training and schooling personnel receive throughout their careers is known as PME (Professional Military Education). Today, it is one of the most important aspects of a successful career.

Since the establishment of the Army and Navy in the 1790s, career progression for officers has received most of the attention from military and civilian leaders. The academies were for many years the only place where officers learned the tools of their trade, but toward the end of the nineteenth century, the military vocation began to be viewed more and more as a profession that required years of education and skill development. The first attempts at officer PME began with the establishment of the Army's Light Artillery School in 1869 and its School of Application for Infantry and Cavalry in 1881. The Navy opened the Naval War College in 1885. It must be noted that most career officers were at best skeptical of these innovations and regarded them as a waste of time, sentiments that may be familiar to some officers even now. Their dismissive attitudes were reflected in the lack of support the schools received. The Naval War College, for example, was first housed in the municipal poorhouse in Newport, Rhode Island, and given no provisions or full-time instructors. After the Spanish-American War revealed the military's severe organizational deficiencies, Secretary of War Elihu Root created the Army War College, and other services followed. Despite discouragements in the early years, the war colleges began to educate officers in the theory and history of warfare. They had their critics, but the success of America's military leadership during World War II is owed in large part to the lessons that senior officers learned at the war colleges.

PME begins immediately after the commissioning ceremony, as new O-1s go off to train for several months or more. In the Marine Corps, O-1s attend a basic officer's course, then complete specialized training in their MOS, while in the Army and Navy, they go directly to a combined course of basic officer skills and branch training. After their basic courses, officers often continue their military educations by attending the Airborne Course, the Ranger Course, the Scout Swimmer, Basic Underwater

Demolition/SEAL course, the DLI (Defense Language Institute), or one of many other schools and courses. Programs of instruction range from a few weeks of Airborne training to a year or more of intensive language study. For the most part, officers can go through these types of schools at any point in the early stages of their careers, but because training is rigorous and time-consuming, and brings extra pay and increased chance for promotion, most officers try to complete as much training as they can early on.

At the intermediate level, after officers have been in the service for eleven years or more and have reached the grade of O-4, they may be selected to attend a command and general staff college. These institutions train officers to command larger units such as battalions and brigades and prepare them for senior staff positions in the headquarters of larger organizations like corps, divisions, or wings.[10] There are a number of schools at this level. The CGSS (Command and General Staff School) at Fort Leavenworth is among the oldest, a successor to the Infantry and Cavalry school founded in 1881. The Navy established its College of Naval Command and Staff in Newport, RI in 1923; the Marine Corps Command and Staff College at Quantico, VA and the Air Command and General Staff College at Maxwell Field, AL developed out of earlier versions dating from the 1920s. In addition, the Armed Forces Staff College at Norfolk, VA, founded in 1946, is a joint service college. Although every school except the joint service college in Norfolk is associated with a specific branch, students may come from all branches of the American forces, and officers from allied military forces also attend.

In recent years, the focus at all the colleges has concentrated increasingly on joint service operations—operations involving, for example, the Air Force working closely with the Army. Each college focuses on its branch specialty, but with an emphasis on how to integrate that specialty into joint operations. This, however, has caused strains. Commanders struggling with a high operations tempo and shortages of personnel need their best officers to deal with service-specific issues, and consequently tend to place a lower priority on joint operations.

After graduating from a Command and Staff College, a few officers go on to study advanced war-fighting from one of the graduate schools run by the services. In the Army, officers study at the SAMS (School of Advanced Military Studies); in the Air Force, at the SAASS (School of Advanced Air and Space Studies), in the Marines, at the SAW (School of Advanced Warfare), and in the Navy, at the NOPC (Naval Operational Planner Course). Some of the programs lead to a master's degree, and all of them prepare officers for further command and staff responsibilities. The goal of the SAMS, for example, is explained, in the somewhat murky language of its Web site, as training officers in the military art and science of planning, preparing and executing full spectrum operations in joint, multinational, and interagency contexts. Curriculum combines integrated study of military history, military theory, and execution-based practical exercises, and enables students to develop cognitive problem-solving skills to overcome tough operational challenges at the tactical and operational levels of war. [The] course emphasizes both command and staff perspectives on military decision making, doctrine, and force employment.[11]

The next level of professional education occurs at the senior level, among officers with sixteen to twenty years of service who are at the O-5 or O-6 pay grade.[12] Officers who reach this level may be chosen for advanced study focusing on the strategic level of warfare. In today's environment, this includes learning how the military works with political leadership, industry and economic bodies, diplomatic organizations, and other parts of American society in its defense of the nation. Programs at this level are taught at the Naval, Army, Air, and Marine Corps War Colleges.[13] Officers may also study at the National War College, part of the National Defense University at Fort McNair in Washington, D.C., which is the joint operations college, similar to the Armed Forces Staff College for intermediate level officers.

It is at this point that officers begin to be marked out for flag level promotions, although only about one-third of the graduates of war colleges go on to become generals or admirals. In addition, at this level, officers begin to interact more extensively with civilian organizations. Some are assigned to fellowships at graduate schools like the Kennedy School of Government at Harvard, others to research positions at the Rand Corporation, or to think tanks and other institutes.[14]

Finally, there are a few courses for general and flag officers. A six-week program called CAPSTONE has since 1986 been mandatory for officers nominated for general or admiral. Students meet with leaders of the various national security organizations as well as members of Congress and leaders of allied governments. They are taught how to handle their future role as public figures, and they learn to interact with the national and international media. Two other courses, the Joint Flag Officer Warfighting Course and Pinnacle, are for higher-level general and flag officers who may command Joint Task Forces or serve as members of the Joint Chiefs of Staff.[15]

A bigger change, in many ways, is the shift toward more professionalism in the NCO and CPO corps. Until well into the twentieth century, NCOs and CPOs were hardly distinguishable from lower enlisted personnel. They lived in the barracks or on ships in small private rooms and their pay was not much more than that of the men. Although they were responsible for training and discipline and for keeping the troops "in line" on the battlefield, they received almost no training themselves, simply learning their roles on the job. During America's twentieth-century wars, NCOs and CPOs were the institutional memory of the military, helping younger troops and new officers adjust to military life. They not only knew the rules and regulations, but they also passed on the culture and traditions of the service. They were often the biggest losers in traditional postwar drawdowns, however, as their pay was cut back and responsibilities diminished.

After World War II, the first Army NCO academies were established in occupied Germany,[16] but they were met with resistance by traditional sergeants, who thought them irrelevant. When one NCO asked his first sergeant for permission to attend one of the schools in Germany, the first sergeant refused him, saying: "You're a combat veteran. You already know everything."[17] (Fortunately, the young sergeant persevered and eventually rose to become the top NCO in the Army.)

By the time the Vietnam War began, the situation had hardly changed. The traditional NCO or CPO was still a "hard-drinking, hard-loving, hard-fighting man"[18] with little formal education and a tough attitude. "Lifers," as career NCOs were labeled, clashed with reluctant citizen warriors, both enlisted personnel and junior officers.[19] Disgusted with the state of the Vietnam-era forces, veteran sergeants eligible for retirement left the service in droves and the Army struggled with crippling shortages. In 1967, the Army created the NCOCC (NCO Candidate Course) in an attempt to increase the number of NCOs available for service in Vietnam. Older NCOs were suspicious of the "shake and bake" sergeants, but they performed well in combat, proving to all that an educated enlisted leadership corps was necessary in the modern army.[20]

The real transformation occurred in the 1970s. The services, recognizing the need for a well-trained, professional enlisted leadership corps in the AVF, raised pay rates and began to establish clearer professional standards for enlisted personnel. The services began to create or revamp schools for NCO and CPO training at the basic, intermediate and senior levels, as well as special academies for E-8 or E-9s, the highest levels of the enlisted corps.

The transition to continuing PME for career enlisted personnel has not been easy or quick. Because of the long-standing emphasis on on-the-job training as well as the weight of institutional culture and tradition, there continues to be resistance to formal education. The first CPO Academy, for example, three weeks of classes on management, administration, and planning, began instruction on selected Navy bases only in 2006. Many CPOs objected to the program, preferring the older "transition" from enlisted sailor to CPO that included informal community activities, fund-raising, learning Navy history, and a ceremony in which new CPOs buried their white sailor hats.[21] But the traditional activities will continue along with formal coursework, and it appears that PME for career enlisted personnel is here to stay.

VETERANS AND RETIREES

Given the arduous working conditions, strict discipline, and relatively low pay of military service, not to mention the constant threat of harm inherent in the job, it is no wonder that Congress has over the years offered many benefits to those who serve. Veterans may be twenty-five-year-olds with just one uneventful term of enlistment, or disabled retirees who participated in one or more of the nation's major wars, but they and their families are eligible for various monetary benefits and services. Official records indicate that there are over 24 million veterans alive today, and three-quarters of them served during a war or official hostility. In total, there are about 63 million veterans and family members who are eligible for some type of veterans' benefits. The commitment to veterans and their families is a long-term one. In 2006, there were still 5 children of Civil War veterans and 440 family members of veterans of the Spanish-American War receiving benefits.[22]

Retirement benefits are viewed by many as deferred compensation rather than pensions, because career servicemembers earn much less than they would in the civilian world. Moreover, military retirees, servicemembers who have put in twenty or more years of service, maintain their military status. They are subject to the UCMJ and can be recalled to active duty in a national emergency, so most retired servicemembers consider their pensions to be continued pay for this "reserve" status.

Two cabinet-level departments are responsible for administering benefits for veterans and retirees: the DoD, whose programs are used by active duty personnel, reservists, noncareer veterans and retirees, and the Department of Veterans Affairs, which deals solely with veterans and their family members. Established in 1930 by President Herbert Hoover, it was formerly known as the VA (Veterans Administration), and is best-known by its original acronym. In 1989, it became a cabinet-level organization, and today the VA is the second-largest cabinet department in the federal government, behind the DoD. Its budget is over $71 billion a year and it employs over 235,000 people.[23]

In spite of its size, or perhaps because of it, most veterans can tell horror stories about dealing with the VA's huge and confusing bureaucracy. The VA administers a bewildering number of programs, and it is almost impossible to determine exactly what an individual veteran might be eligible for without extensive research and consultation. In recent years, however, officials have tried to make the VA more accessible to its users and have improved the quality of services. Long-time vets may not believe it, but these days, some VA services such as medical care have become models for the rest of the nation.[24]

Servicemembers who complete their commitments and separate from the service after less than twenty years of service are eligible for some basic benefits from the VA. The most common of these include transition benefits such as job counseling, a paid move back to their home of record, and unemployment pay; GI Bill education funds; and GI home loans. Disabled veterans are eligible for the basic package plus medical care and disability compensation for themselves and their families. Retirees who have served twenty years or more receive their military pensions in addition to VA benefits.

One of the largest expenditures of the VA and the DoD is for health care for veterans, retirees, and their families. There are several programs through which medical care is provided. First is the network of VA hospitals, clinics, rehab centers, nursing homes, and other facilities, totaling over 1,300 in all. Over 5 million disabled veterans use the VA medical services every year for care that may or may not be specifically related to their disability.

A second category of medical care benefits comes through the CHAMPVA (Civilian Health and Medical Program of the Department of Veterans Affairs). This program, similar to many HMO plans, pays for health care for the families of disabled veterans. Most of the care is received through civilian medical centers, but CHAMPVA pays for it.

A similar HMO-style program is called TRICARE, which is not run by the VA, but by the DoD. It is a health care program for active duty and retired military personnel and their families, and for families of servicemembers killed in action. Like CHAMPVA, it pays for care in civilian medical centers if personnel or family members cannot use a military hospital or clinic. Both CHAMPVA and TRICARE are secondary providers for veterans and retirees who are eligible for Medicare.

The VA and the DoD also administer disability compensation and pension programs, which are distinct and unrelated. The difference is confusing to many people, and the source of much frustration and misunderstanding. The VA compensation program is used by disabled veterans. When a servicemember is injured or develops a medical problem while on active duty, the condition is reviewed by a VA medical board. The VA makes a determination of how disabled the servicemember is, and assigns the disability a percentage—the servicemember is 20 percent disabled, or 60 percent disabled, and so forth. When the servicemember leaves the service, he or she receives monthly tax-free disability compensation from the VA, based on the severity of the disability. It is important to remember that "service-connected" disabilities do not have to be the result of combat or duty-related injury. A servicemember can receive compensation for a knee injury, for example, from playing football or skiing, if he or she is serving on active duty at the time.

Disability compensation is available to anyone who is injured while on active duty, even if the injury occurred in the first few years of service. Retirement pensions, on the other hand, are available only to retirees, and they do not come from the VA but from the DoD. If a servicemember retires after twenty years, he or she receives 50 percent of basic pay, not including housing subsidies and other special pay and bonuses. When servicemembers retire after thirty years, they receive 75 percent of their basic pay.

So far, so good; but the situation gets complicated for retirees who also have a service-related disability. Many retirees have incurred service-related disabilities during active duty, and they receive compensation for these. However, because retirees are still considered to be members of the armed forces, they can go to the VA at any point and apply to have their age-related medical conditions—arthritis, high blood pressure, diabetes—treated as service-connected disabilities even if the conditions began only in retirement. As they get older, many retirees do so, because as disabled veterans, they are eligible for free treatment at VA hospitals, much easier than fighting with "the Hell we call TRICARE," as one user put it. They are also eligible to receive monthly disability compensation payments. Until recently, however, every dollar that disabled retirees received in compensation from the VA reduced their pensions by the same amount. In recent years, veterans groups have pushed to change the ban on "concurrent receipt," as it is officially called, or, in military slang, "double-dipping." In 2003, they finally won the battle, and the ban was dropped for those with disabilities of 60 percent or higher.[25]

The retirement and disability compensation system that exists today is a far cry from that which existed for most of the nation's history. In the early years of the Republic, there was no retirement plan at all, which forced officers and NCOs to stay in the service long after they were able to contribute. It was only in the second half of the nineteenth century that Congress authorized retirement pay for officers, but they had to serve for forty years or reach their early sixties to earn their pensions. In 1885, Congress created a retirement system for NCOs; after thirty years of service they could collect 75 percent of their basic pay.

The system was better than nothing, but it still left many less active and energetic senior personnel filling spaces that ambitious young officers and NCOs should have occupied. In 1945, the retirement laws changed to allow officers and NCOs to retire after twenty years. There were several reasons for the change. First, it was hoped that a twenty-year rule would keep the military forces younger overall than they had been in the past;

second, it compensated for the lower pay that military personnel received comparable to civilian pay; and third, it rewarded personnel for the dangers and sacrifices of military service.[26]

In the 1980s, advocates of a streamlined government led the charge for reform of the military retirement system. Some claimed that it was outdated; Congress had authorized major pay increases that brought military and civilian pay in closer parity, and as the technology and organization of the military had changed, a youthful force was less important. Moreover, as life expectancies increased, military personnel retiring after twenty years could look forward to lucrative second careers in business, government, or as civilian employees of the DoD.[27]

The Military Reform Act of 1986, known as "Redux," cut retirement benefits somewhat; after twenty years, personnel received 40 percent instead of 50 percent of their basic pay. The point was to encourage servicemembers to stay in for thirty or more years. The drawdown of the 1990s changed everything, however. Rather than encouraging personnel to stay in, the DoD paid "exit bonuses" for them to leave. Redux was repealed in 1999. A year later, Congress allowed military personnel to participate in the TSP (Thrift Savings Plan), a 401-K-style retirement plan originally created for civilian government employees. Participation in the TSP enables servicemembers to save for retirement even if they do not stay in the armed forces for the full twenty years, a significant change from the all-or-nothing pension system. The TSP is optional for military personnel, but it is another small step in the "civilianization" of the military system.

The controversy over military retirement, which erupts every few years when a new policy is proposed or a new law passed, generates a lot of heat among defenders of the system and those who want to reform it. Budget cutters worry that government obligations to military retirees will bankrupt the system, while advocates argue that the provisions are necessary to maintain a qualified, ready force, and they point to increasing retention problems as a symptom of government parsimony. Researchers admit, however, that uncertainty about retirement benefits is not the main reason servicemembers decide to leave the service. For most men and women in their 20s, quality of life issues and work tempo are more important factors than retirement pay.[28]

The VA does more than provide monetary compensation for disabled veterans. Several VA programs have enabled veterans, disabled or not, to achieve long-term financial stability and a higher standard of living. Perhaps the most famous of these is the Montgomery GI Bill, an optional but very popular plan that provides funds for college. Servicemembers can enroll in the program when they enlist. They pay into the plan during their first year of service and the VA matches their contributions. During or, more commonly, after their service, they can use the accumulated funds to pay for undergraduate or graduate education.

The VA Home Loan Guaranty is another popular VA program, enabling veterans to purchase homes with no large down payment. Since its inception in 1944, 18 million vets have bought homes with the help of the VA. To use the program, they must apply for a home loan through a bank or mortgage company just like other homebuyers, but the VA will guarantee about $60,000 of the loan. Most lenders will loan up to $250,000 to a veteran without requiring a down payment. If the buyer pays off the loan as required, the VA does nothing. If he or she defaults, and every year about 1 percent of vets using the program do, the VA pays off the loan, assumes ownership of the home, and sells it, usually at a loss.[29]

Both the GI Bill education benefits and the VA home loan program were established as part of the Servicemembers Readjustment Act of 1944. This act, which provided benefits to veterans of World War II, was one of the most significant changes in American policy in the history of the nation, and had among the most far-reaching consequences of any law passed by Congress.

In past wars, soldiers had simply left the armed services and returned home when hostilities ended, but after World War I, the sudden flood of demobilized veterans looking for work put pressure on the economy and government. During the depths of the Depression in 1932, thousands of unemployed World War I vets gathered in Washington, D.C., to demand payment of a bonus promised them in 1924. The government refused to pay, sending troops to disperse the "Bonus Army," and burn the makeshift shelters they had built. Several veterans and family members were killed in the melee, and public opinion turned against the Hoover administration for its shabby treatment of the veterans (although the following year President Franklin Delano Roosevelt also refused to pay the bonus).

During World War II, over 10 million enlisted personnel fought for the country, the vast majority of them citizen soldiers with no intention of staying in the military. Roosevelt, concerned about the effect of such a huge and abrupt demobilization and remembering the Bonus Army, overcame substantial opposition to pass the Servicemembers Readjustment Act. The main provisions of the act, known as the GI Bill, included education benefits, the home loan program, and unemployment pay. In the postwar boom, unemployment pay was dropped, but the education and home loan programs continued with minor changes.

The Servicemembers Readjustment Act enabled millions of veterans from all over the nation to achieve middle class status within their lifetimes, and transformed American society in many ways. Higher education traditionally had been the province of the upper classes, but with veterans streaming into colleges and universities, the education system in America exploded. The infusion of talent and energy into American universities during this period, both from veteran-students and from the many European refugees who took faculty positions, led to the nation's preeminence in science and technology during the postwar decades. After graduation, veterans anxious to settle down to "normal" life bought homes in newly developed suburbs, which they preferred to the farms or city tenements from which so many of them had come. The exodus to suburbia spawned the need for automobiles, the interstate highway system, shopping malls, and other elements of modern life in America. It could not have happened without the GI bill.

Veterans and military retirees are a powerful interest group, and over the years, they have formed many organizations to protect their interests. Many organizations work together in the Military Coalition, an umbrella group of 35 service and veterans groups that lobbies Congress on issues of interest to military personnel and retirees. Some organizations are formed around specific military populations, such as NCOs, women, servicemembers in a specific military branch, or participants in a particular conflict; others are open to all veterans. Many veterans groups are "chartered," which means they are authorized by the VA to help veterans apply for VA benefits. Most large organizations have active community service programs, and many advocate for patriotic causes.

The largest veterans group is the American Legion, formed in 1919 by veterans of World War I. Today it has 2.8 million members and a large auxiliary arm. There are American Legion Posts in every state and in several foreign nations. Another large organization is the Veterans of Foreign Wars, whose members served overseas in any war or campaign with the U.S. forces. Veterans of the Spanish-American and Philippine wars at the turn of the century founded the VFW in 1902, and today it has about 1.9 million members. AMVETS is a group founded by veterans of World War II in 1947 to help veterans negotiate the complexities of the VA. Today, the group boasts 260,000 members and all veterans are eligible to join.

In addition to these large groups, there are dozens of smaller organizations. The Vietnam Veterans of America, for example, founded in 1979, has advocated for the special needs of veterans of that divisive conflict. The group, which counts 45,000 members today, was one of the major proponents of the famous Vietnam Veterans Memorial in Washington, D.C.

CHAPTER 9

WAR

_____

While focusing on aspects of military society like recruitment, quality of life, families and retirement, it can be easy to forget that the primary task of the armed forces is to fight wars. But it is a fact that military personnel spend their time training for combat, and they may well find themselves in conflict situations one or more times in their careers. In most ways, today's soldiers, sailors, airmen, and Marines are better prepared for battle than virtually any other force in American history. They have more sophisticated equipment, better discipline and training, relatively lavish supplies, and advanced medical care. As a highly educated force, they have a sense of why they are fighting and a realistic grasp of the odds of success.

In many other ways, however, servicemembers may find combat more challenging than their predecessors did. Obviously, modern weaponry makes war a terrifying and lethal endeavor, and contemporary asymmetric warfare pits American servicemembers against entire civilian populations in a chaotic, morally ambiguous environment. In addition, contemporary American culture, with its emphasis on individual freedom and choice, has accustomed Americans to believe that they control their own lives and that their lives are inestimably valuable. When incompetence and military bungling result in uncertain deaths, today's servicemembers may be even less likely than soldiers of the past to tolerate it. They must also believe in the cause for which they fight. Whether military or civilian, few Americans are willing to see Americans die, and even fewer are prepared to throw away their own lives for a purpose with which they disagree. Today's military strategists understand that there are serious political consequences of losing American lives in a wasteful war, and a large part of military training, tactics, and strategy involves minimizing casualties to the greatest extent possible.

Today's emphasis on safety and comfort for the troops not only reflects the assumptions and expectations of contemporary American society but also reflects the current status of American servicemembers within the service. They are no longer the mass conscripts of the past, minimally trained citizen soldiers who were sometimes squandered in poorly conceived campaigns. Today's soldiers are valuable professionals, expensively trained, and not easy to replace. The military cannot afford to treat them shabbily.

Regardless of the DoD's attempts to safeguard the lives of U.S. servicemembers, however, the military cannot transform the experience of combat entirely. War is still a fearful and vivid experience, and soldiers can encounter a range of emotions, from panic to euphoria to depression and guilt, as a result of their participation in it. The uncertainty and chaos of battle does not change, no matter how skilled the participants are or how advanced their weaponry is.

WARRIORS TO SOLDIERS

It is a commonplace to observe that warfare has been part of human society since its ancient origins and that armed conflict is somehow "natural" or inevitable. That philosophical question is far beyond the bounds of this survey, but a popular corollary to the idea of war's inevitability, that warfare has always been practiced in more or less the same way, is both relevant to this study and easy to refute. Warfare is not always the same, but rather it is a reflection of the societies that engage in it. In the Western world, warfare has undergone several transformations in the past millennium or two as Western society has changed.

As we have seen, in many important ways the American armed forces owe a great deal to the traditions of European warfare. Traditions of organization, training, and technology in the U.S. forces can be traced back to developments in Europe. At the same time, the American experience of war diverged significantly from the European model. The American citizen soldier model and the submission of the armed forces to civilian control resulted from the Founders' suspicion of military organizations and their desire to maintain a democratic society free of militaristic repression.

Europe, many military historians agree, was an especially bellicose region of the world, and from the early Medieval period on, hardly a decade went by without warfare erupting somewhere on the continent. Warfare in Europe was an accepted and acceptable tool of state policy, used by rulers to seize land, install a friendly ruler in a neighboring state, remove an unfriendly one, or subdue a rebellious province. Monarchs spent much of their time and most of their revenues building armies and navies and conducting warfare. By the eighteenth century, European nation-states had developed professional standards for training, supplying, and commanding their armed forces. Officers all too often attained their positions because of family connections, but soldiers, whether mercenaries or conscripts, were highly trained and disciplined. They were professionals who had drilled and practiced to a point where they overcame the extremes of fear, exhilaration, and despair that accompany every battle. Eighteenth-century armies faced their opponents in ranks (lines) and, upon receiving a bugled order, advanced as a drum beat out a tempo. If fired upon by the enemy, they did not retreat as their comrades fell around them, but continued their steady march until ordered to fire. After firing, they fell back in formation, reloading as another rank took their place.

This fearful discipline, which historian John Lynn calls a "culture of forebearance,"[1] developed along with the use of early musket firearms. Muskets were accurate only at short distances and were less than useless in the hands of untrained men, requiring skill and practice to fire with any hope of success. The line system of advancing, firing, and falling back to reload enabled armies to fire six or more times per minute with the clumsy weapons.

Clearly, the line system required enormous order and restraint. Soldiers practiced not only the advancing and falling back drill, but also the dozen or more steps required to prepare a front-loading musket for use: pouring the powder, ramming the ball down the barrel, lighting the fuse. Every step needed to be done with robotic precision in the heat of battle, as black smoke dimmed the sun and the air filled with the cries of the wounded, the screams of horses, and the drumbeat ordering the soldiers forward.

The line system had another purpose, however; it enabled commanders to control their troops. In European armies, many or most soldiers had been conscripted as part of each region's contribution to the state. Officers rightly feared that soldiers would flee if they had a chance. Soldiers had no ideological identification with what they were doing, nor did they earn wages that would keep them in the army willingly. European conscript soldiers marching forward in rank were given little opportunity to run, but if they tried, an officer or an NCO would be ready with a pistol to stop them.

The American military tradition developed somewhat differently. In the colonial era, white settlers formed themselves into militias to defend their property and communities. The British Crown sent professional soldiers to protect the colonies, but much of the defense of outlying areas lay in the hands of those whose property came under attack. American volunteers fought alongside British professionals in the French and Indian War of 1756, with mixed results; George Washington, an officer in the British forces, thought the poorly disciplined militias a hindrance. But whatever their value to the war effort, volunteer militias based on self-defense were a central part of the earliest thinking about warfare in America.

The tradition of the citizen soldier continued during the Revolutionary War, as militias and professionally trained American soldiers in the Continental Army fought to expel the British from the thirteen original colonies. The Continental Army, under the command of George Washington, was a ragtag affair, always understrength and burdened by overlapping lines of authority from the states and from its founder, the Continental Congress. But the American forces attained a flexibility that the British redcoats could not match. They adopted the guerilla tactics of their Native American adversaries, employed civilian spies and saboteurs, and took advantage of their knowledge of the terrain and climate. Although not as expert in conventional warfare as the British forces, American soldiers had an ideological edge; they understood the cause they were fighting for and knew that the sooner the war ended, the sooner they could resume civilian life.

The Continental Army and Navy were disbanded after the war, and some founders hoped to continue the policy of creating an ad hoc military force when necessary while relying mostly on citizen militias for America's defense needs. As we have seen, this model did not last, and Congress authorized the establishment of permanent armed forces in the 1790s. The ideal of the citizen soldier, however, remained. During peacetime the regular armed forces were small, but when war loomed, calls went out for volunteers. States sent reserve units, both newly created and already established, to augment the federal forces.

By the middle of the nineteenth century, the volunteer system proved incapable of generating the numbers of men needed to fight, and manpower for major conflicts was augmented by the draft. In United States, the notion of conscription was controversial. During the Civil War, the Union draft in New York City was greeted with days of rioting by working-class whites who resented being forced to fight for recently freed slaves. National conscription ran against the tradition of freedom from government interference that was part of the American ideal.

The draft, however, turned out to be necessary as warfare became more industrial. By the Civil War, firearms technology had made warfare somewhat less of a skill than it had been before, and soldiers no longer needed months or years of practice to be effective on the battlefield. Powerful and accurate weapons were being produced in mass quantities in armaments factories. From the Civil War to the Korean War, America's largest wars were fought by millions of men operating automatic weapons, artillery, tanks, and planes across huge battlefields. These were wars of attrition, in which large numbers of relatively unskilled men were sent up against the enemy in bloody slaughter. The side with the largest number of men and the best technology came out the winner.

Americans have debated the political, social, and cultural implications of the draft since its first incarnation in the nineteenth century, and it has been widely accepted only in times of national emergency. Another less frequently discussed issue, however, and one more directly relevant to a discussion of warfare, is the draft's ability to produce a well-trained, motivated fighting force. Are draftees as effective in battle as regular career forces? The evidence from Vietnam suggests that perhaps they are not, but it is impossible to generalize. During World War I, draftees lagged behind the skilled and experienced career fighters, at least at first, but in World War II, conscripted citizen soldiers proved themselves equal not only to regular American troops but also to the highly militarized German and Japanese forces. During the Korean War, draftees proved superior to enlistees in education levels and discipline, and it showed in their superior retention and completion of training. This record contrasts with the Vietnam era when better-educated draftees and draft-motivated enlistees were among the most alienated and opposed to the war. They exhibited the highest levels of indiscipline and were most likely to degrade the morale of their units.

This variance suggests that one factor in the performance of draftees in combat is the larger political picture surrounding the conflict. In a popular war, draftees perform well; in a more divisive conflict like Vietnam, they tend to perform less well. However, there are many other elements influencing the efficiency of draftees compared with career soldiers. One of the more important is the type of war being fought and the technology and skills required. In today's wars, draftees may not perform especially well because modern warfare is extremely complex and requires a great deal of training. The days when a commander could drive unwilling conscripts forward with the flat of his sword, as the Prussian monarch Frederick the Great was said to have done, are long gone. Even the mass armies of the world wars, trained in little more than the rifle, bayonet, and claymore mine, are ancient history. By the mid-1950s, the amount and cost of training a conscript received was not worth the two years of service that the military got out of him, unless the conscript was paid well below market rates for his labor. Underpaid draftees were less likely to reenlist, however, so the opportunity to build on a conscript's brief experience was almost always lost.

The industrial model of warfare began to change in Vietnam. Although Vietnam saw its share of conventional battles, fought with heavy armaments in the style of World War II and Korea, American soldiers in Vietnam were as likely to see unconventional tactics of the type American rebels used during the Revolutionary War. Ambushes, surprise attacks, booby traps, and sabotage were the tactics of Vietnam. Most experts agree that the American forces won every conventional battle they fought but could not adapt quickly enough to the guerilla tactics used by the Vietnamese enemy.

Guerilla tactics in Vietnam required a different type of soldier than the unskilled and unwilling conscript or "draft-motivated" volunteer.

The Vietnam War needed highly motivated, professional troops skilled in small-unit warfare as well as civil affairs techniques. Unfortunately, the armed forces relied on the draft, especially for infantry troops. During Vietnam (and all wars), draftees were the most likely to die in combat because they were the least trained and experienced.

Today's wars continue the trend begun in Vietnam. For the most part, unconventional small-unit fighting has replaced the epic tank, infantry or air battles of the twentieth century. Today's fighters face IEDs, suicide bombers, and a blurring of combatant and noncombatant civilian status, all in a complex political and cultural environment. They need to be able to deal with hostile civilian populations as well as operate complicated electronic equipment. Today's wars are also more likely, at the present time at least, to involve low-level warfare rather than huge national undertakings like World War II, wars that are much less likely to receive consensus support from the American people. While there are strong political and social arguments in favor of conscription, a draft will likely be less than ideal in filling the ranks of today's armed forces.

THE EXPERIENCE OF BATTLE

Regardless whether a servicemember is a draftee or a career soldier with decades of experience in the institution, the experience of combat is likely to be the most vivid of his or her life. Veterans who have been in combat sometimes talk about it, sometimes remain silent for the rest of their lives. But even if they never mention what they have seen to anyone, those experiences are seared in their minds. A man whose combat experience is fifty years in the past will cry at the memory of the friends he lost so long ago. At the same time, the experience of combat is difficult for many soldiers to express even to themselves in their own minds, and many veterans remain unable to articulate or analyze what they went through.[2]

Servicemembers pass through several phases in their adjustment to the experience of war. The first, deployment, is a period of adaptation to military life. In America's twentieth-century wars, soldiers were sent to overseas combat on troop ships, a long and boring voyage that allowed the new soldiers a period of adjustment between training and battle. Transports were so dull that soldiers longed for the voyage to end, and they anticipated combat with a mix of fear and excitement. Regardless, they had enormous confidence in their training and faith that they would succeed. By the end of the voyage, they looked forward to getting to the front and participating in the war, and the enormous military bureaucracy was a source of endless frustration.[3]

Virtually everyone faced with the prospect of combat, whether enthusiastic volunteer or reluctant draftee, wants to acquit himself well in battle, and most soldiers go into battle for the first time with a strong belief in their own competence. Psychiatrist Jules Masserman notes that "faith in personal survival [is] one of the master beliefs undergirding the individual's psychic defense against war's destructiveness";[4] soldiers believe they will not be wounded and they will not die.

The first time soldiers experience battle, however, is a profoundly shocking experience, and for many it is only good training and the desire not to appear cowardly in front of peers that carry the soldier through. Some soldiers freeze, and have to be prodded or forced to move, even to take cover under fire. Many soldiers do not remember the actual events of their first experience under fire because they were so frightened. But if a soldier survives his first battle, he feels enormous pride and relief.[5]

Within a short time, perhaps even a week, a soldier under frequent fire regains the confidence that he lost in the first experience of battle. Soldiers become accustomed to death around them but still do not believe it can happen to them. They conclude that they are especially lucky or that their battle skills are sharp enough to keep them alive.[6] The idea—or illusion— that soldiers control their own fate through their abilities is an important one for the mental state of a soldier.

The first months of a soldier's combat service are his most productive. It is at this point that the soldier takes sensible risks and makes good decisions under stress. In order to maintain their luck, soldiers often develop superstitions and embrace in magical thinking as a way to feel in control. They put stock in their own intuition and instincts, which have indeed developed rapidly in battle: the ability to judge the severity of a wound, or to spot the signs of an ambush or enemy nearby, or to recognize how close an artillery explosion has come.[7]

For many soldiers, combat has a positive side. Some soldiers report that being in combat distills life into its simplest components, so that other extraneous concerns that had seemed important turn out not to be after all. Soldiers also report that the essence of combat—kill or be killed— brings an immediacy to life that does not usually exist. The feeling of being alive, of having a certain kind of elemental power over life and death, can be very intoxicating.

In time, however, soldiers realize that they are not, in fact, invulnerable, and that death can happen to them. The deep emotional recognition that there is an enemy desperately trying to kill them, not in the abstract but in reality, is a shock to most soldiers.[8] They learn to recognize and dread certain enemy weapons and tactics. It is said that artillery is the weapon most feared by ground troops; mines are another horrifying weapon. Their arbitrariness makes artillery and mines especially frightening.[9] As time goes on, soldiers become more fearful and the symptoms of stress emerge as they become more risk-averse.[10] Soldiers gradually lose the idea that they have any control over their fate, and the sense that they are living in a completely different world from the one they left increases.[11] They also gradually lose faith in their abilities, and as they see their friends die, they begin to doubt whether they possess enough intuition to protect them from harm.[12]

Eventually, a soldier who remains in combat long enough will go from believing that death is a remote possibility to believing that death is a certainty. This sense of fatalism, in World War II called the "2000-yard stare," is incipient post-traumatic stress syndrome; perhaps the old phrase "battle fatigue" is more precise, because any soldier with enough combat experience will display it even during battle. Combatants suffering from battle fatigue evince a profound sense of apathy about their own survival, and lose hope that they will come out alive. Indifferent to their fate, they may fail to take necessary steps to protect themselves and are more likely than others to be wounded or killed. Battle fatigue is exacerbated by particularly arduous physical conditions, but military psychiatrists have discovered that after a certain number of days under fire, anyone will suffer from it, regardless of their training, physical and mental makeup, or any other factors.[13] Soldiers and civilians in a war zone learn to recognize the signs of battle fatigue—the 2000-yard stare, the fatigue, expressionless silence and noticeable aging.[14]

In the two world wars, soldiers were deployed for the duration of the war, and so did not know when they would be returning home. In more recent wars, including Iraq and Afghanistan, soldiers serve a specific period of time in the combat theater, and they know when they will be leaving. Soldiers whose return date is approaching often exhibit signs of "short timers syndrome" in which they are extremely cautious, fearful of being wounded or killed, and they begin to detach emotionally from their comrades. Short timers are said to be less interested in helping new soldiers adjust and more interested in protecting themselves.[15]

The experience of battle involves above all, violence and death. For most people, it is deeply unnatural to aim a weapon at another person with the intention of killing, much less to do so repeatedly over an extended period of time. Someone who has never done this cannot truly understand what it is like, but psychologists, sociologists, historians, and others who have studied combat have made some intriguing observations. SLA Marshall, a veteran of World War II and one of the first sociologists to study the behavior of men in combat, argued in his influential book *Men Against Fire: The Problem of Battle Command* that no more than 25 percent of infantry soldiers in battle, even those most experienced and trained, fired their weapons at the enemy in a sustained way, and that in most units, the rate of sustained firing was only 15–20 percent at most. He also described war as essentially a matter of small group cohesion, arguing that men will fight for the sake of their comrades rather than for lofty ideals like patriotism. He even suggests that soldiers are more afraid of killing than of being killed.[16] While a few soldiers enjoy killing from the beginning and feel no remorse for what they are doing, these psychopathic personalities do not make the best soldiers—in fact, "born killers" have so little sense of fear that they are likely to endanger a unit.[17]

However, soldiers do kill in battle, and many of them must do so repeatedly. How do they do it? After World War II, military experts concluded that training methods must focus on breaking down the natural reluctance to kill. Marshall's study of combat veterans changed training methods in the U.S. Army and improved the rate of sustained firing so markedly that during Vietnam War, 95 percent of soldiers fired their weapons during battle.

Combat veteran and author Lt. Col. Dave Grossman has suggested that soldiers go through several stages of response to killing. Before they experience it, they worry if they will be able to perform. As highly trained personnel, however, most of them actually do kill "without even thinking," in Grossman's words. Their training takes over, and they pull the trigger instinctively. After they have done so, they often experience a sense of exhilaration, an adrenaline rush or "combat high." There is a thrill to killing, and although most soldiers are reluctant to admit it, many or even most of them find that there are times when they enjoy it.[18] However, after the elation comes a stage of remorse that can be quite painful; Grossman suggests that "while most modern veterans *have* experienced powerful emotions at this stage, they tend to deny their emotions, becoming cold and hard inside—thus making subsequent killing much easier."[19] Finally, there is the stage of rationalization and acceptance.

Combat makes soldiers coarse in a profound way. Soldiers become desensitized to the death and horror around them, as they must do in order to survive psychologically. With this comes a loosening of the internal rules and limitations that all humans place on themselves and have placed on them by parents, schools, religion, and other socializing institutions. Soldiers begin to see their world as a universe of harsh and divisive moral values, where the old rules are irrelevant. Soldiers begin, for example, to have a relative sense of ownership—to pilfer supplies or equipment that they or their units need.[20] They become careless of destruction, destroying property even when not necessary, especially that belonging to civilians.[21] They begin to treat civilians with less respect, particularly foreigners, whether friend or foe. A recent video clip broadcast on the web site YouTube, for example, shows American soldiers riding in a vehicle, offering young Iraqi boys bottles of water. As the children approach, the vehicle drives off and the boys run after it. The chase goes on for minutes, the soldiers laughing and hooting as the boys tire.

Finally, a soldier carelessly throws a bottle in the direction of the last boy running, but older children dart from the side of the street and snatch the bottle away from the exhausted boy. It is hard to believe that in their civilian lives, these soldiers would be so casually cruel to American children; it is also sobering to consider what impact such thoughtlessness has on civilian impressions of the U.S. armed forces.

Most importantly, war makes soldiers careless with human life. Today, soldiers in Iraq and Afghanistan fight enemies who blend into the civilian population and even pretend to be friendly toward the Americans. Troops must decide instantly whether a car filled with people and approaching a checkpoint is a suicide attack, or whether a family home is actually an insurgent headquarters. Many soldiers in today's wars have faced such decisions, and they almost always choose to err on the side of protecting themselves and their comrades, even if it means shooting the innocent occupants of an automobile or calling down an airstrike on a civilian dwelling. Many incidents involving civilian deaths are ambiguous; it is unclear whether a better course of action was evident at the time. On the other hand, situations that civilian correctly view as atrocities, from the My Lai massacre to the killing of twenty-four civilians at Haditha in November 2005, are more common in war than most Americans like to admit. They are a tragic by-product of the brutalization of combat.

LIFE IN A COMBAT ZONE

During a war, even a global conflict like World War II, most personnel do not experience combat as front line fighting troops, because they are involved in support services of some type. In "traditional" wars, the distinction between front and rear line was fairly sharp. In World War I, for example, soldiers in the front line trenches were in great danger during assaults but were much less so during breaks in the action. Rear line soldiers, by contrast, remained comparatively safe, and those support troops behind the lines were almost as safe as they had been at home. World War II was similar, although the use of aircraft for bombing gave both sides the ability to target civilian population centers as well as military sites. In Vietnam, all American servicemembers in the theater were in some danger because of the popular nature of the war and the guerilla methods used by the enemy, although ground troops patrolling the jungles faced much more danger than the clerks in Saigon offices. In Iraq or Afghanistan today, the front lines are blurred even more; any soldier or civilian employee can be injured or killed by an IED or roadside bomb while traveling outside the protected FOBs.

It is as true today as it was in past wars that combat is not a constant experience but rather an interlude of intense fear and excitement in an otherwise unimaginably boring and uncomfortable existence. As one NCO told reporter Jen Banbury, each day in the Iraq war is "23 hours, 59 minutes of boredom and one minute of hell."[22] The main characteristic that comes through all writing about war is not only the danger of battle, but the extreme discomfort of the time between battles, filled with cold, heat, hunger, fatigue, filth, physical strenuousness, stink, and noise. Whether a soldier is an infantryman carrying a machine gun, a communications specialist or a medic, life on the front lines is extremely unpleasant. This is often the first big shock for new troops going into the combat theater for the first time. They have survived the rigors of basic training, but they cannot adequately prepare for the discomforts of life in the combat zone.

To begin with, combat troops on campaign spend more time exposed to the elements than anyone in almost any other modern job or occupation. American troops experienced the winter rain and damp of northern France in World War I, the tropical heat and humidity of Pacific islands in World War II, the bleak, frozen winters of Korea, and the jungles of Vietnam. Most recently, soldiers and Marines have endured freezing cold and snow in the mountains of Afghanistan and 130-degree heat and blinding sandstorms, known as "shamals" in the deserts of the Middle East.[23] Troops on campaign sleep in hastily dug foxholes, pup tents, or, in Afghanistan, in caves. Even after the fighting ends, personnel in combat zones may live in abandoned or confiscated buildings, tents, metal trailers, or concrete barracks without adequate heat or cooling.

Extreme weather conditions exacerbate another feature of field life: ubiquitous pests and vermin. Soldiers everywhere suffer from lice, or "cooties" in World War I slang, or battle mosquitoes, roaches, and leeches in tropical climates.[24] Other vermin include rats, notorious in the trenches of World War I for eating dead bodies. Not so much has changed; in the Marine camps in the Kuwaiti desert before the Iraq invasion, rats were "scampering around the slumbering Marines" at night, according to reporter Evan Wright.[25] Troops also battle pests they cannot see: bacteria and one-celled organisms that contaminate their drinking water and give them dysentery, or the "krud." Even with the most careful hygiene measures, it is hard to avoid illness; soldiers living in close, primitive quarters have too much exposure to human waste. In Afghanistan, for example, troops battling the Taliban near Kandahar took turns emptying the portable latrines and burning the waste with diesel fuel.[26]

Not all sanitation measures are so distasteful, but bugs spread easily in the filthy environment of combat. In all wars, the absence of bathing and hygiene facilities is an indelible aspect of the combat experience. During World War I, troops who could not remove their boots and change their wet socks for extended periods suffered from trench foot, a condition in which the skin of the ankles and feet peeled off in sheets. Almost a century later, in the 2003 invasion of Iraq, Marines leading the advance to Baghdad wore their heavy MOPP (Mission Oriented Protective Posture) gear to protect against nuclear, chemical, or biological attacks for weeks on end without change of clothes, shower, or even a spray of water to rinse the dust from their faces. It is no wonder that in many photos, the advancing troops appear to be wearing heavy black greasepaint on their faces and necks. Worse, the fine dust of the desert inflames the respiratory system, giving some troops walking pneumonia.[27]

One of the worst aspects of life in a combat zone is the enormous physical effort required for survival. Soldiers and Marines spend more time digging trenches and foxholes, filling and stacking sandbags, and setting up barbed wire perimeters than they do actually firing at the enemy in battle. They build landing strips, improvise bridges, and load war materiel onto trucks and aircraft. Troops also spend a lot of time marching with loads of heavy equipment strapped to their bodies. In the wars of the twentieth century, the official Army pack included seventy pounds or more of equipment. Experienced soldiers tossed out whatever they didn't need, but it took time to learn what was and was not necessary in battle.[28] Today, the pack includes even more equipment than before, such as night-vision goggles and MOPP gear, and can weigh more than 100 pounds. Troops also wear body armor made up of ceramic plates or Kevlar, adding to the weight they must carry.

Predictably, a constant theme running through all soldiers' recollections is fatigue. Studies suggest that troops in combat get at most six hours of sleep a night, and often much less.[29] Veteran combatants learn to go to sleep anywhere, anytime, because they never know when the next opportunity will arise. While on a campaign, troops may not sleep for several days at a time, enduring harsh conditions and brutal physical exertion in a state of extreme exhaustion.

As a result of the discomfort of life in a combat zone, the essentials of life are especially important. Seemingly simple issues like food, shelter, and bathing take on immense significance. As can be imagined, the task of providing food for thousands of physically active young men at the same time is a huge one. Medieval and early modern European armies struggled with the problem, usually allowing soldiers to forage, that is, steal, from local civilians. As armies grew in size, however, foraging could quickly deplete the resources of a region, hindering the ability of the army to function and adding to the plight of the civilians. Commanders developed rationing systems through which they purchased or requisitioned supplies from local traders. In the nineteenth-century U.S. Army, soldiers on the frontier received rations, but they were unappealing—bread, beans, salt pork or beef, and coffee.[30] On their own time, soldiers searched for fresh meat and game or vegetables and fruit, often paying exorbitant prices to civilians who took the opportunity to sell their produce at a hefty profit. If soldiers ate poorly in the field, sailors at sea ate even worse. Their supplies of fresh food quickly disappeared and what was left was wormy hardtack biscuit, green meat, and slimy water. Sailors could not forage or buy fresh produce, and suffered nutritional deficiencies as a result.

By the twentieth century, rations had gotten somewhat better but were far from gourmet. Soldiers behind the lines ate B rations, which were canned and dehydrated foods prepared by cooks in field kitchens. Units tried to set up field kitchens whenever possible, but troops at the front ate prepackaged rations. The famous C rations of World War II included individual portions in cans, such as beef stew, pork and beans, hash, or pasta, and were eaten by soldiers in the combat zone. They were supposed to be for short-term use but in reality soldiers lived on them for weeks at a time.[31] Even worse were the K rations, consumed by those on fast-moving campaigns —unappetizing cans of meat, eggs and cheese, and packaged crackers. These, like the emergency D rations, which consisted of chocolate bars fortified with vitamins, were developed to provide complete nutrition but since most soldiers threw away the parts of the rations they found unappealing, their nutritional benefits were somewhat less than advertised.[32]

Whenever possible, troops during the two world wars were fed from local supplies. These could include fresh vegetables and fruits, dairy products, bread, eggs, and meat. Local items, however, could be unfamiliar and unwelcome. American soldiers in Great Britain and Australia during World War II, for example, hated their meals of mutton, at the time a staple of the British diet but unpalatable to Americans. In spite of all attempts of the Army to provide food for the troops, soldiers did forage whenever they could, sometimes with unhappy results. Very common was the phenomenon of soldiers gorging on fresh produce from an orchard or garden discovered on a march, then suffering from diarrhea as a result.

Commanders knew that food was important for morale, and if they couldn't provide good food on a regular basis, they at least tried to give their men a treat whenever possible. Troops learned that an unusually good meal often meant that a battle would take place the next day.[33] Today, soldiers and Marines on campaign subsist on MREs, which include flameless heaters that use chemical reactions create heat to warm the meals. Food experts at the DoD Combat Feeding Program in Natick, Massachusetts, try hard to make the MREs appetizing, and have developed options such as "Chicken with Salsa and Mexican Rice," "Chicken with Thai Sauce," and "Beef Teriyaki." MREs may not resemble home cooking, but they are by most reports the best military rations in the world. Once the troops return from the field to an established FOB, the quality and variety of food available is similar to that found in dining halls on U.S. bases. Dining facilities make every attempt to offer freshly cooked food, and the exchanges on FOBs stock American-style snacks like corn chips, salsa, and canned soda.

Troops in combat have a higher craving for alcohol than they might otherwise. Drinking plays an important part in helping them to relax and forget at least for a while the bad living conditions, death, and destruction they have seen.[34] Soldiers (and civilians, as well) during World War II were notorious for their drinking—many a fine wine collection secreted away in the cellar of a European estate disappeared down the gullets of thirsty GIs. In Vietnam, soldiers used readily available drugs for the same purpose. Today, troops in Iraq and Afghanistan are not allowed to drink alcohol, and opportunities for clandestine imbibing are limited. This prohibition is, not surprisingly, much resented, but is part of the military's attempt to avoid offending the local population.

Another drive that becomes more intense during war is the desire for sex. The preoccupation with sex is always high among soldiers, mostly single young men away from home who are experiencing frequent episodes of abstinence, but it intensifies in the combat zone.[35] Part of this phenomenon is related to the tough and masculine environment of the military; thoughts of women and sex temporarily mask the harshness of combat.[36] Sex is not merely an antidote to coarse masculinity, however. Rape often accompanies combat, and studies show that rape is most likely right before or after a battle. Military psychiatrists suggest that rape is a way that soldiers can assert power, counteracting the sense of victimization and loss of control that combat brings.[37] Heightened sexuality, today experienced by female as well as male personnel, is viewed by many psychologists as an unconscious effort to stave off the specter of death that hangs over the battlefield. Today's troops have no opportunity to mix with the local population; sexual contact between Americans and women in traditional Islamic societies, whether consensual or not, would inflame local sensibilities and dangerously impede the mission. Male servicemembers do, however, have more access to members of the opposite sex than they used to, because female troops serve alongside them on FOBs. Fraternization is prohibited, but it occurs nonetheless, and female troops are on occasion sent home because they are pregnant. Same-sex relations are not unknown, of course, but are generally even more clandestine than opposite-sex relations. In the absence of regular sexual contact, troops in all wars tend toward more frequent masturbation, an attempt to counteract the boredom and stress of the combat zone.

One of the most vital psychological factors in combat is camaraderie, especially in smaller groups. Soldiers in combat form intense bonds with each other, in some ways stronger than the bonds between family members.[38] Although commanders have been aware of the importance of unit cohesion for centuries, the military's approach to the social structure of units has changed several times, and changes have affected morale and discipline in profound ways. In World War II, for example, soldiers trained and fought with the same units for the duration of the war. They were truly "bands of brothers."[39] During the Vietnam conflict, by contrast, soldiers were sent to Vietnam for 12-month tours to replace other individual soldiers leaving the country. They knew no one in their new units and often were sent directly into combat before bonding with the group in any way. In many cases, new soldiers, without ties of friendship to their comrades, found themselves assigned to the most dangerous missions to preserve the lives of others more integrated into the unit. Not surprisingly, the death rate for newly arriving replacement soldiers was much higher than for soldiers who had survived for a few months and managed to establish friendships.

Adding to the alienation of Vietnam was the disorienting rapidity with which soldiers went from combat to peacetime life back home. When their twelve months were up, soldiers flew from Vietnam to Hawaii to California, a trip lasting twenty-four hours or less. They had no time to reflect on what they had just gone through or to discuss their experiences with buddies, before they were back in civilian life. After World War II, by contrast, soldiers returned home on troop ships, which took several weeks to reach American shores. Soldiers had time to adjust to the idea of going home, first in occupation Europe while waiting for a berth on a troop ship, and second, during the voyage with their friends.

The Vietnam era policy of individual deployment was one of many factors that led to the disintegration of the armed forces, especially the Army, in the 1970s. By the 1980s, the military had realized its mistake and reemphasized the importance of unit cohesion. Today, units train together, deploy to a combat theater, and leave together. The desire of soldiers not to abandon their comrades has an important impact not only on morale and performance on the battlefield but also on reenlistment and attitudes toward the mission. Today, much evidence suggests that while many troops question the mission in Iraq, they participate because they do not want to let their friends down. For the most part, the alienation and resentment of the Vietnam-era soldier has yet to affect today's service-members, even if they personally oppose their assignments. However, unit-based deployments can mean that troops stay on beyond their service commitment if their unit is deployed. The Army's "stop-loss" policy, in which troops are involuntarily kept on active duty beyond their enlistment periods, has been used to keep units together, so that those who leave are not replaced by individual strangers, as was the case in Vietnam.

Camaraderie is an important factor in readiness, but it is also delicate and hard to define. Experts in and out of the military argue about what factors affect esprit de corps and camaraderie for good or ill. One of the most sensitive questions about camaraderie is whether the presence of members of historically excluded groups, such as women or gays, will hurt unit cohesion. These and other questions about the effects of gender on unit cohesion have not been answered conclusively, but there is much less discussion of the matter than there once was. During the 1990s, when increasing numbers of women joined the military, many critics wondered if their presence would hurt unit cohesion. Some believed that women would dilute the fighting spirit that bonded men together, or that men would instinctively protect female members of the unit, to the detriment of the whole. Others argued that physical differences and a widespread belief among male soldiers that women did not contribute their fair share would breed corrosive resentment in gender-integrated units. Some studies showed that gender integration did indeed hurt esprit de corps,[40] fueling debate over the proper role of women in combat.

There is much less talk of the detrimental role of women on unit cohesion these days, at least officially. As women have shared the dangers and hardships of military conflict, they have proven their ability to handle the challenges and bond with male servicemembers.[41] It seems that the issue has faded as a concern of academics and pundits, and most of today's military personnel probably do not remember the acrimonious discussions of a decade ago. A similar trend can be seen with regard to the issue of gay troops. While older career personnel may find the idea of sharing a foxhole with a gay servicemember distasteful, many younger troops seem to have fewer objections. There is no evidence that gay troops behave any differently in combat than heterosexuals.

Many proponents of gender and sexuality integration point to the example of the integration of African-American troops in the military. Similar arguments against racial integration were used in the 1940s by advocates of segregation, but in fact racial integration has been an enormous success. During the late 1960s and early 1970s, integration was put to the test, as racial unrest spread throughout the armed forces all over the world. In the jungles of Vietnam, however, frontline units experienced little or no racial tension. Skin color ceased to matter when units were under attack. As women and gays face danger alongside their straight male comrades, concerns may diminish further. But, as many critics of gender and sexuality integration point out, the first priority of the military must be to its mission, and policymakers must be very careful when considering changes that might interfere with that mission.

Another important factor in wartime morale is the general sense that the military looks after its troops and their families. Attention paid to the comfort and safety of troops while they are deployed, and to the support of family members back home, can reassure servicemembers that the brass cares about them. The DoD seems to be taking this lesson to heart, but not everyone is convinced. In late 2004, for example, when a National Guard soldier challenged Donald Rumsfeld about the lack of armored vehicles in Iraq, many troops agreed that their units were underequipped and that the DoD was to blame. The "stop-loss" policy is another DoD directive that has been widely criticized as a betrayal of trust.

SHELL SHOCK

Soldiers may survive combat more or less physically intact, but their experiences may have a deep and traumatic emotional impact if they continue long enough. PTSD (Post-traumatic stress disorder) is the contemporary name for the reaction to sustained exposure to battle, or, for that matter, to any traumatic experience. In earlier wars, PTSD was known as shell shock or battle fatigue; whatever it is called, it is one of the most common reactions to combat.[42] PTSD manifests itself in a variety of physical and psychological ways. Symptoms include flashbacks; a constant and extreme sense of alertness, jumpiness, or irritability; inability to tolerate crowds of people; insomnia; and sudden "blacking out."[43]

PTSD is most commonly associated with veterans of the Vietnam War, who suffered from it disproportionally compared with the veterans of other wars. According to many studies, in the 1980s, over a decade after the end of American involvement in the Vietnam conflict, 50 percent of Vietnam veterans still had symptoms of PTSD.[44] Some experts suggest that the divisiveness of Vietnam and the public lack of support that most servicemembers perceived was a major cause of PTSD among Vietnam veterans. Others note that the techniques used in basic training to improve fire rates in combat meant that more Vietnam veterans experienced the trauma of killing. Vietnam was also a different type of war, in which civilians and combatants were impossible to tell apart and more soldiers were exposed to morally ambiguous situations or combat atrocities. Finally, the average age of soldiers in Vietnam was 19; in comparison, the average age of combatants in World War II was around twenty-six.

Generally speaking, however, PTSD is a consequence of modern warfare. Unlike preindustrial wars, where battles were short and relatively nonlethal, modern warfare requires that soldiers remain in the intense combat environment for extended periods of time, under fire from much more devastating weaponry than in the past. PTSD was first noticed in the Crimean War of 1854–1856, a European war during which modern artillery was used extensively, as well as in the American Civil War.[45] Physicians noticed that the heavy artillery fire of World War I was especially likely to induce symptoms of PTSD, and by World War II, there was a general consensus that symptoms would appear after exposure to about 200 days of sustained combat.[46]

This makes sense; most experts say that PTSD emerges from a sense of powerlessness and lack of control, the very state that modern combat creates for soldiers. While World War I was notorious for its "shell shock" victims, World War II actually produced a greater proportion of PTSD sufferers. The front lines of World War II were not well-defined trenches as in the earlier war, and units were far more dispersed than they had been in the past. GIs were isolated, unable to see the enemy, and targets of snipers, booby traps and ambushes. In some ways, battle in World War II resembled Vietnam more than it did World War I.[47]

The symptoms of PTSD reflect this sense of powerlessness and fear. Families of veterans watch their loved ones react with violence at an unexpected touch or noise. Some veterans cannot tolerate fireworks displays, or cannot accompany their families on outings. Instinctive behaviors helped soldiers survive in combat, and veterans often have extreme difficulty letting go of those behaviors when they return home.[48]

Military psychiatrists say that PTSD is becoming a major problem among troops returning from Iraq and Afghanistan, and is likely to get worse as time goes on and units are deployed again and again. Treatment of troops suffering from PTSD while deployed focuses on returning the servicemember to his or her unit, a short-term solution with probable long-term consequences.[49] Almost 20 percent of troops returning from contemporary war zones have been diagnosed with PTSD, and the rates of PTSD among veterans of Iraq and Afghanistan may eventually exceed the rates from Vietnam.[50]

CASUALTIES

One of the experiences that separates Americans who have endured combat and those who have not is that war veterans have witnessed some or many of their friends being injured or killed. Perhaps they have even been casualties themselves. When reporting on the outcome of a battle, the military uses the term "casualty" to refer to both the wounded and dead combatants, grouping them together. It may seem to be an imprecise term, but unfortunately some of the wounded may not survive. In warfare, the most significant factor influencing the casualty rate is the lethal power of the weaponry used in battle. Techniques of battlefield medical care, however, affect the survival rate of the wounded.

Modern industrial military technology has vastly increased the numbers of wounded on the battlefield. In World War I, 200,000 Americans sustained injuries, while in World War II, the number rose to almost

672,000.[51] The total number of injured in the Vietnam War was 450,000. In the world wars, most casualties came from artillery fire, but in Vietnam, unconventional warfare techniques caused the most damage.[52] Today, these "unconventional" techniques have become conventional. IEDs, roadside bombs, and mines cause most of the casualties in Iraq and Afghanistan.

Battlefield medical care has changed enormously since the mid-nineteenth century, when nursing pioneers like Florence Nightingale and Clara Barton tended to the wounded in the Crimean and U.S. Civil Wars. In the days of the first industrial wars, few preparations were made for the transportation and care of the wounded, and after large-scale battles, wounded soldiers lay on the battlefield for days without care or help. Even when soldiers managed to find their way to a hospital, nurses and doctors could do little except try to make their patients comfortable. Although physicians used ether and chloroform to sedate patients before amputations, the discovery of germs lay in the future and conditions for the wounded were appalling.

By World War I, sanitary conditions and transportation of the wounded had improved. Motorized ambulance services brought wounded soldiers to hospitals where staffs of trained nurses cared for them, many of them female volunteers anxious to help with the war effort. On the home front, women also prepared bandages and collected other medical supplies. Antibiotics still had not yet been discovered, however, so infection and disease continued to maim and kill.

Penicillin was discovered in 1928, but it was not widely used as an antibiotic until World War II. Along with the use of blood plasma and other medical advances, it saved thousands of lives. Medical staff began to use air evacuation in addition to ambulances to move wounded soldiers from the front lines to hospitals. Statistics from America's twentieth-century wars show the importance of rapid transportation to a hospital. In World War II and the Korean and Vietnam Wars, over a quarter of those wounded in combat died on the battlefield, but if they survived until they were taken to a hospital, fewer than 3 percent passed away.[53]

The lesson of rapid evacuation of the wounded to more fully equipped hospitals shaped medical care and training during the second half of the twentieth century. MASH (Mobile Army Surgical Hospital) units worked in temporary hospitals close to the front lines. Combat medics were trained to stabilize patients so that they could be medevacked, or transported to a hospital by helicopter. MASH units worked on the front lines during battles and suffered from extremely high casualty rates themselves.

This model proved effective during the Vietnam War. In 1993, however, it failed in the short but lethal battle of Mogadishu. There, combat medics stabilized the wounded, but helicopters were not able to land and carry off the wounded because crowds of armed Somalis fired at them as they tried to approach.[54] Unfortunately, the medics had not been trained to provide more sustained care. The lesson of Mogadishu was that in urban warfare, evacuation may not happen immediately.

In the wake of that disaster, the model for providing medical care changed to emphasize more intensive intervention from the time a servicemember is wounded. In Iraq and Afghanistan today, injured soldiers are treated for first by combat medics at BAS (Battalion Aid Stations) or FSTs (Forward Surgical Teams), mobile units of about twenty medical personnel, including physicians, nurses, and combat medics, who drive armored Humvees close to the scene of an attack. The FSTs are equipped with sophisticated equipment normally used in hospital emergency rooms and can keep even severely wounded patients alive for several days if necessary, until evacuation is possible. The wounded are then transported to Combat Support Hospitals in the combat theater. From there they are medevacked to larger hospitals in Germany or Japan and later moved to medical centers in the United States.[55]

The new system, emphasizing not only stabilization but also immediate treatment of serious trauma, has saved many lives in Iraq and Afghanistan. A tragic and unintended side effect, however, has been an increase in the number of permanently disabled soldiers from America's ongoing wars. The percentage of amputees among today's casualties is about twice as high as it was in the past, a result of the lifesaving trauma care wounded soldiers receive and also the body armor today's soldiers wear. Body armor protects soldiers from fatal wounds in the torso, but IEDs continue to tear off arms and legs.[56]

In addition, there are increasing numbers of serious brain injuries among wounded soldiers. In past wars, most soldiers with severe brain trauma died, but today FSTs can save more of them. IEDs also cause brain damage with the force of the blast, damage that is not detected immediately if there is no external wound.

The rehabilitation and care of soldiers wounded in Iraq and Afghanistan is likely to be difficult and expensive. The Army has already established an amputee care center at Brooke Army Medical Center at Fort Sam Houston, Texas, and others are in the works.[57] Brain injuries may be even more problematic. The large percentage of National Guard and Reserve forces that are fighting in Iraq and Afghanistan means that many soldiers with permanent brain injuries are older men and women with families, and the burden of their lifelong care will fall to spouses and children.[58]

If history is any guide, the families of permanently disabled veterans are in for a tough struggle. Rarely have disabled veterans been cared for adequately after the end of hostilities. It was only after World War I that the sheer numbers of injured forced the government to provide some health care and rehabilitation services for disabled veterans.[59] Such efforts proved to be halfhearted, however, and during the 1920s, the sight of homeless amputees begging in the streets was all too common. After World War II, the government was determined not to repeat the dismal performance of the earlier war. The popular General Omar Bradley was given the task of reforming the overwhelmed VA. His leadership went far in improving the awful care veterans received at VA hospitals, and a huge public effort helped even more. Groups like the American Red Cross, the American Legion Auxiliary, and the VA Volunteer Service organized thousands of volunteers to care for injured veterans and reintroduce them to civilian life.[60] Widespread public awareness helped ease the difficulties of reintegration for injured and disabled veterans.

Unfortunately, this lesson was forgotten by the time large numbers of Vietnam War casualties needed help. The VA provided atrocious care to many disabled Vietnam veterans, and the incompetence of VA bureaucrats added to the emotional trauma of veterans' war experiences.[61] The public attitude of indifference or hostility toward veterans did not help. By the 1980s, the situation had improved somewhat, and today the quality of VA medical care is excellent. But the VA continues to be overburdened by the number of veterans needing help. There are long waiting lists for services, and in the past ten years almost 14,000 veterans passed away before their cases were resolved. To make matters worse, many of the facilities for helping disabled veterans currently run by the DoD will be transferred to the VA in the next decade or so, further stressing the system.[62] And while the public has been supportive of the troops, the ongoing burden of caring for disabled veterans has fallen on families and friends rather than on the government or the public at large.

Among the most common and painful recollections of soldiers are the memories of their wounded friends and comrades crying out for help.[63] It is especially painful for soldiers to see the body parts of their friends, and they will go to great lengths to rescue and tend to a wounded comrade, even if there is no hope. Troops treat body parts and the bodies of American servicemembers as if they are caring for themselves.[64]

The care and reverence given to the bodies of dead soldiers is one of the most fundamental elements of military culture in the United States. Soldiers risk their lives to recover the remains of their dead comrades, in many cases suffering additional casualties in the recovery effort. Even decades after hostilities ended in Vietnam, recovery and repatriation efforts continue. According to author Michael Sledge, the government has spent about $1.2 million per body in its efforts to recover the remains of every soldier who died in Southeast Asia.[65]

Soldiers' bodies are returned to the United States from wherever they died, unless the next-of-kin requests otherwise. This policy is not universal by any means. Until recently, British soldiers were buried where they died, in "some corner of a foreign field / That is forever England," as the poet Rupert Brooke put it. In the United States, by contrast, great efforts have been made to bring the bodies of dead soldiers home since the Spanish-American War of 1898, the nation's first major overseas engagement.[66]

In the two world wars, soldiers' bodies were buried in temporary cemeteries near the battlefield, and repatriated after each war ended. In the aftermath of World War I, a lengthy debate over repatriation delayed the process for years; eventually, about 70 percent of families chose to have their loved ones' remains repatriated. The policy was well established by World War II but because of logistical difficulties the first repatriations did not begin until 1947.[67] After 1950, the DoD switched to a "Concurrent Return" policy, in which bodies are embalmed and returned to the United States as quickly as possible.[68] Today, the remains of most dead soldiers are transferred to Dover Air Force Base in aluminum "transfer cases," then returned to the next of kin.

When a soldier dies, his or her next of kin are notified by a Casualty Notification Officer, who arrives at the family's home in formal uniform, usually with a chaplain. The family is given whatever information the officer knows about the death, and counseling is offered. Next, a Casualty Assistance Officer contacts the family and helps the family through the paperwork and other administrative matters. This is especially important for spouses, who are eligible for VA and other benefits.

The funeral of a dead soldier is attended by the Casualty Assistance Officer and other representatives of the servicemember's branch of service. The remains are prepared by specialists at Dover; often, they are not viewable, so they are wrapped in several layers of plastic sheets, white muslin cloth, a green wool blanket, and finally a full dress uniform with the servicemember's medals is pinned carefully on the blanket.[69]

Casualty Notification and Assistance Officers do not have any special training in counseling or grief support, but are assigned the duty from their normal job specialties. The job is tough, and many Assistance Officers find that they become more involved in the lives of the bereaved families than they would have expected. The specialists in Mortuary Affairs are trained to work with the remains of dead servicemembers, but these personnel have among the highest levels of stress from their work of any personnel, including those in combat.[70]

CHAPTER 10

THE MILITARY AND AMERICAN SOCIETY

This examination of life in the armed forces has suggested that in many ways the military subculture is quite distinct from the culture of civilian society. In reality, of course, the two cannot really be separated. They affect each other, and the relationship between military and civilian culture is complex and multi-layered. The number of directions a discussion of military–civilian relations can take is almost infinite; this final chapter will examine four issues that concern many military and civilian observers.

The first question addresses the military's role as an American institution. Should it be required to reflect contemporary American social, cultural, and political values, if necessary through mandate or central decree? Or should the needs of the military mission take precedence even when the resulting structure is objectionable in the eyes of many civilians?

The second issue concerns the image of the military in American culture. How is the military institution, military service, and the individual soldier or veteran portrayed in the news media and in literature and film? How are wars and military service honored and commemorated in American society?

The third question surveys the thorny debate over military–civilian relations in the political sphere. To what extent should the armed forces be able to influence or put pressure on civilian political institutions? What role, if any, should military leadership play in policymaking or effecting social or economic change in civilian society?

The discussion concludes with an examination of the draft and the All-Volunteer Force. Observers agree that the AVF has been a success, but at what cost? Does the American public view military service as a civic obligation, or a profession chosen like any other? And what are the implications for the nation if military service ceases to be a shared responsibility?

These questions cannot be answered in the brief and introductory discussions presented here; at best, the contours of the debates can be laid out as a guide for further investigation. Nevertheless, even a short survey indicates how public perceptions of the role of the military in American society influence all aspects of life in the military, from recruitment and training to retirement and commemoration of the nation's war dead. In the past, American attitudes toward the military have been ambivalent if not downright hostile, and although today the American public is supportive of its soldiers, sailors, airmen, and Marines, there is no consensus about the use of military force as a foreign policy tool or the influence of the military institution on civilian government.

AMERICAN SOCIETY AND THE ROLE OF THE MILITARY INSTITUTION

For many Americans, civilians as well as military personnel, the military is a quintessentially American institution, as closely tied to American identity as any other element of society in the United States. Contemporary American patriotism has a strong pro-military flavor to it, and military culture is thought to be on the more conservative and nationalist side of the scale. On the other hand, because the military has been subordinate to civilian authority since its founding, and military personnel are not supposed to form a separate "caste" in American society, many Americans believe that the military should reflect the values, structures, and demography of civilian society.

At first it may seem obvious that the U.S. armed forces can and do reflect the characteristic strengths and weaknesses of American society. After all, almost all military people come from United States; they grew up in small towns, suburbs, and cities across the nation. They attended American schools, watched American television, and, as workers, played their part in the American economy.

But the military, as this survey shows, is quite different from civilian society in many important respects. Most obviously, the AVF has a distinct demographic profile: younger, more male, healthier, more African-American, better educated, more working and middle class, and more likely to be from the southern and western states. In terms of values, the military is more group-focused, hierarchical and obedience-oriented than civilian society with its emphasis on individualism and private choice. The military is not a democracy; decisions are made by military leaders and passed down through the ranks. Military personnel do not have the same civil liberties as American civilians do. Finally, and most importantly for this discussion, on issues like race, gender, sexual orientation, and religious pluralism, military culture does not always reflect American social trends.

There are solid, practical reasons why the military looks different and behaves differently from civilian institutions. The demographics of the military, especially its youth and its standards of physical and mental functioning, fit its function. The armed forces could not be more inclusive with regard to age or physical and mental capability and still maintain their effectiveness. Their emphases on communal rather than individual values have an important function as well.[1] On the battlefield, obedience, hierarchy, and command decisions are more effective than participation and discussion. Individuals who join the military understand this, or ought to, and the military rigorously culls those who cannot adapt. In short, the military puts its function first when considering who should be allowed to join the military, and justifiably so.

On the other hand, when military values stray too far from those of the civilian world, the danger of a separate military "caste" increases. In recent years, some commentators have noticed a gap between military and civilian values, and they worry about the consequences should the gap grow too large. The self-selected AVF, some experts believe, has the potential to develop into an organization with values far removed from, and even opposed to, those of civilian society. As eighteenth-century opponents of a standing Army were quick to assert, the military values of obedience and hierarchy are very different from the civilian emphasis on democracy and freedom that has been part of America's self-image since its founding. Critics of military society are concerned about the ways that the values of a pluralistic society, such as tolerance for opposing views, the belief in personal choice, and the awareness of individual rights, can be overshadowed by the group ethos of military culture. Over time, critics fear, American civilians and military people might find themselves staring suspiciously at each other over a vast and deep cultural divide. Or worse, democratic traditions in the United States might be eroded. Militarism, "the domination of the military man over the civilian, an undue preponderance of military demands, and emphasis on military considerations, spirit, ideals, and scales of value, in the life of states," might be the unhappy result.[2]

There does seem to be some evidence that military and civilian values are diverging. Youth attitude studies by the military suggest that young people do not like being told what to do, they insist on making their own decisions, and they need to know "why" if they are ordered to do something. These attitudes make military culture all the more strange and uncongenial for them.[3]

Conversely, many career military personnel are uncomfortable with some of the things they see in the civilian world, and they prefer the order and stability of military life. Military bases, while mimicking civilian towns in many ways, are fundamentally quite different from civilian communities in their enforced conformity. The institution has much more control over residents' personal lives and behavior than most civilians would countenance, so the problems of crime and social deviance common to many civilian communities are relatively foreign to military bases. Base communities are, in the words of one writer, "islands of tranquility removed from the seemingly chaotic, crime-ridden civilian environment outside the gates."[4]

A separate military ethos is also fostered by the intergenerational dynamic that characterizes military life; military personnel, especially officers, are somewhat more likely to be the children of military parents.[5] Since the nineteenth century, people who have grown up in the peculiar world of the military find it more congenial than civilians do. By bringing civilians with no military background into the services, institutions like the draft and ROTC once served to balance the inward tendencies of military culture with influences from the outside. The draft has been abolished for over three decades, however, and many universities no longer host ROTC programs, diminishing the civilian "leavening" of military culture advocated by so many earlier experts.[6]

On the other hand, studies also show that Americans admire and appreciate military culture, at least what they understand of it.[7] Moreover, the gap between military and civilian values may well be exaggerated. It is true that some civilians view the military as an exotic and mystifying cult; "to read some of the antiwar stuff currently written about the military, you'd think the Army is like a prison," noted a *Seattle Times* columnist at the beginning of the Iraq war.[8] Most Americans know that the Army is not like a prison, however, and the American public supports the military and its traditions.

Furthermore, many civilian values seep into military culture. The military may tend toward communal values over individual ones, but individualism is impossible to eradicate altogether. One sign of civilian individualism is recruiters' emphasis on the personal benefits to be gained from serving, a "civilianization of the U.S. military ethos," according to some commentators.[9] The emphasis on individualism can be seen among those already serving as well. The recent case of a Roman Catholic officer who refused to serve on duty with women to avoid sexual temptation is an example of individual values clashing with military needs. In his bid to avoid serving with women, the officer received support from Congress, some members of the Catholic hierarchy, and the Family Research Council, a conservative think tank. The officer and his supporters believed that his personal beliefs trumped "functional military necessity"—the requirement that servicemembers perform their duty as

ordered, regardless of their personal preferences. Critics called the officer's supporters "ignorant of or apathetic toward the nation's security
needs," but the case demonstrated the difficult balance between individualism and the rules of the group.[10]

Perhaps the most famous, or notorious, sign of the "civilianization" of
the armed forces is the military's attempt to deal with racism, sexism,
and homophobia in the ranks. Critics of military culture charge that the
services should divest themselves of exclusionary attitudes and policies
and use their unique power to reflect contemporary egalitarian standards
more closely.[11]

However, the use of the military as a "social laboratory," tinker
with traditional social mores, has generated a great deal of controversy.
The institution, many say, should not be experimented with just because
civilians do not approve of its policies. The needs of the service must
come before the public's desire to see the military reflect contemporary
civilian values. If the military must appear backward in its culture and
values in order to maintain discipline and readiness, then so be it.

The first use of the military as a "social laboratory" occurred with the
racial integration of the armed forces in 1948. Critics of the measure
warned that white soldiers, especially those from the segregated South,
would not willingly serve willingly with black soldiers, and morale and
readiness would suffer. As it happened, the dire predictions never came
to pass. Even before President Harry S. Truman mandated integration,
studies conducted among military personnel suggested that most soldiers
would not object to serving with others of different races, and there was
little organized resistance to the change.

The success of integration has suggested to some that inclusion of women
and homosexuals can and should occur in the same way, by centralized
mandate. Many in and out of the military, however, oppose such measures.
The armed forces were integrated not because of a desire for social justice,
but as a simple matter of efficiency; it was more cost-effective to integrate
than to maintain separate facilities for black and white personnel.[12] The
argument for opening combat roles to women and accepting homosexuality
among the troops does not involve at the present time a matter of dire need,
but rather is based on principles of equal treatment. Instead of increasing
military efficiency, critics warn, full inclusion of women and homosexuals
as a sop to political correctness will undermine readiness.[13]

The problems and scandals of the 1990s involving female personnel
indicated to many that the military could not integrate women successfully without damaging readiness and esprit de corps. In more recent
years, however, women have served alongside men without incident,
and it appears that the initial adjustment problems have been largely
overcome.

There is historical precedent for persisting with change through difficult times. In the wake of the civil rights movement in the 1960s, the military suffered through several years of severe racial tension and division, a situation much more harmful to military readiness than the Tailhook and Aberdeen sex scandals. In response, strict policies were put into place to ensure that African-American personnel were treated fairly, and in time the most serious racial tensions abated.[14]

The issue of homosexuality in the military is the latest in this ongoing debate. There is little evidence that the inclusion of homosexuals in the military will damage readiness, and there is much evidence that their exclusion has reduced military capabilities. As noted in Chapter 4, among the gay servicemembers separated from the military in recent years are many Arabic and Farsi language specialists and other highly skilled workers. Military readiness may well dictate the inclusion of homosexuals, just as it should dictate that even conservative Catholic officers serve with women.

IMAGES OF THE MILITARY IN MEDIA AND LITERATURE

Most Americans who are not serving in the armed forces get information about the military the way they learn about other unfamiliar institutions and cultures: through what they read and see in the news or in fictional films and books. Unfortunately, those images are often distorted and incomplete, and are almost as likely to be a reflection of the creators' perspectives as they are to present a window into the world of the military.

The news media are a major source of public impressions of the armed forces, especially during wartime when attention is turned toward military activities. The media have not always been kind to the armed forces, at least to the leadership, and as visual media in particular have become ubiquitous in public life, the services have developed more sophistication in their dealings with them.[15]

There is nothing new, of course, about the role of the media during wartime. During the past century, the media—newspapers and magazines, radio, film, television, and now the Internet—have become an integral part of warfare, used to unite the home front behind the war effort and to squelch dissent, or conversely, to expose poor planning and incompetence.[16]

During World War I, governments on all sides created propaganda of the crudest type to mobilize the civilian population. After the war, such efforts were discredited in the United States and other democratic nations, but the media supported the war effort during World War II as enthusiastically as it had supported World War I.[17] Newspapers and magazines highlighted the American contribution to the global struggle, and film newsreels brought images of war and its devastation to movie audiences. The media acted in concert with the government during both World War II and the Korean War, downplaying blunders and emphasizing the heroism of the citizen soldier.

Many people remember television as the news source that changed everything for the American way of understanding war. During the Vietnam War, television brought uncensored images of carnage to Americans in their homes, hastening widespread disaffection for the conflict. Vietnam was dubbed the "living-room war" in 1966 by *New Yorker* columnist Michael J. Arlen, an expression that captured the immediacy of television images of war.[18] However, some media scholars today discount the role of television in creating opposition to the Vietnam conflict, saying that the impact of television on public attitudes toward the war was overrated and is now "remembered fiction."[19] There may be some truth to this. Studies of news coverage during the era show that the media cooperated with the military during most of the Vietnam War, as it had during the Korean War and World War II. Reporters and anchormen did not question the purpose or importance of the war effort, and reports of antiwar activity were largely unsympathetic.[20] Reporters in Vietnam enjoyed a great deal of freedom in where they went and what they wrote or said, but they supported the administration and reported the military's side of the story. Newsmagazines had gotten somewhat more critical by mid-1967,[21] but, by and large, there does not seem to have been a significant antiwar or antimilitary bias before 1968.

After the Tet offensive in early 1968, however, the media began to turn against the war. Increasingly, the mainstream media questioned its conduct and purpose and wondered whether it could be won. On February 27, 1968, almost a month after the beginning of the Tet offensive, CBS anchor Walter Cronkite broke with tradition to criticize the war and the government's handling of it, opining that "it seems now more certain than ever that the bloody experience of Vietnam is to end in a stalemate."[22]

The March 1968 My Lai Massacre was another moment of transformation in the media portrayal of Vietnam. After My Lai, print media and television reports highlighted morale and discipline problems among the troops, even suggesting widespread disintegration of the military.[23] Relations between the armed forces and the media deteriorated so much that President Richard M. Nixon accused the media of losing the war in Vietnam through its negative and defeatist reporting.[24] The perception that elite papers such as the *New York Times* and the *Washington Post* were (and are still) relentlessly antimilitary continues to be widely held today, but in fact studies suggest that the press' antimilitary bias is part of the "remembered fiction" of the war. The main failures of the Vietnam-era press, according to one study, were its overemphasis on the American role in the war and its corresponding failure to tell the story of the Vietnamese point of view, not its negative portrayal of the armed forces.[25]

Whatever the actual role of the media during the Vietnam War, military leaders perceived it to be largely unfriendly. By the 1980s, as the existence of 24-hour intensive television coverage, known as the "CNN factor," became more important, military leadership had become extremely suspicious of television and print reporters. During American interventions in Grenada and Panama, public affairs officers laid down new rules for reporters covering military news, and the system was perfected during the first Gulf War in 1990–1991.[26] Officers trained in media relations herded groups of journalists through approved areas and gave them small doses of carefully censored information. Public affairs personnel previewed news stories before they were published, and if reporters went out on their own they were accompanied by "minders" who made sure that they saw and heard nothing detrimental to the image military leaders wanted to project. Higher-ranking commanders, who had been young lieutenants and captains during the Vietnam War, were especially suspicious of the elite press, and scoured their coverage for signs of criticism. For its part, the press also seemed to want to prove that it could be patriotic and pro-military, a not entirely successful attempt to erase the image of disloyalty that continued to dog the "liberal" media.

The military's handling of the media during the first Gulf War succeeded, in the sense that coverage was overwhelmingly positive, but it aroused criticisms of censorship. During the wars in Iraq and Afghanistan, military public relations personnel have become even more sophisticated in their handling of the media. Before the Iraq conflict, journalists were "embedded" in combat units and accompanied those units during the fighting. Since 2003, journalists have been embedded in units in Afghanistan as well. Embedded journalists have been able to report exactly what occurred as it happened, so there is a sense of vivid realism and truthfulness in their stories. Moreover, as military officials had suspected, there was little danger of the embedded journalists reporting negative stories. Rather, they tended to try to make their units look good[27] not only so that they would continue to be able to interview and gather information, but also because they began to identify with their units. Criticism was muted, but the immediacy of information came at the cost of deeper analysis.[28] While the system has helped produce positive coverage, the quality of war journalism may have suffered.

The military has also begun an ambitious campaign to use the Internet to get its message out directly. The DoD maintains an extensive web presence, centered on news and information about current military activities, all carefully coordinated to present military activities in a positive light. Individual branches also maintain their own Web sites. Finally public relations personnel are trained to deal not only with the American media but also with the less friendly media of other nations.

Literature, such as films, novels, poems, and plays, is another source of enduring images of war and the military. Societies have always reflected on their armed conflicts through literature, and those reflections often become the "truth" about war. As one literary scholar explains, "literature about war becomes the war remembered."[29] Much classical war literature portrays combat in a way that may seem somewhat abstract to modern eyes. From Beowulf to the Iliad to Shakespeare, themes of heroism in battle, courage and manliness, and personal sacrifice predominate. Battle in the preindustrial age is usually portrayed as a personal endeavor in which the most courageous warrior wins or dies with honor. The hero may undergo personal struggles, but rarely does he question his obligation to fight, the cause for which he is fighting, or the intrinsic value of combat itself.

The epic style of warrior literature inevitably changed with the transformation of warfare in the industrial age. Many critics believe that the first modern American war novel was Stephen Crane's *Red Badge of Courage* (1895), in which a young man wrestles with his feelings of fear and cowardice in the face of battle.[30] In *Red Badge of Courage*, the protagonist is overwhelmed by the chaos of industrial warfare; the novel centers on his inner experience rather than the grand sweep of the war. The focus on the individual soldier as antihero became a common theme in twentieth-century war literature. After the trauma of World War I, novelists, poets, and playwrights from all nations told stories of naivety and disillusionment, the incompetence of high command, the alienation of soldiers from civilian life, and the psychological effects of combat. But they also told of the intense bonding among soldiers and the thrill of battle. Some novels, such as the German writer Ernst Junger's *Storm of Steel* (1920), highlighted the intensity of war in a positive way.[31] In the 1920s and 1930s, the first war films appeared. Dealing mostly with World War I, early war cinematography tended to have a pacifist message. The films *All Quiet on the Western Front* (1930) and *A Farewell to Arms* (1932), like the novels from which they were adapted,[32] told of young men exhausted and alienated by the senseless war.

During World War II, the film industries of the combatant countries participated in the war effort by producing films designed to encourage young men to enlist and boost the morale of the home front. Cinema soldiers were heroic, the war effort was just, and the enemy was clearly evil. John Wayne, who starred in such films as *Flying Tigers* (1942) and *The Fighting Seabees* (1944), was one of the iconic stars of patriotic filmmaking.

Immediately after the war ended, however, a new genre of war film emerged. Called film noir, these films dispensed with the patriotism and purpose of wartime cinema. Films like *The Best Years of Our Lives (1946)* highlighted the reality of postwar life for many veterans: maladaptation to civilian culture, mental and physical injuries from the war, survivors' guilt, alcoholism, and violence. In *The Third Man* (1949), the chaos of postwar Europe is the backdrop to a story of corruption and evil perpetrated by American veterans. Film noir shows a bleak world of no values or standards, where nothing is as it seems, a reflection of the disorientation of a society moving from war to peace.[33]

Like film noir, many novels of the immediate postwar period, such as Norman Mailer's *The Naked and the Dead* (1948), showed soldiers as flawed, even repellent individuals, implicitly rejecting wartime boosterism. But by the Cold War of the 1950s, a new crop of films and novels again portrayed war in simpler terms. In films like John Wayne's *Sands of Iwo Jima (1949),* soldiers were honorable and brave, even if, like Wayne's character Sergeant Stryker, they were hard-bitten men of few words. Many war and military films of the 1950s and early 1960s had anticommunist themes, even when ostensibly dealing with earlier wars; the didactic tone of such films is no surprise given the political climate of the times.

As the war in Vietnam grew more divisive in the 1960s, pro-war films lost their mass appeal. For example, *The Green Berets* (1968), a film about Vietnam starring John Wayne, was a box-office failure, while more cynical films like *M*A*S*H* (1970) appealed to wider audiences through their antimilitary and antiwar critiques. *M*A*S*H* was set during the Korean War; viewers knew its true theme was Vietnam, but most mainstream films and literature had not yet begun to assess the Vietnam experience directly.

After several years of neglect, the topic of Vietnam came to the attention of writers and filmmakers, and by the 1980s, a torrent of works had been produced. *Apocalypse Now* (1979) was one of the first major films of the Vietnam War, followed by *Platoon* (1986), *Full Metal Jacket* (1987), and many others. None of these films portray the Vietnam War as anything but a disaster for those involved.

In 1978, two of the first examinations of Vietnam veterans came to the public eye: the film *The Deer Hunter* and Ron Kovac's memoir *Born on the Fourth of July,* which was made into a film in 1989. Both deal with the traumatic return of veterans who cannot find their way in civilian society. During the next decade, a host of films, from *Rambo* (1982) to *Lethal Weapon* (1987), depicted Vietnam veterans as outsiders, albeit sympathetic, even heroic ones. Novelists such as Tim O'Brien have dealt with the lasting effects of Vietnam service on those who returned. In television programming, the character of the disturbed Vietnam veteran has become such a staple that it is now a cliché; the animated comedy *The Simpsons* pokes fun at conventional portrayals of troubled veterans in the character of Principal Skinner and his flashbacks from the war.

Literary critic Katherine Kinney has suggested that a common theme of the literature and cinema of the Vietnam War is the destruction of Americans by other Americans, either physically through friendly fire or "fragging" (troops murdering their commanders), or in an emotional or spiritual sense. Artistic treatments of Vietnam tend to show men undergoing a transition from naïve and idealistic boys before the war, to soldiers adapting to the strange world of combat, to veterans who are afflicted with loneliness and alienation from family and friends, guilt, loss of faith, problems related to PSTD, and secrets held from that divisive time.[34] The self-destruction, according to Kinney, can be seen as a symbol of the breakdown of important elements of American identity: the United States as "world hegemon" and the traditional hierarchies of gender and race.[35] Whether or not Vietnam was a war in which America destroyed its own, it is certainly remembered that way in written literature, film, and television.

The armed conflicts of the post–Cold War era have not produced a crop of distinctive literature as yet, but thousands of journalistic accounts, memoirs, and autobiographies of participants have been published in recent years. Some, like *Blackhawk Down,* the story of the 1993 peace-keeping operation in Somalia, have become minor classics. Generally speaking, however, the amount of literature created in the aftermath of any war is directly related to the size, trauma, and divisiveness of the conflict. Thus, World War I produced an enormous amount of literature in Great Britain, while the Vietnam War had a similar effect in the United States.

Since the use of the Internet has become widespread, we may be seeing a new way to understand the experience of war and its aftermath. Printing houses have always published selected memoirs and autobiographies of soldiers, even soldiers' diaries and letters, but now any interested reader can find thousands of wartime blogs posted on the Web. These accounts vary in quality but may add immediacy and authenticity to the representations of soldiers' experiences available through traditional media.[36]

A third way that war is understood and remembered is through war memorials. Physical or temporal spaces dedicated to war help the nation form its memory not only of war and soldiers but also of the American story itself. The creation of war memorials in the United States has always been controversial, with many different groups in society fighting for a voice in each memorial's conception and design.[37] Many Americans assume that the federal government has been responsible for this public function, but in fact for most of the nation's history, private groups have pushed to create war memorials. Because the public is so involved in the memorialization process, there have always been different understandings of the role of memorials. Should they recognize the contributions of a specific group or remember veterans as a whole? Should they attempt to create national identity or honor the service of soldiers? Glorify war or warn against it?

Until the Civil War, the tradition of memorializing wars was not an enduring part of American culture. Memorials for specific war leaders had only local interest and tended to be neglected after those with direct memory of the individual or the conflict passed away. The Civil War changed this. In 1866, the federal government established a series of cemeteries for the Union dead, not only for officers but also for enlisted men.[38] In 1890, the government took over responsibility for the Confederate cemeteries as well. Local groups erected memorials to the men who had died in the war, remembering for the first time the common soldier as well as the war leader. At the same time, public interest in the Revolutionary War increased. Equestrian themes and classical styles in Revolutionary and Civil War memorials harked back to ancient Greece and Rome, and made war seem glamorous and exciting.[39]

After World War I, the government became more involved in memorialization. In 1923, Congress created the ABMC (American Battle Monuments Commission) to oversee public commemoration sites. The ABMC built huge cemeteries for the war dead, mostly in France and Belgium. Graves in military cemeteries were marked with identical headstones and included no sign of rank, region of origin, or social class. Race, however, continued to be a barrier; separate cemeteries were created for black and white soldiers. Interestingly, there was little interest in memorials after World War II; a plan to build a War Museum near Washington, D.C., as a way of explaining the war never got off the ground. The familiar Iwo Jima memorial, depicting U.S. Marines raising a flag on the island of Iwo Jima, recalls World War II most vividly but is actually a memorial to all Marines who have died serving their country since 1775.

The most famous of all American war memorials is probably the Vietnam War memorial. In 1979, Jan C. Scruggs, a Vietnam veteran who was deeply moved by the film *The Deer Hunter,* began a movement to create a memorial for the troops who died during the war. He contributed several thousand dollars of his own money and within two years collected funds totaling over $8 million. In a contest held to choose a design for the memorial, 21-year-old Yale student Maya Lin submitted the winning idea, a long wedge of black granite with the names of all the American war dead engraved on it in the chronological order in which they died.

It caused a sensation; many in the Reagan Administration, especially Secretary of the Interior James Watt, hated it, and insisted that a "traditional" representational statue be placed nearby. But in spite of the controversy over the design, the Vietnam War memorial was completed by 1982, less than a decade after the end of America's involvement in the war. It is now the most visited site in Washington, D.C., and is universally recognized as a great work of public art.[40]

In the 1990s the ABMC, with the support of Congress, began work on memorials for the Korean War and World War II. The expansive World War II memorial, located on the Washington Mall between the Lincoln Memorial and the Washington Monument, is the newest war memorial, dedicated in 2004. Opinion is divided; while admirers enjoy its parklike openness, detractors find it bombastic and overdone. One critic calls it "vainglorious, demanding of attention and full of trite imagery."[41] Like other commemorations of America's military history, the World War II memorial has generated its share of heated discussion and controversy.

There are as yet no memorials to the veterans of Iraq and Afghanistan, of course, but the memorialization of those conflicts is likely to be very interesting. The war in Afghanistan, coming in the wake of the September 11 attacks, has generally been widely supported by the American public. Not so the Iraq war. In public opinion polls, a majority of Americans now say that the war in Iraq was a mistake, and many support immediate withdrawal of U.S. forces. On the other hand, critics of the war have taken great pains to separate their opposition to the war from their support for the troops. Support for the actual men and women fighting overseas is nearly universal. In fact, it could be said that the real memorial to these troops are the millions of "Support the troops" car magnets and banners that plaster the surfaces of American shops, homes, and cars.

It is especially fascinating, therefore, that for most Americans, life goes on with almost no real evidence that the United States is at war. Fewer and fewer Americans know anyone in the military, and fewer and fewer will countenance their own family members serving. In the absence of genuine and widespread involvement in the military, civilian America has elevated servicemembers to "the top of the nation's moral hierarchy," as Andrew Bacevich writes. "The character and charisma long ago associated with the pioneer or the small farmer—or carried in the 1960s by Dr. King and the civil-rights movement—has now come to rest upon the soldier."[42] When the troops do come home, many with real physical and mental problems resulting from their war service, American society may not be able to maintain its facile adulation. It will be a real challenge, then, to "support the troops."

THE INFLUENCE OF THE MILITARY ON CIVILIAN SOCIETY

The institutional armed forces and the ideal of military service have exerted a great deal of influence on American society since the founding of the nation. Of course, war itself will affect any society in devastating ways; an extended conflict on national soil can almost destroy a nation, as was the case for Germany after World War I, and Great Britain never regained its world power status after its tribulations during World War II. Thankfully, the United States has not yet experienced such a massive trauma, but even in peacetime, the military leaves its mark on civilian society in ways not always understood by the public. Of particular significance is the influence of military leadership on civilian policymaking and politics.

Civil–military relations, or the interchange between civilian government and military leadership, is, like the principle of church–state separation, an topic that emerges in public debate with some frequency. According to American tradition, the military should keep away from politics; it is supposed to remain under strict civilian control and is prohibited from meddling in government affairs. In reality, however, military leaders cannot ignore politics altogether because their organizations are directly affected by the decisions of civilian political leaders. Furthermore, the president and Congress must have a clear understanding of military capabilities if they are to deploy troops in combat. Civilian authorities depend on the military for advice and guidance.

But how much input is too much? Can top officers step over the line from legitimate communication to advocacy, pressure, even coercion of civilian leaders? As scholar and career officer Richard D. Hooker writes, "how to keep the military strong enough to defend the states and subservient enough not to threaten it is the central question in civil–military relations."[43]

This debate has gone on throughout American history. There have been times when military leaders have overstepped their bounds, such as Gen. Douglas MacArthur's defiance of President Truman over military strategy in Korea. Since the Vietnam War, however, the question has assumed greater importance. One of the major debates about the Vietnam debacle has been over the role of the military in determining strategy in that conflict. Did President Johnson and his cabinet tie the hands of the military for domestic political reasons, or was the JCS too supine to speak up and give strong warnings about the direction of the war?

Even today scholars differ on the answer to this question, but many agree that the Johnson administration's policymaking hierarchy did not allow the JCS a great deal of input into policy even if it had wanted to offer a strong critique. Secretary of Defense Robert McNamara had his own civilian advisors on whom he relied, and the JCS stood outside his close circle. To correct this imbalance, the 1986 Defense Reorganization Act strengthened the role of the JCS in policymaking, establishing the Chairman of the JCS the "primary military adviser to the president." When Gen. Colin Powell became Chairman of the JCS (1989–1993) he began to use his access to the president to give much sterner advice— advice that he and others of his generation wished that the Vietnam-era JCS had been able to provide. "I had been appalled at the docility of the Joint Chiefs of Staff," Powell wrote in his autobiography, "fighting the war in Vietnam without ever pressing their political leaders to lay out clear objectives for them."[44]

Unlike his predecessors, Powell insisted that four conditions be met before American military power could be used by civilian authorities. First, national interests must be at stake; second, objectives must be clearly laid out; third, overwhelming force must be used; and fourth, the American public must be solidly behind the effort. These conditions clearly show the impact of Vietnam on Powell's thinking; none of them were met in the Vietnam conflict.

As commonsensical as it appeared to be, however, the Powell Doctrine also implied that the military would not carry out the president's orders if a proposed military action did not meet the four conditions. This could be interpreted as an act of insubordination,[45] but in the wake of the success-ful 1991 Gulf War, few objected to what was widely seen as a necessary and welcome exorcism of the ghosts of Vietnam.

A few years later, civil–military relations were again challenged. When newly elected president Bill Clinton tried to change the military's policy toward gays in the service, military leaders, including Powell, defied him. It was not a matter of vital national security policy, but the issue poisoned Clinton's already troubled relationship with the military and, many commentators have argued, weakened Clinton's freedom to use the military as he saw fit.[46]

Not only do the attitudes of military leaders toward civilian authorities influence civil–military relations, but those of civilian leaders toward the military can have a similar effect. The troubled relationship between Bill Clinton and the armed forces was not a result of Clinton being antimili-tary per se, but, egged on by conservative media pundits, many in the military community viewed his personal history and policy decisions as insulting toward military society. Clinton was already unpopular with many in and around the military because of his open avoidance of the draft during the Vietnam War. Early missteps, like the gays in the military fiasco and the popular image of Hillary Clinton as an elite feminist policy wonk out of touch with regular Americans, made Clinton one of the most unpopular presidents with the military in the nation's history. He bears a great deal of responsibility for this, but the Republican Party used his missteps to bolster its own pro-military image. During the 1990s, the Republican Party was perceived by many Americans to be the party of the armed forces; it had taken control of the southern states, original home to about 40 percent of the military personnel,[47] and it generally was more supportive of military issues, such as military pay raises and increased appropriations, than the Democratic Party.[48]

This maneuvering was well within the bounds of normal political partisanship, but some incidents crossed an important line. When North Carolina senator Jesse Helms said in 1994 that if Clinton visited military bases in North Carolina, he had "better have a bodyguard," many felt that the pandering had gone too far.[49] Likewise, when Zell Miller, a conservative Democrat, said in a speech at the 2004 Republican National Convention that any president should be pro-military and that soldiers are more important to American freedom than the press, some saw a worrying move toward militarism on the part of civilian leaders.[50]

By the end of the 1990s, some commentators worried that the armed forces and the Republican Party were too close, and the military was losing its neutrality. As the Iraq and Afghanistan conflicts drag on, that view seems to be becoming less prevalent, especially after high-ranking military officers have criticized the Bush administration's policy in Iraq. In April 2006, for example, a half-dozen retired generals publicly demanded the resignation of Donald Rumsfeld for his mistakes. While many welcomed the "generals' revolt" for its attention to the problems of the Iraq war, others warned that it set a dangerous precedent of military opposition to civilian leadership. In January 2007, a group enlisted soldiers presented Congress with a petition asking that Congress "support the prompt withdrawal of all American military forces and bases from Iraq." This "Appeal for Redress from the War in Iraq" may be largely symbolic, but it too raises the same issues of military involvement in political affairs.[51]

One lesson of these examples of military participation in political debates is that beauty is in the eye of the beholder. Many of those who supported the military's resistance to allowing gays to serve in the military, and who applauded Helms' comments, were appalled by the generals' criticism of Rumsfeld and Bush. Others who labeled the military an undemocratic and homophobic institution because of the gay issue applauded the generals when they spoke out. In fact many noted that the generals should have spoken out earlier, while they were still on active duty. The soldiers who signed the "Appeal for Redress" have received almost universal sympathy and support, and almost no one has pointed out the potential conflict for abuse when soldiers participate in policymaking.

Another lesson is that the line between the military having too much or too little say in civilian affairs is blurry and shifts according to circumstance. Not only do historical events like the Vietnam War influence the public's notion of how much criticism is appropriate, but also civilian authorities may request more or less input from military leaders at different times. Over the course of the twentieth century, and especially during and after World War II, presidents expected military leaders to advise them not just on military capabilities, but on broader national and international matters in which the military might have a role. President John F. Kennedy requested that military officers "prepare themselves to take active roles in the policy-making process."[52] As it happened, he himself did not use the military in this way, nor did his successor, but the growing complexity of military affairs meant that military leaders would possess knowledge and expertise that no civilian could match.

In recent years, the military has embraced its expanded role in policy-making with programs at the War Colleges and the National Defense University in relevant areas like information technology, resources management, and international diplomacy. Civilian leaders may or may not heed the advice of military leaders, but officers at the highest levels of the military are better prepared than ever before to consider the diplomatic, economic, sociocultural, and political impact of military actions, and integrate those perspectives into their knowledge of tactics, strategy, and other military considerations.

THE AVF AND AMERICAN SOCIETY

In the thirty-plus years it has existed, the AVF has unquestionably succeeded in producing an outstanding military force. A decade after it was implemented, the armed services were better qualified, trained, and equipped to defend the United States than virtually any other military force in American history. There is no reason to question this success. Even if the current wars in Iraq and Afghanistan do not end with the results American policymakers want, the AVF has performed up to and even exceeded expectations.

As has been discussed earlier, the volunteer nature of the AVF is the key to its own success. Today's complex military affairs cannot be left to inexperienced draftees, and training is so expensive that it is not worth forcing unenthusiastic conscripts to serve two years or less. The modern military is much better as a professional force than as a conscript service.[53]

Even so, the AVF is troublesome to many Americans. Aside from the danger of the AVF developing into a subculture at odds with civilian society, observers are concerned about two additional issues, which are separate from each other but related. First is the perception that the defense burden being borne by low-income Americans, who have fewer choices than more affluent young men and women. Second is the long-term implication for society if those who have more life choices fall into the habit of avoiding service to their nation. Citizenship, critics say, carries responsibilities as well as rights, and the better-off seem to be in danger of forgetting this.

In response to these concerns, some experts over the years have called for a return to compulsory national service of some sort. In 1988, the Democratic Leadership Council embraced such a proposal. Charles Moskos, one of the nation's leading experts on military affairs, has long been an advocate of national service, as have many others involved in military affairs. Proponents of national service see it as "an obligation incurred because of one's membership in a community"[54] and wish to see the obligation shared by everyone. Although the idea lost much of its resonance during the drawdowns of the 1990s, by 2004 there was a renewed discussion of national service. Among others, Charles Rangel, a Congressional representative from New York, called for a return to the draft. His bill was defeated in Congress by an overwhelming margin, but it served its purpose of bringing the issue to public attention.

For the most part, these and others calling for a return to national service are suggesting that young people be required either to serve in the military or to perform some kind of civilian service. The goal of such proposals is not so much to deal with the manpower needs of the military as to redress the alleged imbalances that the AVF has created. In the past year or so, however, with the Iraq and Afghanistan wars squeezing the military's capacity ever tighter, there has been a renewed discussion of a return to the military draft to fill the ranks of the military, which, some experts fear, is in danger of becoming a new "hollow force."[55] This is a different species of animal from the idea of national service as a part of citizenship, and its merits depend on how well or poorly a draft would serve the interests of the military. By contrast, the "citizenship" idea of national service is designed to serve the interests of society as a whole by mitigating the unfairness of the AVF and sparking a sense of citizenship among more affluent young people.

But are the problems caused by the AVF serious enough to warrant such a measure? We can begin with the argument that the AVF is unfair. Critics characterize the AVF as a working-man's army, in which youths without the resources available to the more affluent middle classes are forced to look to military service for college funding, health care, retirement, and other elements of a stable lifestyle. In return, they must face the possibility of being wounded or dying in war. Facing death for one's nation, critics say, should not be a function of how rich or poor one is. This burden should be shared more equally.

Maybe so, opponents respond. But aside from the practical point that the draft does not produce as capable a military force as the AVF, the draft also did not equalize military service the way some proponents might think it did. After the total mobilization of World War II, the draft in the twentieth century allowed for many deferments based on education and occupation. These deferments were not simply "white man's privilege;" the creators of the draft, concerned with the Soviets' apparent lead in the Cold War technology race, did not want to prevent young people from entering science and technology–related careers, so they allowed deferments for young people studying or working in certain scientific and technological fields.[56] And the rules excluded those in the lowest mental categories from being conscripted, because these people were especially difficult to train and discipline.

As a result, the draft was in fact not demographically fair and did tend to conscript lower-income young men. During the Korean and Vietnam wars, casualties were higher for draftees, a disproportionate number of whom were low-income and African-American. A new national service might avoid such unfairness by not allowing deferments or exclusions, but the original rationales for excusing individuals from service—either for occupation or for low mental category—still exist.

Furthermore, many defenders of the AVF point out that while it may be unfair that young people from lower-income families must join the military to pay for college, the fact remains that the military *is* a path to college and even post-secondary education for many young Americans. While affluent Americans may cringe at the trade-off between a college education and the possibility of facing combat, many lower-income Americans count on the military as an avenue to a better life. If a draft were reinstituted, some argue, some young people who would choose to join the military would be denied a chance for upward mobility; their spots would be taken, in the name of fairness, by more affluent draftees.

The biggest argument against the class injustice criticism of the AVF is that the AVF actually does not recruit from the most vulnerable classes in American society. The AVF is rather choosy about who it accepts (see Chapter 1), and military recruits are on average better educated, more law-abiding, and healthier than their peers in the civilian world. It is true that the geographical origins of recruits are not equally spread across the country. Servicemembers are more likely to come from the South, and less likely to hail from New England, but all fifty states and American territories contribute to the AVF.

It is also true that the AVF does not tend to draw recruits from the wealthiest groups in America, and this fact leads to the second argument in favor of national service. This argument points out that since the beginning of the AVF in 1973, affluent Americans have not had to consider national service as a possibility. Proponents of national service say that military service should be seen as "an obligation incurred because of one's membership in a community,"[57] to be borne equally by all. It has been argued that when everyone is equally eligible for military service, national leaders, who come from the most privileged classes of society, may be less likely to send the nation to war.

National service also may enrich a sense of American identity and common purpose at a time when many Americans seem to be focusing on their differences rather than their similarities. Service provides a shared experience for people who otherwise have little in common.

In addition to shaping group values and identity, military service also helps form personal identity. Many Americans who were drafted remember the experience as valuable one, even when they admit that they did not exactly enjoy their military service. They recall that the military introduced them to people from different walks of life, people whom they otherwise would never have had an opportunity to know. "You learn arrogance in the Ivy League," says a former army lieutenant who graduated from Princeton and is now a Harvard graduate student. "You learn humility in the Army, because some guy from a college you've never heard of knows a lot more than you do."[58]

Proponents and opponents of national service alike would probably agree that military service exudes a masculine mystique. Military personnel are as susceptible to this mystique as anyone else—perhaps more so, because they actually go and sign up. In a 1989 study, 50 percent of the Marine recruits polled at Camp Pendelton claimed to have joined the Marines because of images they saw in John Wayne movies.[59] Although military personnel suffer through basic training, they often react passionately against suggestions that it be made easier. Marines, especially, value their experiences, seeing them as rites of passage to masculine adulthood. "They believe that other soldiers in other, softer services achieve such manhood cheaply and have no hold on authenticity," notes one expert.[60]

Civilians are also susceptible to this mystique. It faded during Vietnam, when long hair was in vogue and signs of traditional masculinity were out of style. Avoiding military service carried no stigma. But years later some men began to rethink their dismissal of military service. As early as 1981, journalist Michael Blumenthal, who had avoided the draft by deliberately inflaming his asthma, wrote about his peers who had served: "I'm not at all sure that they didn't turn out to be better *men*, in the best sense of the word."[61] Blumenthal suggested that perhaps there was something to be gained from military service. "It has to do with learning that life involves more than being concerned with—indeed, being obsessed by—our own skins."[62] Others in the early 1980s began to notice the same thing. "I thought anyone who was in the Army was crazy," a 28-year-old told a reporter in 1982. "But now I have a dream about being in the Army and going to Vietnam...I'm doing the things that men are expected to do and doing them well. Men who have been in the service seem to have done more than me. There's a tinge of awe...."[63]

During the Gulf War almost a decade later, Roger Rosenblatt reflected on his Vietnam deferments: "Looking back, I wish I had chosen [to serve]. I'm not talking about mere guilt—though there's plenty of that. I'm not even talking about national duty....I'm talking about the moral logic that says, or in my opinion ought to say: Everybody's war, everybody's risk." And in 2003, a young lawyer reflecting on the events of September 11 wrote that examples of military honor "have made many Americans, including me, beam with pride. But at the same time, I have never felt so ashamed—ashamed that I myself have failed to serve my country. Speaking to friends and peers, I've discovered that I'm not alone in feeling this sense of guilt."[64]

Some critics of military service, however, note that the emphasis on masculinity implies a devaluation of women. "War, and the prospect of war while in peacetime, is at least partly responsible for the subordinate position of women in society in all periods,"[65] writes psychoanalyst Theodore Nadelson. Historians of war and gender note that military service during war transforms notions of masculinity and femininity. Contemporary advocates of gender integration in the armed services argue that expanding women's role will also expand notions of women's equality in public life in general. As long as women do not defend society, it is argued, they will not be perceived as fully deserving of equality.

The question of the role of the armed forces in American society is a complex one, and the issues raised here are just a few of the ones confronting military personnel and civilians alike. Nevertheless, in spite of widespread disapproval of the war in Iraq, public support for America's military forces remains firm. The armed forces today are one of the nation's most respected institutions, and military service has been part of the lives of millions of Americans.

APPENDIX: U.S. MILITARY RANKS AND UNITS

Modern U.S. Military Ranks

Pay Scale	Army	Air Force	Marines	Navy and Coast Guard
Commissioned Officers				
**	General of the Army	General of the Air Force		Fleet Admiral
O-10	Army Chief of Staff	Air Force Chief of Staff	Commandant of the Marine Corps	Chief of Naval Operations
	General	General	General	Commandant of the Coast Guard
				Admiral
O-9	Lieutenant General	Lieutenant General	Lieutenant General	Vice Admiral
O-8	Major General	Major General	Major General	Rear Admiral (Upper Half)
O-7	Brigadier General	Brigadier General	Brigadier General	Rear Admiral (Commodore)
O-6	Colonel	Colonel	Colonel	Captain
O-5	Lieutenant Colonel	Lieutenant Colonel	Lieutenant Colonel	Commander
O-4	Major	Major	Major	Lieutenant Commander
O-3	Captain	Captain	Captain	Lieutenant
O-2	1st Lieutenant	1st Lieutenant	1st Lieutenant	Lieutenant, Junior Grade
O-1	2nd Lieutenant	2nd Lieutenant	2nd Lieutenant	Ensign

Warrant Officers

W-5	Master Warrant Officer 5		Chief Warrant Officer 5	Master Warrant Officer
W-4	Warrant Officer 4		Chief Warrant Officer 4	Warrant Officer 4
W-3	Warrant Officer 3		Chief Warrant Officer 3	Warrant Officer 3
W-2	Warrant Officer 2		Chief Warrant Officer 2	Warrant Officer 2
W-1	Warrant Officer 1		Warrant Officer	Warrant Officer 1

Non-Commissioned Officers

Special	Sergeant Major of the Army	Chief Master Sergeant of the Air Force	Sergeant Major of the Marine Corps	Master Chief Petty Officer of the Navy
E-9	Command Sergeant Major	First Sergeant (Chief Master Sergeant)	Sergeant Major	Master Chief Petty Officer
	Sergeant Major	Chief Master Sergeant	Master Gunnery Sergeant	
E-8	First Sergeant	First Sergeant (Senior Master Sergeant)	First Sergeant	Senior Chief Petty Officer
	Master Sergeant	Senior Master Sergeant	Master Sergeant	
E-7	Sergeant First Class	First Sergeant (Master Sergeant)	Gunnery Sergeant	Chief Petty Officer
		Master Sergeant		
E-6	Staff Sergeant	Technical Sergeant	Staff Sergeant	Petty Officer First Class
E-5	Sergeant	Staff Sergeant	Sergeant	Petty Officer Second Class
E-4	Corporal		Corporal	Petty Officer Third Class

Enlisted Personnel

E-4	Specialist	Senior Airman		
E-3	Private First Class	Airman First Class	Lance Corporal	Seaman

E-2	Private	Airman	Private First Class	Seaman Apprentice
E-1	Private (Recruit)	Airman Basic	Private	Seaman Recruit

The table shows current ranks in the U.S. military service branches, but it can also serve as a fair guide for the entire twentieth century. Ranks in foreign military services may vary significantly, even when the same names are used. Many European countries use the rank Field Marshal, for example, which is not used in the United States.

Blank indicates there is no rank at that pay grade.

**Ranks used infrequently during wartime.

Used by permission of Professor Emil Pocock, Professor of History and American Studies, Eastern Connecticut State University.

Unit Size (U.S. Army in the Late-Twentieth Century)

Unit	Approximate Personnel	Composition	Typical Commander
Army	100,000	2+ corps, HQ	General
Corps	30,000+	2+ divisions	Lieutenant General
Division	15,000+	3 brigades, HQ, support units	Major General
Brigade	4,500+	3+ regiments, HQ	Brigadier General
Regiment	1,500+	2+ battalions, HQ	Colonel
Battalion	700	4+ companies, HQ	Lieutenant Colonel
Company	175	4 platoons, HQ	Captain
Platoon	40	4 squads	Lieutenant
Squad	10		Staff Sergeant

The size, composition, and leadership of military units vary with time, place, and circumstances. The composition of fully authorized units (reflected in this table) will vary, especially during in periods of active engagement. Use this as a general guide for the late-twentieth century U.S. Army. The composition of foreign military units may deviate considerably from U.S. practices.

Used by permission of Professor Emil Pocock, Professor of History and American Studies, Eastern Connecticut State University.

NOTES

INTRODUCTION

1. Department of Defense, *Quadrennial Defense Review Report* (Washington, D.C.: U.S. Government Printing Office, September 30, 2001), iii.

2. Peter Karsten, ed., *The Military in America: From the Colonial Era to the Present* (New York: Free Press, 1986), 59.

3. Ibid., 96.

4. George Q. Flynn, *Conscription and Democracy: The Draft in France, Great Britain, and the United States* (Westport, CT and London: Greenwood Press, 2002), 75.

5. Sheila Nataraj Kirby and Harry J. Thie, *Enlisted Personnel Management: A Historical Perspective* (Santa Monica, CA: Rand, 1996), xvi.

CHAPTER 1

1. Chad Fifer, "Advertising Solutions for the U.S. Military's Recruitment Problems," *The Simon,* March 30, 2005.

2. Navy Recruiting Command, "CNRC Stats," http://www.cnrc.Navy.mil/.

3. Edward M. Coffman, *The Old Army* (New York: Oxford University Press, 1986), 13.

4. Ibid., 14.

5. Allan Millett and Peter Maslowski, *For the Common Defense: A Military History of the United States of America,* rev. & expanded ed. (New York: Free Press, 1994), 277.

6. Coffman, *The Old Army,* 14.

7. U.S. General Accounting Office, *Military Recruiting: DOD Needs to Establish Objectives and Measures to Better Evaluate Advertising's Effectiveness* (Washington, D.C.: U.S. Government Printing Office, 2003).

8. Dave Griffiths, "Atten-Hut! The Army's Ad Business Is Up for Grabs," *Business Week,* November 17, 1986.

9. Leonard Shyles and John E. Hocking, "The Army's 'Be All You Can Be' Campaign," *Middle East Review* 16, no. 3 (Spring 1990): 369–83.

10. Philip H. Dougherty, "Advertising; Campaign By Ayer," *New York Times,* December 24, 1980.

11. Ibid.

12. Bill Keller, "The Pentagon: Now It's Not Just 'I Want You' But 'You Need Us,'"*New York Times,* January 19, 1985.

13. Ibid.

14. Griffiths, "Atten-Hut!"

15. Ibid.

16. Philip H. Dougherty, "Advertising; Marines Switch Recruiting Theme Line," *New York Times,* October 11, 1984.

17. Keller, "The Pentagon."

18. Stefan Wray, "Cross Into the Blue: Austin's GSD&M Markets Air Force," *Iconmedia.org,* April 8, 2003, http://www.iconmedia.org/articles/article 007.php.

19. Staff Sgt. Alicia K. Borlik, "Recruitment Ads: New Strategies, New Messages," *American Forces Information Service,* June 8, 2004.

20. Beth Snyder Bulik, "Operation Army Advertising," *American Way Magazine,* September 1, 2003.

21. James Dao, "Ads Now Seek Recruits for 'An Army of One,'" *New York Times,* January 10, 2001.

22. Lucian K. Truscott IV, "Marketing an Army of Individuals," *New York Times,* January 12, 2001.

23. John Leo, "New Slogan Belies What the Army Really Is," January 15, 2001, www.johnleo.com/2001/01/15/new-slogan-belies-what-the-army-really-is/.

24. Ibid.

25. Thomas E. White, Secretary of the Army, "Special Briefing on Army Recruiting Results," September 4, 2001, http://www.defenselink.mil/tran scripts/2001/t09052001_t904army.html

26. Holly Selders, "Recruiting the Next Generation: You Can Do It," May 11, 2006, *Lifelines Services Network,* http://www.lifelines.navy.mil/lifelines/Military Life/JoiningtheNavy/Recriuter/RECRUITINGTHENEXTGENERATION

27. Ibid.

28. Lev Grossman. "The Army's Killer App: Game Designers go to Boot Camp to Perfect the Video Game the Military Uses to Entice New Recruits," *Time* 165, no. 9 (February 28, 2005): 43.

29. Ibid.

30. Gaming Is More Than Just Play for Military Services," *infowars.com,* July 8, 2006, http://www.infowars.com/articles/military/gaming_more_than_play_for_mil_services.htm.

31. "Army Uses NASCAR in Recruiting Effort," November 26, 2004, http://gnn.tv/headlines/283/Army_Uses_NASCAR_in_Recruiting_Effort.

32. Matt Crossman, "Exploring the NASCAR–Navy Relationship," Reprinted from *Sporting Times* in the *Navy Recruiter,* April 2006.

33. "Army Uses NASCAR in Recruiting Effort."

34. James W. Crawley, "Gentlemen, Rethink Your Logos: The Coast Guard and the Marines Are Dropping NASCAR Sponsorships," *Richmond Times Dispatch,* November 15, 2006.

35. Richard J. Newman, et al., "A Few Good Women,"*U.S. News and World Report* 129, no. 1 (July 3, 2000): 8.

36. National Research Council, Committee on the Youth Population and Military Recruitment, Paul Sackett, and Anne S. Mavor, eds., "Attitudes, Aptitudes, and Aspirations of American Youth: Implications for Military Recruiting" (Washington, D.C.: National Academy Press, 2003), 219.

37. Wayne Specht, "Air Force Offering Incentives in Its Effort to Find Recruiters,"*Stars and Stripes,* July 2, 2006.

38. U.S. General Accounting Office, *Military Recruiting.*

39. "Basic Recruiter Course," *Marine Corp Recruiting Command,* https://www.marines.usmc.mil/RS/BRC/BRCs.htm.

40. Sackett and Mavor, "Attitudes, Aptitudes, and Aspirations of American Youth," 224.

41. Marine Corps Command, "Marines Wanted for duty," www.usmc.mil/marinelink/mcn2000.nsf/main5.

42. Sackett and Mavor, "Attitudes, Aptitudes, and Aspirations of American Youth," 218.

43. Damien Cave, "Growing Problem for Military Recruiters: Parents," *New York Times,* June 3, 2005.

44. Tommy Nguyen, "School Recruiters Meet Resistance," *The Christian Science Monitor,* December 19, 2003.

45. George Fisher, "Power Over Principle," *New York Times,* September 7, 2002.

46. Denny Boyles, "New Battle Lines Separate Military Recruiters, Foes," *Fresno Bee,* February 26, 2007.

47. Transcript, "Talk of the Nation" with Neal Conan, National Public Radio, May 10, 2005.

48. Michael Bronner, "The Recruiters' War," *Vanity Fair,* September 2005.

49. Bruce R. Orvis, Narayan Sastry and Laurie L. McDonald, "Military Recruiting Outlook: Recent Trends in Enlistment Propensity and Conversion of Potential Enlisted Supply" (Santa Monica, CA: Rand, 1996).

50. Robert H. Barrow, "Understand Core Motivation of America's Youth for Joining Military Forces," *Tampa Tribune,* January 23, 2000.

51. Orvis, Sastry, and McDonald, "Military Recruiting Outlook," 41–42.

52. Barrow, "Understand Core Motivation."

53. Sackett and Mavor, "Attitudes, Aptitudes, and Aspirations of American Youth," 208.

54. Kurt Andersen, "In Washington: Missionary," *Time* 123 (May 14, 1984): 9.

55. Jeremy Kirk, "At Manhattan Recruiting Center, Attacks Pique Enlistment Interest," *Stars and Stripes,* July 2, 2006.

56. Kirby and Thie, *Enlisted Personnel Management,* xxii.

57. Coffman, *The Old Army,* 331.

58. See William L. Hauser, *America's Army in Crisis: A Study in Civil–Military Relations* (Baltimore, Johns Hopkins University Press, 1973).

59. Martin Binkin, *America's Volunteer Military: Progress and Prospects* (Washington, D.C.: Brookings Institution, 1984), 8.

60. Jim Mannion, "Pentagon Defends Quality of Military Recruits," *Agence France Presse*, October 10, 2006.

61. David McLemore, "Immigrant Soldiers Serve the U.S.," *Dallas Morning News*, November 28, 2006.

CHAPTER 2

1. Peter Thompson, *An Insider's Guide to Military Basic Training: A Recruit's Guide of Advice and Hints to Make It Through Boot Camp*, 2nd ed. (Universal Publishers, 2003), 6.

2. James Woulfe, *Into the Crucible* (Novato, CA: Presidio Press, 2000), 23-24.

3. James Kitfield, "Boot Camp Lite," *Government Executive Magazine*, February 1, 1998.

4. Rhonda Burke, "New GQ Drills Bring Additional Realism, Intensity to Boot Camp," *Navy Newsstand*, October 1, 2002, www.news.navy.mil.

5. Daniel Da Cruz, *Boot*, Reprint (New York: St. Martin's Press, 1987), 43.

6. Thompson, *An Insider's Guide to Military Basic Training*, 46–55.

7. Da Cruz, *Boot*, 69.

8. Ibid.

9. Kitfield, "Boot Camp Lite."

10. J.F. Leahy, *Honor, Courage, Commitment: Navy Boot Camp* (Annapolis, MD: Naval Institute Press, 2002), x–xi.

11. Thompson, *An Insider's Guide to Military Basic Training*, 131.

12. Ibid., 132.

13. Jim Garamone, "Tougher Sailors from the Start," Armed Forces Press Service, January 9, 2004.

14. Francis O'Connor, "Injuries During Marine Corps Officer Basic Training," *Military Medicine*, July 2000, 1.

15. Pat Dev, "We Are All Volunteers in this Army," February 2006, http://onlyvolunteers.blogspot.com

16. Dennis Drehner, "Death Among U.S. Air Force Basic Trainees, 1956 to 1996," Military Medicine, December 1999.

17. Leahy, *Honor, Courage, Commitment*, 183.

18. Woulfe, *Into the Crucible*, 25.

19. P. J. Budahn, *What to Expect in the Military: A Practical Guide for Young People, Parents and Counselors* (Westport, CT: Greenwood Press, 2000), 8.

CHAPTER 3

1. Jeffrey A. McNally, *The Adult Development of Career Army Officers* (New York: Praeger, 1991).

2. *The History of Officer Social Origins, Selection, Education and Training Since the Eighteenth Century: An Introductory Bibliography* (Colorado Springs, CO: U.S. Air Force Academy Library, 1996), 336.

3. Nathaniel Fick, *One Bullet Away: The Making of a Marine Officer* (Boston: Houghton Mifflin, 2005).

4. See, for example, William H. McMichael, *The Mother of All Hooks: The Story of the U.S. Navy's Tailhook Scandal* (New Brunswick, NJ: Transaction Publishers, 1997).

5. Michael R. Belknap, *The Vietnam War on Trial: The My Lai Massacre and the Court-Martial of Lieutenant Calley* (Lawrence: University Press of Kansas, 2002).

6. Michael Bilton and Kevin Sim, *Four Hours in My Lai* (New York: Viking, 1992).

7. Oretha D. Swartz, *Service Etiquette,* 4th ed. (Annapolis, MD: Naval Institute Press, 1988).

8. Martin L. Van Creveld, *The Training of Officers: From Military Professionalism to Irrelevance* (New York: Free Press, 1990).

9. Joseph J. Ellis, *School for Soldiers: West Point and the Profession of Arms* (New York: Oxford University Press, 1974), 94.

10. David Lipsky, *Absolutely American: Four Years at West Point* (New York: Vintage, 2004).

11. Van Creveld, *The Training of Officers,* 2.

12. Ellis, *School for Soldiers.*

13. Office of the Dean, United States Military Academy at West Point, "Educating Future Army Officers for a Changing World," December 23, 2006, http://www.dean.usma.edu/academics.cfm, 7.

14. Van Creveld, *The Training of Officers,* 13.

15. Stephen E. Ambrose, *Duty, Honor, Country: A History of West Point* (Baltimore: Johns Hopkins University Press, 1999).

16. James S. Robbins, *Last in Their Class: Custer, Pickett and the Goats of West Point* (New York: Encounter Books, 2006).

17. Peter Karsten, *The Naval Aristocracy: The Golden Age of Annapolis and the Emergence of Modern American Navalism* (New York: Free Press, 1972).

18. William B. Skelton, *An American Profession of Arms: The Army Officer Corps, 1784–1861* (Lawrence: University Press of Kansas, 1992).

19. Robert F. Collins, *Reserve Officers Training Corps: Campus Pathways to Service Commissions,* 1st ed. (New York: Rosen Pub. Group, 1986).

20. Carol Barkalow with Andrea Raab, *In the Men's House: An Inside Account of Life in the Army by One of West Point's First Female Graduates* (New York: Poseidon Press, 1990); Sharon H. Disher, *First Class: Women Join the Ranks at the Naval Academy* (Annapolis: Naval Institute Press, 1998); and Judith Stiehm, *Bring Me Men and Women: Mandated Change at the U.S. Air Force Academy* (Berkeley: University of California Press, 1981).

21. Susan D. Hosek, *Minority and Gender Differences in Officer Career Progression* (Santa Monica, CA: Rand, 2001).

CHAPTER 4

1. Robert E. Harkavy, "Thinking About Basing," *Naval War College Review* 58, no. 3 (Summer 2005): 13–45.

2. James R. Blaker, *United States Overseas Basing: An Anatomy of the Dilemma* (New York: Praeger, 1990), 21.

3. Ibid., 57.

4. Ibid., 29.

5. "Base Realignment and Closure (BRAC)," globalsecurity.org, September 11, 2005, http://www.globalsecurity.org/military/facility/brac.htm.

6. John D. Banusiewicz, "Conference Addresses Issues Raised by 2005 BRAC Results" *American Forces Press Service*, May 3, 2006, http://www.defenselink.mil /news/May2006/20060503_5003.html.

7. Leonard Wong and Stephen Gerras, *CU@ The FOB: How the Forward Operating Base Is Changing the Life of Combat Soldier* (Carlisle, PA: Strategic Studies Institute, Army War College, 2006), 1.

8. Edward M. Coffman, *The Old Army*, 313.

9. William A. Dobak, *Fort Riley and Its Neighbors: Military Money and Economic Growth, 1853–1895* (Norman: University of Oklahoma Press, 1998), 5.

10. I have written about the reaction against U.S. military bases overseas in *American Soldiers Overseas: The Global Military Presence* (Westport, CT: Praeger, 2004).

11. For a clear example of this, see Catherine Lutz's examination of Fayette-ville, North Carolina, host to Fort Bragg. Catherine Lutz, *Homefront: A Military City and the American Twentieth Century* (Boston: Beacon Press, 2001).

12. See Shirley A. Gilley, *Closing Down the American Base at Adak, Alaska: The Social and Psychological Trauma of Relocating Military Families* (Lewiston: Mellen University Press, 1997).

13. Ronald B. Bailey and Earl R. Wingrove, III, "Effects of the DoD Drawdown on Small Business: Supporting Material for Adjusting to the Drawdown: Report of the Defense Conversion Commission" (Bethesda, MD: Logistics Management Institute; Washington, D.C.: Department of Defense, 1993).

14. "Office of Economic Adjustment," September 18, 2006, http://www.oea. gov/oeaweb.nsf/Home?OpenForm

15. Louis Jacobson, "There Is Life After a Military Base Closes," *National Journal* 32, no. 17 (April 22, 2000): 1292; Mark A. Hooker and Michael M. Knetter, "Measuring the Economic Effects of Military Base Closures," *Economic Inquiry* 39, no. 4 (October 2001): 583–99.

16. Ralph Vartabedia, "Base Closings Often Leave Live Explosives, Polluted Lands," *Seattle Times*, April 12, 2005.

17. Jim Carlton, "Another Shade of Green: Army Aids Nature Lovers," *Wall Street Journal*, January 24, 2007.

18. "MCB Camp Lejeune, N.C.," http://www.lejeune.usmc.mil/mcb/ index.asp.

19. "Team Bliss," https://www.bliss.army.mil/

20. "Call to Duty: Boots on the Ground," http://pao.hood.army.mil/

21. "Welcome to Fort Bragg: 'Home of the Airborne,'" http://www.bragg. army.mil/

22. "Ramstein Air Base," http://www.bragg.army.mil/

23. "U.S. Marines in Japan," http://www.okinawa.usmc.mil/

24. See Martha Summerhayes, *Vanished Arizona: Recollections of the Army Life of a New England Woman* (Chicago: Lakeside Press, 1939).

25. Edward Coffman, *The Regulars: The American Army 1898–1941* (Cambridge, MA: Belknap Press of Harvard University Press, 2004), 296–98, 365–67.

26. Ibid., 324–71.

27. Military Housing: Opportunities that Should be Explored to Improve Housing and Reduce Costs for Unmarried Junior Servicemembers (Washington, D.C.: U.S. General Accounting Office, 2003), http://purl.access.gpo.gov/GPO/LPS37308.

28. John Benner, "Military Aims to Improve Base Housing— and Morale; Private Sector Assists Renewal of Family Units," *Washington Post,* November 13, 2003.

29. Ellen Romano, "Uncle Sam Wants You to Manage His Housing," *Journal of Property Management* 64, no. 2 (March–April 1999): 30–36.

30. Peter Skirbunt, " Defense Commissary Agency Has 140-Year History, 231-Year Heritage," *The Military Family Network,* September 29, 2006, http://www.emilitary.org/article.php?aid=8195.

CHAPTER 5

1. Elaine Donnelly, "Army Consultant Hits 'Masculinist Culture,'" *Insight on the News* 13, no. 15 (April 28, 1997): 29–30.

2. Kirby and Thie, *Enlisted Personnel Management,* 2.

3. "Army Technology-Patriot Missile-Air Defense System," July 15, 2006, http://www.army-technology.com/projects/patriot/.

4. Sandra Jontz, "Exercises Will Help Determine Whether 'Light' Is Right for Army," *Stars and Stripes,* August 24, 2000.

5. Charlie Coon, "EUCOM Exercise Employs New Warfare Tactics," *Stars and Stripes,* May 30, 2005.

6. Steve Mraz, "MPS Prep One Final Time in Germany Before Taking on the Real Thing," *Stars and Stripes,* July 10, 2005.

7. Charlie Coon, "U.S. Seeking to Aid Africa Without Massive Footprint," *Stars and Stripes,* July 17, 2005.

8. Fred Knapp, "Cobra Gold Troops Win Hearts and Minds with Medical, Dental Care," *Stars and Stripes,* May 30, 2001.

9. Ben Murray, "Training Center Creates Illusion to Help GIs Prepare for Real Battle," *Stars and Stripes,* January 30, 2005.

10. Seth Robson, "Good Pay Attracts Many Role Players," *Stars and Stripes,* March 23, 2006.

11. "Subject: Report on Staff Trip to Army Training Facilities," *Defense and the National Interest,* July 25, 2006, http://www.d-n-i.net/fcs/trip_rpt_army_tng.htm.

12. Gordon Witkin, "The Fall and Rise of the Fourth Division,"*U.S. News & World Report* 97 (September 17, 1984): 28.

13. Seth Robson, "Tank Crews Qualify for Gunnery Duties," *Stars and Stripes,* December 8, 2003.

14. Murray, "Training Center Creates Illusion to Help GIs Prepare for Real Battle."

15. Jeremy Kirk, "Apache Copter Training Helps Soldiers in Air, on Ground," *Stars and Stripes,* February 15, 2002.

16. Scott Schonauer, "Spangdahlem Pilots, Crews Feel 'Surge' of a Hectic Week," *Stars and Stripes,* March 12, 2005.

17. Charlie Coon, "Communications Is Focus of Combined Endeavor 2006," *Stars and Stripes,* May 7, 2006.

18. Marni McEntee, "No Room for Slow Moves in Airlift Exercise," *Stars and Stripes,* March 16, 2002.

19. Jennifer H. Svan, "U.S., JASDF Units Practice Gate-Guard Duty at Misawa," *Stars and Stripes,* March 18, 2005.

20. Jan Wesner Chiles, "Yongsan Training Gives PAOs Practice in Dealing with the News Media," *Stars and Stripes,* March 29, 2002.

21. Rick Emert, "54th Engineers Training for Iraq Return," *Stars and Stripes,* April 3, 2005.

22. Senate Armed Services Committee, "Sen. Carl Levin Holds a Hearing on the Current and Future Readiness of the Army and Marine Corps," Washington, D.C., February 17, 2007. Transcript: Congressional Quarterly.

23. William S. Cohen, Department of Defense, *Report of the Quadrennial Defense Review,* (Washington, D.C.: U.S. Government Printing Office, September 30, 1997), 32.

24. Ron Harris, "Combat Deaths Reflect Changing Role of Guard. Their Presence in Iraq Represents the Largest Long-Term Deployment of the Nation's Reserves in 50 Years," *St. Louis Post Dispatch,* July 24, 2005.

25. John O. Marsh, Jr., "Personnel: Active and Reserve Forces," *Annals of the American Academy of Political and Social Science* 517 (September 1991): 100.

26. Rick Emert, "Tool Time for Reserve, Guard Troops in Germany," *Stars and Stripes,* August 6, 2002.

27. David Wood and Harry Esteve, "National Guard Stretched to the Limit," *The Sunday Oregonian,* June 12, 2005.

28. David Josar, "From Weekend Warrior to Full-Time Fighter. Some Reservists Sent to Iraq Question Equity in Deployments, Treatment," *Stars and Stripes,* October 18, 2003, Special Series: 5.

29. Sarah Kershaw, "Governors Tell of War's Impact on Local Needs," *New York Times,* July 20, 2004.

30. Harris, "Combat Deaths Reflect Changing Role of Guard."

31. Matt Kelley, "Contractors, Military in 'Bidding War,'" *USA TODAY,* July 31, 2005.

32. Public Broadcasting Service, "Frequently Asked Questions," PBS, June 21, 2005, Jul 25, 2006, http://www.pbs.org/wgbh/pages/frontline/shows/warriors/faqs/.

33. William D. Hartung, "Outsourcing Is Hell," *The Nation* 278, no. 22 (June 7, 2004): 6.

34. U.S. Government Accounting Office, *Rebuilding Iraq: Actions Needed to Improve Use of Private Security Providers* (Washington, D.C.: U.S. Government Accounting Office, 2005).

35. Joseph Giordono, "Contractors Do More than Sling Troops' Chow," *Stars and Stripes,* March 10, 2003.

36. Doug Brooks, "Thinking Big: War Inc," *Boston Globe,* October 19, 2003.

37. Ibid.

38. Public Broadcasting Service, "Frequently Asked Questions."

39. P.W. Singer, "Nation Builders and Low Bidders in Iraq," *New York Times,* June 15, 2004.

40. U.S. Government Accounting Office, *Rebuilding Iraq.*

41. Leslie Wayne, "America's For-Profit Secret Army," *New York Times,* October 13, 2002.

42. Seymour M. Hersh, "Torture at Abu Ghraib," *New Yorker,* May 10, 2004.

43. Bureau of Labor Statistics, U.S. Department of Labor, "Federal Government, Excluding the Postal Service," *Career Guide to Industries,* 2006–07 ed., July 25, 2006, http://www.bls.gov/oco/cg/cgs041.htm.

44. Coffman, *The Regulars,* 71–72.

45. Ibid., 86.

46. Martin Binkin and Mark J. Eitelberg, *Blacks and the Military, (Studies in Defense Policy)* (Washington, D.C.: Brookings Institution Press, 1982), 14.

47. Ibid., 24.

48. Ibid., 35.

49. Aline O. Quester and Curtis L. Gilroy, "Women and Minorities in America's Volunteer Military," *Contemporary Economic Policy* 20, no. 2 (April 2002): 111–21.

50. Binkin and Eitelberg, *Blacks and the Military,* 51.

51. Quester and Gilroy, "Women and Minorities in America's Volunteer Military," 119.

52. Charles C. Moskos and John Sibley Butler, *All That We Can Be: Black Leadership and Racial Integration the Army Way* (New York: Basic Books, 1996), 7.

53. Margaret C. Harrell *Barriers to Minority Participation in Special Operations Forces* (Santa Monica, CA: Rand, 1999), 85.

54. Margaret C. Harrell, Megan K. Beckett, Chiaying Sandy Chien, and Jerry M. Sollinger, *The Status of Gender Integration in the Military: Analysis of Selected Occupations* (Santa Monica, CA: Rand, 2003).

55. Kim Field and John Nagl, "Combat Roles for Women: A Modest Proposal," *Parameters* 31, no. 2 (Summer 2001): 74.

56. Leora N. Rosen, Paul D. Bliss, Kathleen A. Wright, and Robert K. Gifferd, "Gender Composition and Group Cohesion in U.S. Army Units: A Comparison Across Five Studies," *Armed Forces & Society* 25, no. 3 (Spring 1999): 365–77.

57. Judith Hicks Stiehn, "Army Opinions About Women in the Army," *Gender Issues* 16, no. 3 (Summer 1998): 88.

58. Jennifer Boldry, Wendy Wood, and Deborah A. Kashy, "Gender Stereotypes and the Evaluation of Men and Women in Military Training," *Journal of Social Issues* 57, no. 4 (Winter 2001): 689–706.

59. Donnelly, "Army Consultant Hits 'Masculinist Culture,'" 29–30.

60. Juanita M. Firestone and Richard J. Harris, "Sexual Harassment in the U.S. Military: Individualized and Environmental Contexts," *Armed Forces & Society* 21, no. 1 (Fall 1994): 25–44; Leora N. Rosen and Lee Martin, "Sexual Harassment, Cohesion, and Combat Readiness in U.S. Army Support Units," *Armed Forces & Society*, 24, no. 2 (Winter 1997): 221–45.

61. Firestone and Harris, *Sexual Harassment in the U.S. Military: Individualized and Environmental Contexts*, 25–44.

62. Sharon Cohen, "Women Take on Major Battlefield Roles," *Associated Press Online,* December 3, 2006.

63. Gail Burton, "Report: More Gay Linguists Discharged than First Thought," *Associated Press*, January 13, 2005.

64. Donna Miles, "Homosexual Discharge Rates Drop," *American Forces Press Service*, February 27, 2005.

CHAPTER 6

1. Jeremy Kirk, "Slot Machines Pay MWR Bills, But Some Worry About Effects on Servicemembers," *Stars and Stripes*, March 18, 2001.

2. Anthony Burgos, "Cappuccino, Aerobics, Weight Rooms, Salad Bars ... Welcome to Today's Navy," *Stars and Stripes*, January 6, 2002.

3. Terry Boyd, "Outdoor Rec Program Set to Keep Baumholder Busy," *Stars and Stripes*, December 5, 2005.

4. Seth Robson, "MWR Surveys Soldiers in S. Korea About Favorite Off-Duty Activities," *Stars and Stripes*, December 28, 2004.

5. Seth Robson, "Army Improving Korea Area I Base Bars so Soldiers Will Party on Post," *Stars and Stripes*, January 29, 2005.

6. Joseph Giordono, "Recreational Activities Program Shows Yokosuka Sailors a REAL Good Time," *Stars and Stripes*, January 27, 2002.

7. Greg Tyler and Joe Giordono, "Bases Hope Added Activities Keep Troops from Mischief," *Stars and Stripes*, December 29, 2002.

8. Burgos, "Cappuccino, Aerobics, Weight Rooms, Salad Bars ... Welcome to Today's Navy."

9. USO, "History of the USO," http://www.uso.org/whoweare/ourproud-history/historyoftheuso/.

10. Mason Booth, "America's Veterans Honored Daily by Red Cross Services," American Red Cross, November 8, 2002, http://www.redcross.org/news/af/veterans/021108veterans.html

11. University of Maryland University College, http://www.umuc.edu/index.html

12. Rick Emert, "At Home or at War, Degree Opportunities Never Out of Reach for Servicemembers," *Stars and Stripes*, July 10, 2005.

13. Phaedra Brotherton, "eArmyU Improves Educational Access for Soldiers: But HBCUs May Be Missing Out Due to Distance Learning Incapacity," *Black Issues in Higher Education* 19, no. 1 (February 28, 2002): 32–35.

14. Ibid., 32–35.

15. Seth Robson, "2nd ID Orientation Will Feature More South Korean Culture," *Stars and Stripes*, February 10, 2005.

16. Robert M. Bray, Mary Ellen Marsden, John R. Herbold, and Michael R. Peterson, "Progress Toward Eliminating Drug and Alcohol Abuse Among U.S. Military Personnel," *Armed Forces and Society* 18 (Summer 1992): 476–95.

17. Ibid., 479.

18. Ibid., 485.

19. Ibid., 486.

20. Sean E. Cobb, "Army, Air Force in Europe Battling Sharp Rise in Use of Club Drug Ecstasy," *Stars and Stripes*, January 27, 2002.

21. Allison Batdorff, "CNFJ Calls for 'Period of Reflection' After Fatal Beating," *Stars and Stripes*, January 8, 2006.

22. Greg Tyler and Joe Giordono, "Eye on Alcohol," *Stars and Stripes*, December 29, 2002.

23. Ibid.

24. Allison Batdorff, "CNFJ Issues Restrictions at Yokosuka in Bid to Curb Alcohol Abuse," *Stars and Stripes*, January 21, 2006.

25. Seth Robson, "Army Uses Activities, Education in Bid to Curb Alcohol Abuse in Korea's Area I," *Stars and Stripes*, December 19, 2004.

26. Ibid.

27. T.D. Flack, "Drinking Problems Decrease in Korea," *Stars and Stripes*, December 29, 2002.

28. Sandra Jontz, "Navy: No Second Chances for Drug Users, Alcohol Abusers," *Stars and Stripes*, September 17, 2005.

29. Sandra Jontz, "Navy Mulls Big Increase in Number of Sailors Screened for Drugs," *Stars and Stripes*, January 13, 2006.

30. James W. Crawley, "Military Sees Drug Use Rise Despite Tests and Warnings," *San Diego Union-Tribune*, July 29, 2002.

31. Paul von Zielbauer, "For U.S. Troops at War, Liquor Is Spur to Crime," *New York Times*, March 13, 2007.

32. Kendra Helmer, "Easy, Queasy Money: Cash, Health Risks Part of Philippine Sex Trade," *Stars and Stripes*, June 17, 2001.

33. Equality Now, *Annual Report 2003*, www.equalitynow.org.

34. Franklin Fisher, "Ban Is Lifted on Top Cat Club, Near Camp Humphries," *Stars and Stripes*, November 5, 2005.

35. Jeff Schogol, "Patronizing a Prostitute Is Now a Specific Crime for Service-members," *Stars and Stripes*, January 7, 2006.

36. David Allen, "Troops Mixed on Anti-Prostitution Proposal," *Stars and Stripes* September 25, 2004.

37. Helmer, "Easy, Queasy Money: Cash, Health Risks Part of Philippine Sex Trade."

38. Carlos Bongioanni and Dendra Helmer, "With or Without Visiting U.S. Troops, Sex Trade Is Thriving in Philippines," *Stars and Stripes*, June 18, 2001.

39. David Allen and Chivomi Sumida, "General Gets an Earful from Okinawa Governor," *Stars and Stripes*, August 13, 2003.

40. Erik Slavin, "Kadena Civilians Who Run Afoul of Law Face Swift Punishment from KDAP," *Stars and Stripes*, February 15, 2005.

41. Diana B. Henriques, "Captive Clientele: Financial Advice, at a Price," *New York Times*, July 20, 2004.

42. J.D. Heyman, "Stealing from Soldiers: After Serving, Some in the Military Come Home to Find Their Savings Gone," *People Weekly*, October 18, 2004.

43. Thomas Watkins, "Thousands of U.S. Troops Are Being Held Back from Overseas Duty Because of Debt," Associated Press Financial Wire, October 19, 2006.

44. Leo Shane III, "New Programs Offer Servicemembers Better Financial Advice," *Stars and Stripes*, February 17, 2006.

CHAPTER 7

1. Mady Wechsler Segal, "The Military and the Family as Greedy Institutions," *Armed Forces and Society* 13, no. 1 (Fall 1986): 9–38.

2. Cynthia Enloe, *Does Khaki Become You? The Militarization of Women's Lives* (Boston: Pandora, 1988).

3. D.M. Lagrone, "The Military Family Syndrome," *American Journal of Psychiatry* 135 (1978): 1040–43.

4. Casey Wardynski, *Military Compensation in the Age of Two-Income Households: Adding Spouses' Earnings to the Compensation Policy Mix* (Santa Monica, CA: Rand, 2000).

5. James A. Martin, Leora N. Rosen, and Linette R. Sparacino, eds., *The Military Family: A Practice Guide for Human Service Providers* (Praeger Publishers, 2000), 7.

6. Ellen McGowan Biddle, *Reminiscences of a Soldier's Wife* (Philadelphia: Press of J.B. Lippincott Company, 1907), 104.

7. Lydia Sloan Cline, *Today's Military Wife: Meeting the Challenges of Service Life*, 5th rev. ed. (Mechanicsburg, PA: Stackpole Books, 2003), 216.

8. United States, Office of the Chief of Staff, U.S. Army, Headquarters, Department of the Army, *White Paper, The Army Family 1983* (Washington, D.C.: U.S. Government Printing Office, 1983).

9. Gail L. Zellman, Anne S. Johansen, and Lisa S. Meredith, *Improving the Delivery of Military Child Care: An Analysis of Current Operations and New Approaches* (Santa Monica, CA: Rand, 1992).

10. Cardell S. Hunter, *Measuring the Impact of Military Family Programs on the Army* (Carlisle Barracks, PA: U.S. Army War College, 1987).

11. Lizette Alvarez, "Long Iraq Tours Can Make Home a Trying Front," *New York Times*, February 23, 2007.

12. Meredith Leyva, *Married to the Military: A Survival Guide for Military Wives, Girlfriends, and Women in Uniform* (New York: Fireside, 2003), 38.

13. Cline, *Today's Military Wife,* 99.

14. "Department of Defense Education Activity," http://www.dodea.edu/

15. Cline, *Today's Military Wife,* 217.

16. Martin, Rosen, and Sparacino, *The Military Family,* 45.

17. Sydney J. Freedberg Jr., "On Writers: An Officer's Kid on Unfamiliar Terrain," *National Journal* 33, no. 24 (June 16, 2001): 1824.

18. Elfrieda Berthiaume Shukert and Barbara Smith Scibetta, *War Brides of World War II* (Novato, CA: Presidio, 1988), 7.

19. Bok-Lim C. Kim and Michael R. Sawdey, *Women in Shadows: A Handbook for Service Providers Working with Asian Wives of U.S. Military Personnel* (LaJolla, CA: National Committee Concerned with Asian Wives of U.S. Servicemen, 1981).

20. Donna Miles, "Bicultural Marriages," *Soldier,* June 1989.

21. Ibid.

22. Ji-Yeon Yuh, *Beyond the Shadow of Camptown: Korean Military Brides in America* (New York: New York University Press, 2002), 173–85.

23. Jennifer Hickes, "When Race Makes no Difference: Marriage and the Military," *Social Forces* 83, no. 2 (December 2004): 731–58.

24. Kim and Sawdey, *Women in Shadows,* 17.

25. Seth Robson, "Area I to Offer Cultural Classes for Non-American Spouses," *Stars and Stripes,* July 6, 2004.

26. Manuel Roig-Franzia, "A Base Rocked by Violence: Deaths at Fort Bragg Stir Questions on Counseling, Army Culture," *Washington Post,* August 2, 2002.

27. Peter J. Mercier and Judith D. Mericer, eds., *Battle Cries on the Home Front: Violence in the Military Family* (Springfield, IL: C.C. Thomas, 2000), 9; William Walker, "Slayings Shock U.S. Army Base," *Toronto Star,* July 27, 2002.

28. Mark Thompson, "The Living Room War," *Time* 143, no. 21 (May 23, 1994): 48–52.

29. Ibid.

30. Paul B. Paulus, Dinesh Nagar, Timothy S. Larey, and Luz M. Camacho, "Environmental, Lifestyle, and Psychological Factors in the Health and Well-Being of Military Families," *Journal of Applied Social Psychology* 26 (1996): 2070.

31. Mercier and Mercier, *Battle Cries on the Home Front.*

32. Thompson, "The Living Room War."

33. Linda D. Kozaryn, "Task Force Calls for Crackdown on Domestic Violence," *American Forces Press Service,* March 9, 2001.

34. Thompson, "The Living Room War."

CHAPTER 8

1. Sheila Natarai Kirby and Harry J. Thie, "'Managing' the Enlisted Force: Whistling in the Wind?" *Armed Forces & Society* 24, no. 4 (1998): 567–88.

2. Tom Philpott, "Military Update: DoD Seeks Upgrade in Promotion Policies," *Stars and Stripes*, May 5, 2005.

3. Kirby and Thie, "'Managing' the Enlisted Force: Whistling in the Wind?"

4. Sandra Jontz, "GAO Report Blasts Air Force, Navy Re-enlistment Bonus Procedures," *Stars and Stripes*, November 27, 2002.

5. Lisa Burgess, "Army Reinstates Bonus for Active-Duty GIs Who Re-enlist While in War Zones," *Stars and Stripes*, December 19, 2003.

6. Leo III Shane, "GI Bill Benefits Might Extend to Spouses if Soldiers Re-enlist," *Stars and Stripes*, September 11, 2005.

7. Steve Liewer, "Re-enlisting? Army Tightens Rules, Suspends Programs as Ranks Swell," *Stars and Stripes*, January 26, 2003.

8. "Before the Board," *Military-net.com*, http://www.military-net.com/education/mpdbefore.html.

9. "Army to Begin Accelerating Officer Promotions," *Stars and Stripes*, May 19, 2002.

10. Center for Strategic and International Studies, Study Group on Professional Military Education, *Professional Military Education: An Asset for Peace and Progress* (Washington, D.C.: CSIS, March 1997), 6.

11. "Advanced Military Studies Program," http://www-cgsc.army.mil/sams/amsp/, October 11, 2006.

12. Ibid., 41.

13. Ibid., 42.

14. Ibid., 43.

15. Ibid., 44.

16. David W. Hogan, Jr., Arnold G. Fisch, Jr., and Robert K. Wright, Jr., *The Story of the Noncommissioned Officer Corps: The Backbone of the Army* (Washington, D.C.: Center of Military History, United States Army, 2003).

17. Daniel K. Elder, "Educating Noncommissioned Officers," Fort Riley, KS: July 1999, http://www.ncohistory.com.

18. Richard Halloran, "New Breed of Sergeants: Less Spit, More Polish," *New York Times*, September 3, 1987.

19. Hogan, Fisch, and Wright, *The Story of the Noncommissioned Officer Corps*, 27.

20. Elder, "Educating Noncommissioned Officers."

21. Sandra Jontz, "Navy to Open Its First CPO Academy," *Stars and Stripes*, March 30, 2006.

22. "Department of Veterans Affairs Fact Sheet," May 2006, http://www.vba.va.gov/benefit_facts/index.htm.

23. "Fact Sheet: Facts About the Department of Veterans Affairs, May 2006, http://www1.va.gov/opa/fact/vafacts.asp.

24. Phillip Longman, "The Best Care Anywhere," *Washington Monthly*, January–February 2005.

25. "Concurrent Receipt Pay Becomes Reality," Defense Finance and Accounting Service, December 16, 2003, http://www.dfes.mil/news/2003pressreleases/pressrelease0357.html.

26. Robert S. Dudney, "Behind New Furor Over Military Pensions," *U.S. News & World Report* 96 (January 9, 1984): 61–63.

27. Ibid.

28. Sydney Freedberg, Jr., "Smart Salute," *National Journal* 31, no. 5 (1999): 264.

29. "Fact Sheet: Facts About the Department of Veterans Affairs."

CHAPTER 9

1. John A. Lynn, *Battle: A History of Combat and Culture* (Cambridge, MA: Westview Press), 2004.

2. Gerald F. Linderman, *The World Within War: America's Combat Experience in World War II* (Cambridge: Harvard University Press, 1999), 2.

3. Ibid., 4.

4. Ibid., 7.

5. Peter S. Kindsvatter, *American Soldiers: Ground Combat in the World Wars, Korea, and Vietnam* (Lawrence: University Press of Kansas, 2003), 77.

6. Ibid., 79.

7. Linderman, *The World Within War,* 58–9.

8. Ibid., 13.

9. Ibid., 18.

10. Kindsvatter, *American Soldiers,* 81.

11. Linderman, *The World Within War,* 16.

12. Ibid., 63.

13. Michael D. Gambone, *The Greatest Generation Comes Home: The Veteran in American Society* (College Station: Texas A&M University Press, 2005), 40.

14. Linderman, *The World Within War,* 26.

15. Kindsvatter, *American Soldiers,* 91.

16. S.L.A. Marshall, *Men Against Fire: The Problem of Battle Command in Future War* (New York: Morrow, 1947).

17. Theodore Nadelson, *Trained to Kill: Soldiers at War* (Baltimore: Johns Hopkins University Press, 2005), 55.

18. Ibid., 92.

19. Dave Grossman, *On Killing: The Psychological Cost of Learning to Kill in War and Society* (Boston: Little, Brown, 1995), 237.

20. Linderman, *The World Within War,* 77.

21. Ibid., 83.

22. Jen Banbury, "Night Raid in Bagdad," in *Boots on the Ground: Stories of American Soldiers from Iraq and Afghanistan,* Clint Willis, ed. (New York: Thunder's Mouth Press, 2004), 268.

23. Evan Wright, *Generation Kill: Devil Dogs, Iceman, Captain America and the New Face of American War* (New York: G. P. Putnam's Sons, 2004), 16.

24. Kindsvatter, *American Soldiers,* 42.

25. Wright, *Generation Kill,* 16.

26. Evan Wright, "Not Much War, but Plenty of Hell," in *Boots on the Ground: Stories of American Soldiers from Iraq and Afghanistan,* Clint Willis, ed. (New York: Thunder's Mouth Press, 2004), 134.

27. Wright, *Generation Kill,* 16.

28. Kindsvatter, *American Soldiers,* 37.

29. Ibid., 34.

30. Robert M. Utley, *Frontiersmen in Blue: The United States Army and the Indian, 1848–1865* (Lincoln: University of Nebraska Press, 1967), 36.

31. Peter Schrijvers, *The Crash of Ruin: American Combat Soldiers in Europe During World War II* (New York: New York University Press, 1998), 158.

32. Ibid., 158.

33. Ibid., 161.

34. Ibid., 167.

35. Nadelson, *Trained to Kill,* 149.

36. Schrijvers, *The Crash of Ruin,* 178–79.

37. Nadelson, *Trained to Kill,* 154.

38. Ibid., 29.

39. Stephen Ambrose, *Band of Brothers: E Company, 506th Regiment, 101st Airborne from Normandy to Hitler's Eagle's Nest* (New York: Simon & Schuster, 2001).

40. Leora N. Rosen, Paul D. Bliss, Kathleen A. Wright, and Robert K. Gifferd, "Gender Composition and Group Cohesion in U.S. Army Units: A Comparison Across Five Studies," *Armed Forces & Society* 25, no. 3 (Spring 1999): 365–77.

41. M. C. Devilbiss, "Gender Integration and Unit Deployment: A Study of G.I. Jo," *Armed Forces & Society* 11 (Summer 1985): 540; Margaret C. Harrell and Laura L. Miller, *New Opportunities for Military Women: Effects upon Readiness, Cohesion, and Morale* (Santa Monica: CA: Rand, 1997), 95.

42. J.M.W. Binneveld, *From Shell Shock to Combat Stress: A Comparative History of Military Psychiatry* (Amsterdam: Amsterdam University Press, 1997).

43. Aphrodite Matsakis, *Vietnam Wives: Facing the Challenges of Life with Veterans Suffering Post-Traumatic Stress,* 2nd ed. (Baltimore, MD: The Sidran Press, 1996).

44. Nadelson, *Trained to Kill,* 90.

45. Ronald J. Glasser, *Wounded: Vietnam to Iraq* (New York: George Braziller, 2006), 85.

46. Gambone, *The Greatest Generation Comes Home,* 40.

47. Ibid.

48. Nadelson, *Trained to Kill,* 91.

49. Gregg Zoroya, "Psychologist: Navy Faces Crisis; Military Needs Mental Health Workers, Commander Says," *USA Today,* January 17, 2007.

50. "Long, Repeated Tours in Iraq Are Taking a Mental Toll on Soldiers," *Cox News Service,* November 15, 2006.

51. Gambone, *The Greatest Generation Comes Home,* 38.

52. Glasser, *Wounded,* 28.

53. Ibid., 27.

54. Ibid., 34.

55. Ibid., 22.

56. Ibid., 45.

57. Ibid., 48.

58. Ibid., 82.

59. Gambone, *The Greatest Generation Comes Home*, 8.

60. Ibid., 41.

61. Ron Kovic, *Born on the 4th of July* (New York: McGraw-Hill, 1976).

62. Glasser, *Wounded*, 49.

63. Nadelson, *Trained to Kill*, 97.

64. Ibid., 95.

65. Michael Sledge, *Soldier Dead: How We Recover, Identify, Bury, and Honor Our Military Fallen* (New York: Columbia University Press, 2005) 93.

66. Sledge, *Soldier Dead*, 36.

67. Ibid., 173.

68. Ibid., 41.

69. Ibid., 225.

70. Ibid., 61.

CHAPTER 10

1. Richard D. Hooker, Jr., "Soldiers of the State: Reconsidering American Civil–Military Relations," *Parameters* 33, no. 4 (2003): 4.

2. William Pfaff, "The Praetorian Guard," *The National Interest* 42 (Winter 2000): 57.

3. Matthew J. Morgan, "Army Recruiting and the Civil–Military Gap," *Parameters* 31, no. 2 (2001): 101.

4. Ibid.

5. John Lehman, "An Exchange on Civil–Military Relations," *The National Interest* 36 (Summer 1994): 24.

6. Don M. Snider, Robert F. Priest, and Felisa Lewis, "The Civilian–Military Gap and Professional Military Education at the Precommissioning Level," *Armed Forces & Society* 27, no. 2 (Winter 2001): 249.

7. Hooker, "Soldiers of the State: Reconsidering American Civil–Military Relations."

8. James F. Vesely, "The Gap Between Spit Shines and Sandals," *Seattle Times*, March 16, 2003.

9. Morgan, "Army Recruiting and the Civil–Military Gap."

10. Ibid.

11. Amy Waldman, "Strangers in Uniform," *Utne Reader* 14, no. 80 (March–April 1997): 65–67.

12. Charles Moskos, "From Citizens' Army to Social Laboratory," *The Wilson Quarterly* 17, no. 1 (1993): 83.

13. Sean Paige, "Military Might," *Insight on the News* 16, no. 21 (2000): 10.

14. See Charles C. Moskos and John Sibley Butler, *All That We Can Be: Black Leadership and Racial Integration the Army Way* (New York: Basic Books, 1996).

15. Sam C. Sarkesian and Robert E. Connor, Jr., *The U.S. Military Profession into the Twenty-First Century: War, Peace and Politics* (Portland, OR: Frank Cass, 1999).

16. Michael S. Sweeney, *The Military and the Press: An Uneasy Truce* (Evanston, IL: Northwestern University Press, 2006).

17. Mark Connelly and David Welch, *War and the Media: Reportage and Propaganda, 1900–2003* (New York: I.B. Tauris and St. Martin's Press, 2005).

18. For a discussion of this thesis, see Michael J. Arlen, *Living-Room War* (New York: Viking, 1969).

19. Connelly and Welch, *War and the Media*, xiii.

20. Todd Gitlin, *The Whole World Is Watching: Mass Media in the Making and Unmaking of the New Left* (Berkeley: University of California Press, 1980, 2003).

21. Charles C Moskos, John Allen Williams, and David R. Segal, eds., *The Postmodern Military: Armed Forces After the Cold War* (New York: Oxford University Press, 2000), 5.

22. For a look at Cronkite's analysis of the war, see Walter Cronkite, *A Reporter's Life* (New York: A.A. Knopf, 1996).

23. Moskos, Williams, and Segal, *The Postmodern Military*, 4.

24. William M. Hammond, *Reporting Vietnam: Media and Military at War* (Lawrence: University Press of Kansas, 1998), ix.

25. Moskos, Williams, and Segal, *The Postmodern Military*, 274-5.

26. Robert Wiener, *Live from Baghdad: Making Journalism History Behind the Lines* (New York: St. Martin's Griffin, 1992).

27. Connelly and Welch, *War and the Media*, iv.

28. Howard Tumbler and Jerry Palmer, *Media at War: The Iraq Crisis* (London, Thousand Oaks, CA, and New Delhi: Sage Publications, 2004), 26.

29. Nadelson, *Trained to Kill*, 105.

30. Stephen Crane, *Red Badge of Courage* (New York: Random House, 2000).

31. Ernst Junger, *Storm of Steel*, trans. Michael Hofmann (New York: Penguin Classics, 2004).

32. Erich Maria Remarque, *All Quiet on the Western Front* (New York: Vintage, 2005); Ernest Hemingway, *A Farewell to Arms* (New York: Scribner, 1995).

33. Gambone, *The Greatest Generation Comes Home*, 155.

34. Emmett Early, *The War Veteran in Film* (Jefferson, NC and London: McFarland & Company, Inc., Publishers, 2003), 9.

35. Katherine Kinney, *Friendly Fire: American Images of the Vietnam War* (Oxford: Oxford University Press, 2000), 4.

36. See, for example, Colby Buzzell, "My War," 2004-2005, http://cbftw.blogspot.com/.

37. G. Kurt Piehler, *Remembering War the American Way* (Washington, D.C.: Smithsonian Institution Press, 1995), 2.

38. Ibid., 51.

39. Ibid., 86.

40. Kristin Ann Hass, *Carried to the Wall: American Memory and the Vietnam Veterans Memorial* (Berkeley: University of California Press, 1998).

41. Tom M. Keane, Jr., "WWII Memorial Fails Both Past and Present," *Boston Globe,* June 25, 2004.

42. Andrew Bacevich, "Warrior Politics," *Atlantic Monthly* 299, no. 4 (May 2007): 26

43. Hooker, "Soldiers of the State: Reconsidering American Civil–Military Relations."

44. Colin L. Powell, with Joseph E. Persico, *My American Journey* (New York: Ballantine Books, 2003), 464.

45. Pfaff, "The Praetorian Guard."

46. Ibid.

47. Michael Lind, "Bush's Martyrs: Michael Lind Reveals Who Is Really Fighting in Iraq: Southerners Who, Unlike the Secularized Puritans of the American North-East and the Pacific Coast, Believe in Dying for Their Country," *New Statesman* 133, no. 4677 (2004): 20.

48. Hooker, "Soldiers of the State: Reconsidering American Civil–Military Relations."

49. See, for example, David M. Bland, "G.O.P. Should Check Helms' Competence," Letters, *New York Times,* November 29, 1994.

50. Cathy Young, "Martial Vices: Zell Miller's un-American View of the Armed Forces," *Reason* 36, no. 7 (2004): 17.

51. Bacevich, "Warrior Politics."

52. Hooker, "Soldiers of the State: Reconsidering American Civil–Military Relations."

53. Charles Rangel, "Should the Draft Be Reinstated? With U.S. Forces Stretched Thin and Many Reservists on Full-Time Duty, Some Urge a Draft for Reasons of Fairness and Practicality. Opponents Say It's Unnecessary and Dangerous," *Time* 162, no. 26 (2003): 101.

54. Meyer Kestnbaum, "Citizenship and Compulsory Military Service: The Revolutionary Origins of Conscription in the United States," *Armed Forces & Society* 27, no. 1 (2000): 7.

55. Michael Hedges, "With Army Stretched Thin, Could the U.S. Respond to a New Crisis? Retired General Says Deployments Put America in 'Strategic Peril,'" *The Houston Chronicle,* October 29, 2006.

56. Morris Janowitz, "American Democracy and Military Service," *Society* 35, no. 2 (1998): 39.

57. Kestnbaum, "Citizenship and Compulsory Military Service: The Revolutionary Origins of Conscription in the United States."

58. Waldman, "Strangers in Uniform."

59. Nadelson, *Trained to Kill,* 9.

60. Ibid., 25.

61. Michael Blumenthal, "Of Arms and Men," *New York Times,* January 11, 1981.

62. Ibid.

63. Michael Norman, "To Some, Call to Arms is but an Echo," *New York Times* May 31, 1982.

64. Kenneth Lee, "Repaying the Debt," *The American Enterprise* 14, no. 5 (2003): 12.

65. Nadelson, *Trained to Kill,* 140.

BIBLIOGRAPHY

Ackley, Charles Walton. *The Modern Military in American Society: A Study in the Nature of Military Power*. Philadelphia: Westminster Press, 1972.

Aichinger, Peter. *The American Soldier in Fiction, 1880–1963: A History of Attitudes Toward Warfare and the Military Establishment*. Ames: Iowa State University Press, 1975.

Alt, Betty Sowers, and Bonnie Domrose Stone. *Campfollowing: A History of the Military Wife*. New York: Praeger, 1991.

Ambrose, Stephen E. *Duty, Honor, Country: A History of West Point*. Baltimore: Johns Hopkins University Press, 1999.

Appy, Christian G. *Working-Class War: American Combat Soldiers and Vietnam*. Chapel Hill and London: University of North Carolina Press, 1993.

Armentrout, L. Eve. *Farms, Firms & Runways: Perspectives on U.S. Military Bases in the Western Pacific*. Imprint Pubns, 2000.

Astor, Gerald. *The Right to Fight: A History of African Americans in the Military*. Novato, CA: Presidio, 1998.

Atkinson, Rick. *In the Company of Soldiers: A Chronicle of Combat*. 1st ed. New York: Henry Holt and Co., 2004.

———. *The Long Gray Line: The American Journey of West Point's Class of 1966*. Boston: Houghton Mifflin, 1989.

Baker, Anni. *American Soldiers Overseas: The Global Military Presence*. Westport, CT: Praeger, 2004.

Baldwin, W.C. *Four Housing Privatization Programs: A History of the Wherry, Capehart, Section 801, & Section 802 Family Housing Programs in the Army*. Alexandria, VA: US Army Corps of Engineers, Office of History, 1996.

———. *A History of Army Peacetime Housing*. Alexandria, VA: US Army Corps of Engineers, Office of History, 1993.

Banning, Kendall. *Annapolis Today*. 6th ed. Annapolis, MD: United States Naval Institute, 1968.

Barkalow, Carol, with Andrea Raab. *In the Men's House: An Inside Account of Life in the Army by One of West Point's First Female Graduates*. New York: Poseidon Press, 1990.

Belenky, Gregory. *Contemporary Studies in Combat Psychiatry*. Westport, CT: Greenwood Press, 1987.

Benton, Jeffrey C. *Air Force Officer's Guide*. 33rd ed. Mechanicsburg, PA: Stackpole Books, 2002.

Berg, Norman E. *Regret to Inform You: Experiences of Families Who Lost a Family Member in Vietnam*. Central Point, OR: Hellgate Press, 1999.

Berryman, Sue E. *Military Enlistment Process: What Happens in It and Can It Be Improved.* Santa Monica, CA: Rand, 1983.

Biddle, Ellen McGowan. *Reminiscences of a Soldier's Wife.* Philadelphia: Press of J.B. Lippincott Company, 1907.

Bilton, Michael and Kevin Sim. *Four Hours in My Lai.* New York: Viking, 1992.

Binkin, Martin. *America's Volunteer Military: Progress and Prospects.* Washington, D.C.: Brookings Institution, 1984.

Binkin, Martin, and Mark J. Eitelberg. *Blacks and the Military* (Studies in Defense Policy). Washington, D.C.: Brookings Institution Press, 1982.

Binneveld, J.M.W. *From Shell Shock to Combat Stress: A Comparative History of Military Psychiatry.* Amsterdam: Amsterdam University Press, 1997.

Blaker, James R. *United States Overseas Basing: An Anatomy of the Dilemma.* New York, Westport, CT, and London: Praeger, 1990.

Bluhm, Jr., Col. Raymond K., and Col. James B. Motley. *The Soldier's Guidebook.* Washington and London: Brassey's, 1995.

Bonn, Keith E. *Army Officer's Guide.* 49th ed. Mechanicsburg, PA: Stackpole Books, 2002.

Boot, Max. *The Savage Wars of Peace: Small Wars and the Rise of American Power.* Basic Books, 2003.

Bourke, Joanna. *An Intimate History of Killing: Face-to-Face Killing in Twentieth-Century Warfare.* New York: Basic Books, 1999.

Bourne, Peter G. *Men, Stress, and Vietnam.* Boston: Little, Brown, 1970.

Brewer, C.W. *How to Win ROTC Scholarships: An In-Depth, Behind-the-Scenes Look at the ROTC Scholarship Selection Process.* 1st ed. Fort Bragg, CA: Lost Coast Press, 2000.

Bryant, Clifton D. *Khaki-Collar Crime: Deviant Behavior in the Military Context.* New York and London: The Free Press, 1979.

Budahn, P.J. *What to Expect in the Military: A Practical Guide for Young People, Parents and Counselors.* Westport, CT: Greenwood Press, 2000.

Buddin, Richard, and Phuong Do. *Assessing the Personal Financial Problems of Junior Enlisted Personnel.* Santa Monica, CA: Rand, 2002.

Buddin, Richard, Carole Roan Gresenz, Susan D. Hosek, Marc Elliot, and Jennifer Hawes-Dawson. *An Evaluation of Housing Options for Military Families.* Santa Monica, CA: Rand, 1999.

Builder, Carl H. *Command Concepts: A Theory Derived from the Practice of Command and Control.* Santa Monica, CA: Rand, 1999.

Cameron, Craig M. *American Samurai: Myth, Imagination, and the Conduct of Battle in the First Marine Division, 1941–1951.* Cambridge: Cambridge University Press, 1994.

Carhart, Tom. *West Point Warriors: Profiles of Duty, Honor, and Country in Battle.* New York: Warner Books, 2002.

Caylor, John S., Thomas G. Sticht, and William B. Armstrong. *Cast-Off Youth: Policy and Training Methods from the Military Experience.* Westport, CT: Praeger Publishers, 1987.

Chambers, John Whiteclay, II. *To Raise an Army: The Draft Comes to Modern America.* New York: Free Press, 1987.

Cline, Lydia Sloan. *Today's Military Wife: Meeting the Challenges of Service Life.* 5th rev. ed. Mechanicsburg, PA: Stackpole Books, 2003.

Coffman, Edward M. *The Old Army: A Portrait of the American Army in Peacetime, 1784–1989*. New York: Oxford University Press, 1986.

———. *The Regulars: The American Army, 1898–1941*. Cambridge, MA and London: The Belknap Press of Harvard University Press, 2004.

Cohen, Eliot A. *Supreme Command: Soldiers, Statesmen, and Leadership in Wartime*. New York: Free Press, 2002.

Collier, Peter. *Medal of Honor: Portraits of Valor Beyond the Call of Duty*. New York: Artisan, 2003.

Collins, Robert F. *Reserve Officers Training Corps: Campus Pathways to Service Commissions*. 1st ed. New York: Rosen Publishing Group, 1986.

Connell, Royal W. *Naval Ceremonies, Customs, and Traditions*. 6th ed. Annapolis, MD: Naval Institute Press, 2004.

Connelly, Mark, and David Welch. *War and the Media: Reportage and Propaganda, 1900–2003*. London and New York: I.B. Tauris and St. Martins Press, 2005.

Cooperman, Stanley. *World War I and the American Novel*. Baltimore: Johns Hopkins University Press, 1967.

Cornum, Rhonda. *She Went to War: The Rhonda Cornum Story*. Novato, CA: Presidio Press, 1992.

Crossley, A., and C. A. Keller. *The Army Wife Handbook: A Complete Social Guide*. Sarasota, FL: ABI Press, 1993.

Cutler, Thomas J. *The Bluejacket's Manual*. Centennial ed. Annapolis, MD: Naval Institute Press, 2002.

Da Cruz, Daniel. *Boot*. Reprint, New York: St. Martin's Press, 1987.

Dansby, Mickey R., James B. Stewart, and Schuyler C. Webb. *Managing Diversity in the Military*. New Brunswick, NJ and London: Transaction Publishers, 2001.

Dinter, Elmar. *Hero or Coward: Pressures Facing the Soldier in Battle*. London and Totowa, NJ: Frank Cass, 1985.

Dionne, E.J., Jr., Kayla Meltzer Drogosz, and Robert E. Litan, eds. *United We Serve: National Service and the Future of Citizenship*. Washington, D.C.: Brookings Institution Press, 2003.

Disher, Sharon H. *First Class: Women Join the Ranks at the Naval Academy*. Annapolis, MD: Naval Institute Press, 1998.

Dobak, William A. *Fort Riley and Its Neighbors: Military Money and Economic Growth, 1853–1895*. Norman: University of Oklahoma Press, 1998.

Downs, Frederick. *The Killing Zone: My Life in the Vietnam War*. New York: Berkley Books, 1978.

Eales, Anne Bruner. *Army Wives on the American Frontier: Living by the Bugles*. Boulder, CO: Johnson Books, 1996.

Early, Emmett. *The War Veteran in Film*. Jefferson, NC and London: McFarland & Company, Inc., Publishers, 2003.

Ellis, John. *Eye-Deep in Hell; Trench Warfare in World War I*. 1976. Reprint, Baltimore: Johns Hopkins University Press, 1989.

———. *The Sharp End: The Fighting Man in World War II*. New York: Charles Scribner's Sons, 1980. Also published as *On the Front Lines: The Experience of War Through the Eyes of the Allied Soldiers in World War II*. New York, Chichester, Brisbane, Toronto, and Singapore: John Wiley and Sons, 1991.

Ellis, Joseph J. *School for Soldiers: West Point and the Profession of Arms.* New York: Oxford University Press, 1974.

Ender, Morten G., ed. *Military Brats and Other Global Nomads: Growing Up in Organization Families.* Westport, CT: Praeger Publishers, 2002.

Endler, James R. *Other Leaders, Other Heroes: West Point's Legacy to America Beyond the Field of Battle.* New York: Praeger, 1998.

English, John A. *On Infantry.* New York: Praeger, 1981.

Enloe, Cynthia. *Does Khaki Become You? The Militarization of Women's Lives.* London and Boston: Pandora, 1988.

Erenberg, Lewis A., and Susan E. Hirsch, eds. *The War in American Culture: Society and Consciousness During World War II.* Chicago: University of Chicago Press, 1996.

Estes, Kenneth W. *The Marine Officer's Guide.* 6th ed. Annapolis, MD: Naval Institute Press, 1996.

Exum, Andrew. *This Man's Army: A Soldier's Story from the Front Lines of the War on Terrorism.* New York: Gotham Books, 2004.

Fenner, Lorry, and Marie deYoung. *Women in Combat: Civic Duty or Military Liability?* Washington, D.C.: Georgetown University Press, 2001.

Fick, Nathaniel. *One Bullet Away: The Making of a Marine Officer.* Boston: Houghton Mifflin, 2005.

Fleming, Thomas J. *The Officers' Wives.* Garden City, NY: Doubleday, 1981.

Flynn, George Q. *Conscription and Democracy: The Draft in France, Great Britain, and the United States.* Westport, CT and London: Greenwood Press, 2002.

———. *The Draft, 1940–1973.* Lawrence: University Press of Kansas, 1993.

Foner, Jack D. *Blacks and the Military in American History: A New Perspective.* Westport, CT: Praeger Publishers, 1974.

———. *The United States Soldier Between Two Wars: Army Life and Reforms, 1865–1898.* New York: Humanities Press, 1970.

Francke, Linda Bird. *Ground Zero: The Gender Wars in the Military.* New York: Simon & Schuster, 1997.

Franke, Volker. *Preparing for Peace: Military Identity, Value Orientations, and Professional Military Education.* Westport, CT: Praeger, 1999.

Fredland, J. Eric, Curtis L. Gilroy, Roger D. Little, and W.S. Sellman, eds. *Professionals on the Front Line: Two Decades of the All-Volunteer Force.* Washington and London: Brassey's, 1996.

Fuller, Louise Lawrence. *Army Wives: Veterans Without Glory.* Bloomington, IN: 1st Books, 2001.

Gabriel, Richard A. *The Painful Field: The Psychiatric Dimension of Modern War.* Contributions in Military Studies, number 75. New York, London, and Westport, CT; Greenwood Press, 1988.

Gabriel, Richard A., and Paul L. Savage. *Crisis in Command: Mismanagement in the Army.* New York: Hill and Wang, 1978.

Gambone, Michael D. *The Greatest Generation Comes Home: The Veteran in American Society.* College Station: Texas A&M University Press, 2005.

Gardiner, Juliet. *Overpaid, Oversexed, and Over Here: The American GI in World War II Britain.* New York: Canopy Books, 1992.

Gilley, Shirley A. *Closing Down the American Base at Adak, Alaska: The Social and Psychological Trauma of Relocating Military Families.* Lewiston, ME: Mellen University Press, 1997.

Glad, Betty, ed. *Psychological Dimensions of War.* Newbury Park, London, and New Delhi: Sage Publications, 1990.

Glasser, Ronald J. *Wounded: Vietnam to Iraq.* New York: George Braziller, 2006.

Goldstein, Joshua S. *War and Gender : How Gender Shapes the War System and Vice Versa.* Cambridge: Ca mbridge University Press, 2001.

Graham, Herman. *The Brothers' Vietnam War: Black Power, Manhood, and the Military Experience.* Gainesville: University Press of Florida, 2003.

Gray, J. Glenn. *The Warriors: Reflections on Men in Battle.* Introduction by Hannah Arendt. New York: Harper & Row, Publishers, 1970.

Griffith, Robert K., Jr. *Men Wanted for the U.S. Army: America's Experience with an All-Volunteer Army Between the World Wars.* Westport, CT: Greenwood Press, 1982.

Grossman, Dave, Lt. Col. *On Killing: The Psychological Cost of Learning to Kill in War and Society.* Boston, New York, Toronto, and London: Little, Brown, 1995.

Hammond, William M. *Reporting Vietnam: Media and Military at War.* Lawrence: University Press of Kansas, 1998.

Harkavy, Robert. *Bases Abroad: The Global Foreign Military Presence.* Oxford and New York: Oxford University Press, 1989.

Harrell, Margaret C. *Invisible Women: Junior Enlisted Army Wives.* Santa Monica, CA: Rand, 2000.

———. *Barriers to Minority Participation in Special Operations Forces.* Santa Monica, CA: Rand, 1999.

Harrod, Frederick S. *Manning the New Navy: The Development of a Modern Naval Enlisted Force, 1899–1940.* Greenwood Press, 1978.

Hauser, William L. *America's Army in Crisis: A Study in Civil–Military Relations.* Baltimore: Johns Hopkins University Press, 1973.

Hedges, Chris. *War Is a Force that Gives Us Meaning.* Oxford and New York: PublicAffairs Ltd., 2002.

———. *What Every Person Should Know About War.* New York: Free Press, 2003.

Hellmann, John. *American Myth and the Legacy of Vietnam.* New York: Columbia University Press, 1986.

Helmer, John. *Bringing the War Home: The American Soldier in Vietnam and After.* New York: Free Press; London: Collier Macmillan, 1974.

Henderson, C.J., and Jack Dolphin. *Career Opportunities in the Armed Forces.* New York: Checkmark Books, 2003.

Henderson, Kristin. *While They're at War: The True Story of American Families on the Homefront.* New York: Houghton Mifflin, 2006.

Henderson, William Darryl. *Cohesion: The Human Element in Combat: Leadership and Societal Influence in the Armies of the Soviet Union, the United States, North Vietnam, and Israel.* With an introduction by Charles C. Moskos. Washington, D.C.: National Defense University Press, 1988.

Hendin, Herbert, and Ann Pollinger Haas. *Wounds of War: The Psychological Aftermath of Combat in Vietnam.* New York: Basic Books, 1984.

Herbert, Melissa S. *Camouflage Isn't only for Combat: Gender, Sexuality, and Women in the Military*. New York: New York University Press, 2000.

Higonnet, Margaret R. *Behind the Lines: Gender and the Two World Wars*. New Haven, CT: Yale University Press, 1987.

The History of Officer Social Origins, Selection, Education and Training Since the Eighteenth Century: An Introductory Bibliography. Colorado Springs, CO: U.S. Air Force Academy Library, 1996.

Hogan, David W., Jr., Arnold G. Fisch, Jr., and Robert K. Wright, Jr. *The Story of the Noncommissioned Officer Corps: The Backbone of the Army*. Washington, D.C.: Center of Military History, United States Army, 2003.

Holm, Jeanne. *Women in the Military: An Unfinished Revolution*. Novato, CA: Presidio Press, 1993.

Holmes, Richard. *Acts of War: Behavior of Men in Battle*. 1st American ed. New York: Free Press, 1985.

Hosek, James R. *Married to the Military: The Employment and Earnings of Military Wives Compared with Those of Civilian Wives*. Santa Monica, CA: Rand, 2002.

Hosek, Susan D., *Minority and Gender Differences in Officer Career Progression*. Santa Monica, CA: Rand, 2001.

Houppert, Karen. *Home Fires Burning: Married to the Military—for Better or Worse*. New York: Ballantine Books, 2001.

Hunter, Cardell S. *Measuring the Impact of Military Family Programs on the Army*. Carlisle Barracks, PA: U.S. Army War College, 1987.

Hutchhausen, Peter. *America's Splendid Little Wars: A Short History of U.S. Military Engagements: 1975–2000*. New York: Viking, 2003.

Hynes, Samuel. *The Soldiers' Tale: Bearing Witness to Modern War*. New York: Allen Lane, 1997.

Janowitz, Morris. *The Professional Soldier: A Social and Political Portrait*. New York: Free Press, 1960, prologue added in 1974.

Jason, Philip K., ed. *Fourteen Landing Zones: Approaches to Vietnam War Literature*. Iowa City: University of Iowa Press, 1991.

Ji-Yeon Yuh. *Beyond the Shadow of Camptown: Korean Military Brides in America*. New York: New York University Press. 2002.

Karsten, Peter, ed. *The Military in America: From the Colonial Era to the Present*. New York: Free Press, 1986.

———. *The Naval Aristocracy: The Golden Age of Annapolis and the Emergence of Modern American Navalism*. New York: Free Press, 1972.

———. *Soldiers and Society: The Effects of Military Service and War on American Society*. Grass Roots Perspectives on American History, number 1. Westport, CT and London: Greenwood Press, 1978.

———. *The Training and Socializing of Military Personnel*. New York: Garland Publishing, 1998.

Keegan, John. *The Face of Battle*. New York: Viking, 1976.

Keegan, John, and Richard Holmes, with John Gau. *Soldiers: A History of Men in Battle*. Foreword by Frederick Forsyth. New York: Viking, 1986.

Keene, Jennifer. *Doughboys, The Great War, and the Remaking of America*. Baltimore: Johns Hopkins University Press, 2001.

Kellett, Anthony. *Combat Motivation: The Behavior of Soldiers in Battle.* Boston: The Hague; London: Kluwer, Nijhoff, 1982.

Kennedy, David M. *Over Here: The First World War and American Society.* Oxford, New York, Toronto, and Melbourne: Oxford University Press, 1980.

Kennedy, Gregory C., and Keith Neilson, eds. *Military Education: Past, Present, and Future.* Westport, CT: Praeger, 2002.

Kennett, Lee. *G.I.: The American Soldier in World War II.* New York: Charles Scribner's Sons, 1987.

Kim, Bok-Lim C., and Michael R. Sawdey. *Women in Shadows: A Handbook for Service Providers Working with Asian Wives of U.S. Military Personnel.* LaJolla, CA: National Committee Concerned with Asian Wives of U.S. Servicemen, 1981.

Kinney, Katherine. *Friendly Fire: American Images of the Vietnam War.* Oxford: Oxford University Press, 2000.

Kirby, Sheila Nataraj, and Harry J. Thie. *Enlisted Personnel Management: A Historical Perspective.* Santa Monica, CA: Rand, 1996.

Klein, Stephen P., Jennifer Haws-Dawson, Thomas Martin. *Why Recruits Separate Early.* Santa Monica, CA: Rand, 1991.

Kovic, Ron. *Born on the 4th of July.* New York: McGraw-Hill, 1976.

Lande, Nathaniel. *Dispatches from the Front: A History of the American War Correspondent.* New York: H. Holt, 1995.

Landers, James. *The Weekly War: Newsmagazines and Vietnam.* Columbia and London: University of Missouri Press, 2004.

Lanning, Michael Lee, Lt. Col. (Ret.). *The African-American Soldiers: From Crispus Attucks to Colin Powell.* Secaucus, NJ: Carol Publishing Group, 1997.

Laurence, Janice H., and Peter F. Ramsberger. *Low-Aptitude Men in the Military: Who Profits? Who Pays?* Westport, CT: Praeger Publishers, 1991.

Leahy, J.F. *Honor, Courage, Commitment: Navy Boot Camp.* Annapolis, MD: Naval Institute Press, 2002.

Leon, Philip W. *Bullies and Cowards: The West Point Hazing Scandal, 1898–1901.* Westport, CT: Greenwood Press, 2000.

Leslie, Paul, ed. *The Gulf War as Popular Entertainment: An Analysis of the Military–Industrial Media Complex.* Lewiston, ME: E. Mellen Press, 1997.

Leyva, Meredith. *Married to the Military: A Survival Guide for Military Wives, Girlfriends, and Women in Uniform.* New York: Fireside, 2003.

Linderman, Gerald F. *Embattled Courage: The Experience of Combat in the American Civil War.* New York: Free Press; London: Collier Macmillan, 1989.

———. *The Mirror of War: American Society and the Spanish-American War.* Ann Arbor: University of Michigan Press, 1974.

———. *The World Within War: America's Combat Experience in World War II.* Cambridge: Harvard University Press, 1999.

Lipsky, David. *Absolutely American: Four Years at West Point.* New York: Vintage, 2004.

Lomperis, Timothy J. *"Reading the Wind": The Literature of the Vietnam War.* Durham, NC: Duke University Press, 1987.

Lutz, Catherine. *Homefront: A Military City and the American Twentieth Century.* Boston: Beacon Press, 2001.

Lynn, John A. *Battle: a History of Combat and Culture*. Cambridge, MA: Westview Press, 2004.

Mann, Monroe. *To Benning and Back: The Making of a Citizen Soldier—My Journals of Daily Life in U.S. Army Basic Training and Officer Candidate School, from Private to Second Lieutenant, from First Call to Lights Out, and Yes, Everything in Between*. Bloomington, IN: Unlimited Publishing, 2002.

March, James G., and Robert Weissinger-Baylon, eds. *Ambiguity and Command: Organizational Perspectives on Military Decision Making*. Boston: Pitman, 1986.

Mardis, Jaime. *Memos of a West Point Cadet*. New York: David McKay Company, Inc., 1976.

Margiotta, Franklin D., ed. *The Changing World of the American Military*. Cambridge, MA: Westview Press, 1979.

Marshall, S. L. A. *Men Against Fire: The Problem of Battle Command*. New York: Morrow, 1947. Reprint. Norman: University of Oklahoma Press, 2000.

———. *Pork Chop Hill: The American Fighting Man in Action, Korea, Spring, 1953*. New York: Morrow, 1956.

Martin, James A., Leora N. Rosen, and Linette R. Sparacino, eds. *The Military Family: A Practice Guide for Human Service Providers*. Westport, CT: Praeger Publishers, 2000.

Martin, Ralph G. *The G.I. War, 1941–1945*. Boston and Toronto: Little, Brown, 1967.

Mason, Robert. *Chickenhawk: Back in the World: Life After Vietnam*. New York: Viking Press, 1983.

Matsakis, Aphrodite. *Vietnam Wives: Facing the Challenges of Life with Veterans Suffering Post-Traumatic Stress*. 2nd ed. Baltimore, MD: The Sidran Press, 1996.

Matthews, Lloyd J., ed. *The Future of the Army Profession*. Boston: McGraw-Hill, 2002.

Mays, Josephine D. *Black Army Brat*. 1st ed. New York: Vantage Press, 1976.

McCarthy, Kevin F., Jess Malkin, Georges Vernez, and Michael Dardia. *The Effects of Military Base Closures on Local Communities: A Short-Term Perspective*. Santa Monica, CA: Rand, 1996.

McCormick, David. *The Downsized Warrior: America's Army in Transition*. New York and London: New York University Press, 1998.

McClure, Peggy, ed. *Pathways to the Future: A Review of Military Family Research*. Scranton, PA: Military Family Institute, Marywood University, 1999.

MacGregor, Douglas A. *Transformation Under Fire: Revolutionizing How America Fights*. Westport, CT and London: Praeger, 2003.

McNally, Jeffrey A. *The Adult Development of Career Army Officers*. New York: Praeger, 1991.

Mercier, Peter J., and Judith D. Mercier, eds. *Battle Cries on the Home Front: Violence in the Military Family*. Springfield, IL: C.C. Thomas, 2000.

Mermin, Jonathan. *Debating War and Peace: Media Coverage of U.S. Intervention in the Post-Vietnam Era*. Princeton, NJ: Princeton University Press, 1999.

Mershon, Sherie, and Steven Schlossman. *Foxholes and Color Lines: Desegregating the U.S. Armed Forces*. Baltimore and London: Johns Hopkins University Press, 2003.

Meyer, Edward C. *Who Will Lead?: Senior Leadership in the United States Army*. Westport, CT: Praeger, 1995.

Miller, Wayne Charles. *An Armed America, Its Face in Fiction: A History of the American Military Novel.* New York: New York University Press, 1970.

Millett, Allan R. *The General: Robert L. Bullard and Officership in the United States Army, 1881–1925.* Westport, CT: Greenwood Press, 1975.

———. *Semper Fidelis: The Story of the United States Marine Corps.* rev. and expanded ed. New York: Free Press, 1991.

Millett, Allan, and Peter Maslowski. *For the Common Defense: A Military History of the United States of America.* rev. and expanded ed. New York: Free Press, 1994.

Montor, Karel, ed. *Ethics for the Junior Officer: Selected Cases from Current Military Experience.* Annapolis, MD: Naval Institute Press, 2001.

Moon, Katharine. *Sex Among Allies: Military Prostitution in U.S.–Korean Relations.* New York: Columbia University Press, 1997.

Moskin, J. Robert. *The U.S. Marine Corps Story.* 3rd ed. New York: McGraw-Hill, 1992.

Moskos, Charles C., Jr. *The American Enlisted Man: The Rank and File in Today's Military.* New York: Russell Sage Foundation, 1970.

———. *Public Opinion and the Military Establishment.* Beverly Hills, CA: Sage Publications, 1971.

Moskos, Charles C., Jr., and Frank R. Wood, eds. *The Military: More than Just a Job?* Washington, D.C.: Pergamon-Brassey's International Defense Publishers, 1988.

Moskos, Charles C., Jr., and John Whiteclay Chambers II. *The New Conscientious Objection: From Sacred to Secular Resistance.* New York: Oxford University Press, 1993.

Moskos, Charles C., Jr., and John Sibley Butler. *All That We Can Be: Black Leadership and Racial Integration the Army Way.* New York: Basic Books, 1996.

Moskos, Charles C., Jr., John Allen Williams, and David R. Segal, eds. *The Postmodern Military: Armed Forces After the Cold War.* New York and Oxford: Oxford University Press, 2000.

Motley, Mary Penick. *The Invisible Soldier: The Experience of the Black Soldier, World War II.* Foreword by Howard Donovan Queen. Detroit: Wayne State University Press, 1975.

Murphy, Mary Kay Connors, and Carol Bowles Parker. *Fitting in as a New Service Wife.* Harrisburg, PA, Stackpole Books, 1966.

Myers, Thomas. *Walking Point: American Narratives of Vietnam.* New York and Oxford: Oxford University Press, 1988.

Nacy, Michele J. *Members of the Regiment: Army Officers' Wives on the Western Frontier, 1865–1890.* Westport, CT: Greenwood Press, 2000.

Nadelson, Theodore. *Trained to Kill: Soldiers at War.* Baltimore: Johns Hopkins University Press, 2005.

The Naval Officer's Guide. 11th rev. ed. Annapolis, MD: Naval Institute Press, 1998.

Neiberg, Michael S. *Making Citizen-Soldiers: ROTC and the Ideology of American Military Service.* Cambridge, MA: Harvard University Press, 2000.

Nichols, Boone. *Airman's Guide.* 6th Rev ed. Mechanicsburg, PA: Stackpole Books, 2004.

Parks, David. *GI Diary.* Washington, D.C.: Howard University Press, 1984.

Patton, Gerald W. *War and Race: The Black Officer in the American Military, 1915–1941.* Westport, CT: Greenwood Press, 1981.

Piehler, G. Kurt. *Remembering War the American Way.* Washington, D.C., and London: Smithsonian Institution Press, 1995.

Pois, Robert A. *Command Failure in War: Psychology and Leadership.* Bloomington: Indiana University Press, 2004.

Radine, Lawrence B. *The Taming of the Troops: Social Control in the United States Army.* Westport, CT: Greenwood Press, 1977.

Regan, Geoffrey. *Blue on Blue: A History of Friendly Fire.* New York: Avon Books, 1995.

Rickey, Don, Jr. *Forty Miles a Day on Beans and Hay: The Enlisted Soldier Fighting the Indian Wars.* Norman: University of Oklahoma Press, 1963.

Rimmerman, Craig A., ed.*Gay Rights, Military Wrongs: Political Perspectives on Lesbians and Gays in the Military.* Garland Publishing, 1996.

Robbins, James S. *Last in their Class: Custer, Pickett and the Goats of West Point.* New York: Encounter Books, 2006.

Rush, Robert. *Enlisted Soldier's Guide.* 6th ed. Mechanicsburg, PA: Stackpole Books, 2003.

Sackett, Paul, and Anne S. Mavor. *Attitudes, Aptitudes, and Aspirations of American Youth: Implications for Military Recruiting.* Washington, D.C.: National Academy Press, 2002.

Sandars, C.T. *America's Overseas Garrisons: The Leasehold Empire.* Oxford and New York, Oxford University Press, 2000.

Sarkesian, Sam C., and Robert E. Connor, Jr. *The U.S. Military Profession into the Twenty-First Century: War, Peace and Politics.* London and Portland, OR: Frank Cass, 1999.

Sarkesian, Sam C., ed. *Combat Effectiveness: Cohesion, Stress, and the Volunteer Military.* Vol. 9. Sage Research Progress Series on War, Revolution, and Peace-keeping. Beverly Hills and London: Sage Publications, 1980.

———. *Soldiers, Society, and National Security.* Boulder, CO: L. Rienner Publishers, 1995.

Schneller, Robert J. *Breaking the Color Barrier: The U.S. Naval Academy's First Black Midshipmen and the Struggle for Racial Equality.* New York: New York University Press, 2005.

Schrijvers, Peter. *The Crash of Ruin: American Combat Soldiers in Europe During World War II.* New York: New York University Press, 1998.

Segal, David R. *Recruiting for Uncle Sam: Citizenship and Military Manpower Policy.* Lawrence: University Press of Kansas, 1989.

Segal, David R., and Mady Wechsler Segal. *Peacekeepers and Their Wives: American Participation in the Multinational Force and Observers.* Westport, Ct: Greenwood Press, 1993.

Shay, Jonathan. *Achilles in Vietnam: Combat Trauma and the Undoing of Character.* New York, London, Sydney, Tokyo, and Singapore: Scribner, 1995.

Shea, Nancy. *The Army Wife.* New York: Harper & Row, 1954.

Shukert, Elfrieda Berthiaume, and Barbara Smith Scibetta. *War Brides of World War II.* Novato, CA: Presidio, 1988.

Skelton, William B. *An American Profession of Arms: The Army Officer Corps, 1784–1861.* Lawrence: University Press of Kansas, 1992.

Sledge, Michael. *Soldier Dead: How We Recover, Identify, Bury, and Honor Our Military Fallen.* New York: Columbia University Press, 2005.

Snyder, R. Claire. *Citizen-Soldiers and Manly Warriors: Military Service and Gender in the Civic Republican Tradition.* Lanham, MD: Rowman & Littlefield Publishers, 1999.

Stallings, Laurence. *The Doughboys: The Story of the AEF, 1917–1918.* New York, Evanston, and London: Harper & Row, 1963.

Stiehm, Judith. *Bring Me Men and Women: Mandated Change at the U.S. Air Force Academy.* Berkeley: University of California Press, 1981.

———. *It's Our Military, Too! Women and the U.S. Military.* Philadelphia: Temple University Press, 1996.

Stouffer, Samuel A., *Studies in Social Psychology in World War II.* 4 vols. Vol. 1, *The American Soldier: Adjustment During Army Life*; Vol. 2, *The American Soldier: Combat and Its Aftermath.* Princeton, NJ: Princeton University Press, 1949.

Sturdevant, Saundra Pollack, and Brenda Stoltzfus. *Let the Good Times Roll: Prostitution and the U.S. Military in Asia.* New York: New Press, 1993.

Swartz, Oretha D. *Service Etiquette.* 4th ed. Annapolis, MD: Naval Institute Press, 1988.

Sylvester, Judith L. *Reporting from the Front: The Media and the Military.* Lanham, MD: Rowman & Littlefield, 2005.

Thie, Harry J., *A Future Officer Career Management System.* Santa Monica, CA: Rand, 2001.

Thompson, Peter. *An Insider's Guide to Military Basic Training: A Recruit's Guide of Advice and Hints to Make It Through Boot Camp.* 2nd ed. Boca Raton, FL: Universal Publishers, 2003.

Thrall, A. Trevor. *War in the Media Age.* Cresskill, NJ: Hampton Press, Inc., 2000.

Truscott, Mary R. *Brats: Children of the American Military Speak Out.* 1st ed. New York: E. P. Dutton, 1989.

U.S. Army Infantry School. *Ranger Handbook.* Boulder, CO: Paladin Press, 1992.

Utley, Robert M. *Frontiersmen in Blue: The United States Army and the Indian, 1848–1865.* Lincoln: University of Nebraska Press, 1967.

Van Creveld, Martin L. *The Training of Officers: From Military Professionalism to Irrelevance.* New York: Free Press, 1990.

Volkin, Michael C. *The Ultimate Basic Training Guidebook.* Booklocker.com, 2004.

Watson, Peter. *War on the Mind: The Military Uses and Abuses of Psychology.* New York: Basic Books, 1978.

Weigley, Russell F. *History of the United States Army.* New York: Macmillan Publishing Co., 1967.

Wertsch, Mary Edwards. *Military Brats: Legacies of Childhood Inside the Fortress.* New York: Harmony Books, 1991.

Westheider, James E. *Fighting on Two Fronts: African Americans and the Vietnam War.* New York and London: New York University Press, 1997.

Williams, Cindy, ed. *Filling the Ranks: Transforming the U.S. Military System.* Cambridge: The MIT Press, 2004.

Willis, Clint, ed. *Boots on the Ground: Stories of American Soldiers from Iraq and Afghanistan.* New York: Thunder's Mouth Press, 2004.

Woulfe, James. *Into the Crucible.* Novato, CA: Presidio Press, 2000.

Wright, Evan. *Generation Kill: Devil Dogs, Iceman, Captain America, and the New Face of American War.* New York: Putnam Publishing Group, 2004.

Zellman, Gail L., Anne S. Johansen, and Lisa S. Meredith.*Improving the Delivery of Military Child Care: An Analysis of Current Operations and New Approaches.* Santa Monica, CA: Rand, 1992.

INDEX

ABOUT THE AUTHOR

ANNI BAKER is Associate Professor of Modern European History at Wheaton College in Norton, Massachusetts. She is the author of two other books, including *American Soldiers Overseas* (Praeger, 2004).